IF I DON'T MAKE IT, I LOVE YOU

Survivors in the Aftermath of School Shootings

Edited by
AMYE ARCHER & LOREN KLEINMAN

Foreword by
FRED GUTTENBERG
founder of Orange Ribbons for Jaime

Skyhorse Publishing

Skyhorse Publishing books may be purchased in bulk at special discounts for sales promotion, corporate gifts, fund-raising, or educational purposes. Special editions can also be created to specifications. For details, contact the Special Sales Department, Skyhorse Publishing, 307 West 36th Street, 11th Floor, New York, NY 10018 or info@skyhorsepublishing.com.

Skyhorse® and Skyhorse Publishing® are registered trademarks of Skyhorse Publishing, Inc.®, a Delaware corporation.

Visit our website at www.skyhorsepublishing.com.

10 9 8 7 6 5 4 3 2 1

Library of Congress Cataloging-in-Publication Data is available on file.

Cover design by Daniel Brount
Cover photo by Getty Images

ISBN: 978-1-5107-7296-0
Ebook ISBN: 978-1-5107-4650-3

Printed in China

> *"We're all survivors. Even those not at the school that day. We all had to find a way to heal."*

ALICIA GRAVES was the former editor in chief at Umpqua Community College's (UCC) student-run newspaper, *The Mainstream*. She was working on a class paper when the shooting at UCC took place at Snyder Hall.

Complete digital archive for *If I Don't Make It, I Love You* available at www.ifidontmakeitthebook.com. Archive includes additional images and essays not represented in the book, including a corresponding discussion guide for educators.

CONTENTS

THE FINAL SECONDS
by Fred Guttenberg

MY DAUGHTER, JAIME, was killed at Marjory Stoneman Douglas (MSD) High School in Parkland, Florida, on February 14, 2018. What I remember of that day was the typical morning chaos: the kids bustling past my wife and me, a rushed breakfast, the dogs barking, trying to get ready for work myself. Still running late. But it's what I *can't* remember about that morning that haunts me. Did I tell my kids I loved them as they ran out the door? *Did I stop to tell Jaime I loved her? Jesse, my son?* It wasn't supposed to be the last time. I sent two kids to school that day; only one of them came home.

The day after Jaime's murder I attended a vigil in Parkland. I spoke at the mayor's request. While I didn't prepare, I had a lot I needed to say. I told the crowd at the vigil I felt broken. But I realized I wasn't alone in my brokenness. I realized that people would help me heal. It's the greatness of people that gives me the strength and inspiration to move forward.

Jaime was the strongest person I knew, and she fought for her life until the last second. She ran down the hall from an active shooter until a single gunshot ended her life. I don't know if she died instantly or if she suffered, but I think about her final seconds every second of my life.

Grief doesn't get easier. Even with time. I'm reminded every holiday, on Mother's Day, Father's Day, birthdays, and through the echo of dance recitals that Jaime isn't here. But I've learned so much about myself since her death. I'm strong and resilient. And I learned the same is true for those affected by gun violence. I've seen communities come together before Congress fighting for change. I've seen networks of survivors comforting one another through grief. I've heard parents, siblings, and friends of the murdered share their stories over and over again. I've watched this current generation march to end gun violence. My life's purpose and mission now is to fight to reduce gun violence in our country. To prevent this from happening to another parent's child.

In this collection of stories, you will meet people like me: parents grieving their child. You will meet students who *just* made it, friends who survived, teachers who acted, and the families and communities who supported them. One thread holds these stories together: resilience. Since Jaime's death, I have been welcomed into and surrounded by a community whose strength I could never have imagined. The resilience of this community can never be broken. We will continue to fight. We are parents. We are sons and daughters. We are students. We are teachers. We are friends. We are the change. And these are our stories.

Fred and Jaime Guttenberg. To donate in Jaime's memory,
please visit orangeribbonsforjaime.org.

INTRODUCTION
by Roger S. Friedman, PhD

IN THE FIFTY-TWO years since a sniper calmly took the elevator to the top of the University of Texas Library Tower in Austin in 1966, shot and killed fourteen people, and wounded thirty-one others, more than seventy mass shootings have occurred on America's school grounds and university campuses. This new form of public human disaster has resulted in hundreds of deaths, many more wounded and countless traumatized surviving family members, first responders, police officers, and witnesses. The frequency of such tragedies has increased since 1996, with twenty-nine multi-victim shootings occurring in just the past fifteen years. You don't have to be a combat veteran to be exposed to violent trauma in America. Hardly. We have learned a dreadful lesson this past half century, that trauma can occur in formerly safe and even sacred public spaces, and any of us, including our friends, neighbors, and our kids, can be victims.

If I Don't Make it, I Love You pulls together, for the first time, the voices of several generations of survivors from twenty-one school shootings beginning with Santa Fe High School in Santa Fe, Texas on May 18, 2018, and concluding with August 1, 1966 at the University of Texas, at Austin. The book includes first-person narratives from Columbine High School, Sandy Hook Elementary

School, Virginia Tech University, Marjory Stoneman Douglas High School, and from lesser reported tragedies at New River Community College, Thurston High, and Bard College at Simon's Rock, among others. There are over eighty contributors, including students who have escaped shootings in their own schools, parents who have lost children, children who have lost parents, teachers who have lost students, writers and journalists covering these events, gun violence advocates, and doctors offering medical treatment. These original narratives, some describing experiences just weeks after shootings and some reflecting after decades, provide vivid personal documentation of how trauma affects child and adult survivors—and how human beings, over generations, find ways to lead their lives in the face of haunting traumatic memories and troubling real-time reminders. These brave storytellers describe in great detail the steps forward and backward that occurred in their varied journeys of recovery and the range of strategies they've used to cope with making meaning of the trauma they've experienced.

An adult mental health counselor, who was a child when her father, a much-loved teacher at Columbine, was killed in that shooting in 1999, describes how in college she found her way into psychology and eventually received a master's in psychology. Her first job out of graduate school was working with offenders of violent domestic crime, and more than a decade later she is still working in this setting. "I never expected what I found. A room of men from different backgrounds, some wearing business attire, some in jeans, none in wifebeater shirts and . . . no face tattoos." She reflects that shortly after starting this new work, "it hit me. I'm the teacher like Dad, and these men are students who need me. I finally found where I belonged, in a room full of convicted felons, offering the same things Dad did to those 'tough kids' he so often sought out: kindness and encouragement without judgment and an opportunity to work hard to improve their lives."

One teenage survivor of a shooting at her high school in Maryland says that months after the incident, when she put on the sweatshirt she had worn that day, ". . . my back broke out in hives, like my body was rejecting it." A Thurston High School student survivor writes, "I fall to the ground. I stare at my hand thinking, I should put that between my legs and apply pressure but then I can't figure out how to move. I look at my friend and say, *I've been shot*, and he says *yeah, me too.* Months later, he says we never had that conversation." A teacher who helped protect dozens of students during the Sandy Hook massacre describes a moment a week later when she stopped at a Starbucks on the way to a funeral. She says she cried as she saw the staff ". . . at Starbucks were wearing our school colors, green and white, in honor of Sandy Hook Elementary School. It took me half a day to realize those were their regular uniforms."

The residual memories and reminders of trauma stay with us for a lifetime. A survivor shot through the hand at New River Community College in 2013, worries the effects of her injury will prevent her from holding her newborn son's bottle: "Now, five and a half years later, I'm sitting on my bed. It's 1:00 a.m. and I'm staring at our new baby. A boy. He doesn't know it yet, but his life is already affected by gun violence. Specifically, school shootings."

Even after decades, survivors struggle with how vulnerable they are and how their priorities are different from those of peers who do not share their traumatic experience. A parent who lost a child at Sandy Hook sits in frustration through a PTA meeting when others are arguing about the distribution of donations, and she finally can't stop herself from shouting out, "At least you have your children!" The sister of a victim killed at Virginia Tech wrestles with deactivating her dead brother's cell phone, "Not more than eight weeks following your murder, we received a letter addressed to you stating that your cell phone service was going to be deactivated because of your death. . . . Your cell phone recording was all we had left of your voice. I pay ten dollars extra each month to keep your account active. I'd pay anything to hear your voice."

In addition to this painful frustration about never again fitting into society if you are a trauma survivor, there is a hopeful theme that emerges from these narratives. A decade after her younger brother had been killed at Sandy Hook, his teenage sister says that "seeing my dad work for gun violence prevention for so long and so tirelessly is amazingly inspiring to me and makes me proud to be part of this family. My parents showed me that when things are wrong you stand up and fix them because it's what absolutely needs to be done." What we hear in the more recent voices of the contributors to this book is an escalating, more political and hopeful response to the long-term effects of trauma. What half a century ago were viewed by society and survivors themselves as "accidents or private mental health problems" that individuals and institutions should best deal with in silence, is now being redefined as a public health disaster that demands an outspoken narrative, political organizing, and social action. The survivors, with the help of family members, progressive political leaders, and the communication power of the Internet, are leading this redefinition of the problem and, in so doing, are fostering social change while also finding important communal ways to heal.

Today survivors from different shootings, across the country and across the past fifty years, are connecting with each other through groups like The Rebels Project (Columbine Rebels), Columbine Memorial, Sandy Hook Promise, Survivors Empowered (Aurora Theater shooting), Koshka Foundation (Virginia Tech), March for Our Lives (Parkland), Safe and Sound Schools (Sandy Hook), Swim for Nick (Parkland), and Everytown for Gun Safety (Sandy Hook). The March for Our Lives movement, with leadership from Parkland survivors and their families, organized a student-led demonstration in support of tighter gun control that took place on March 24, 2018. Two hundred thousand people marched in Washington, D.C., alone, and there were over eight hundred similar events occurring throughout the United States and around the world on the same day. In September 2018, March for Our Lives organizers began focusing on the midterm elections and broadcast the following banner on their website to millions:

VOTE FOR OUR LIVES!

Now is the time for the youth vote to stand up to the gun lobby
when no one else will.

On November 6th, we can elect morally just leaders who will
help us end gun violence in the U.S.

On November 6th, we can change the country.

November 6: Save the date, save America.

We learn from these personal reflections that trauma is not just an event that takes place some time in the past. It is the imprint left by that experience on our brain, body, and relationships for years and perhaps generations. The survivors teach us that both private and public remedies are needed to cope with their traumatic stress. To feel that you are not alone is the first and most basic step in healing. They discuss how family support and clinical help can be useful in the immediate aftermath of such terrifying experiences and that there is no "right" way to cope with trauma. They eloquently express how important it is to form lasting connections with other survivors and build a capacity to manage dark memories and unsettling symptoms that can recur unexpectedly throughout their lives. As many of the survivors are now adults and some parents them-selves, finding positive meaning in the public tragedies they experienced is the biggest challenge they face.

It has been a unique personal experience for me to hear the voices of a new generation of survivors of public school shootings—who, no longer isolated from each other and much more socially conscious, no longer see the rampage of gun violence in America as a private problem to quietly manage, but rather as a public epidemic that demands a public response—and most importantly, they believe they can lead this public response with proud flags waving. I am of an "older generation" of school shooting survivors. My best childhood friend, Paul Sonntag, and his girlfriend, Claudia Rutt, were killed on August 1, 1966, during what we now know was the first incident of public school shootings in the mod-ern era at the University of Texas at Austin. Paul, Claudia, and I were eighteen years old that summer, and thought we would be heading off to college in just a few weeks. The story of how this inexplicable loss as a teenager haunted me throughout adulthood, and the important connection I maintained with the Sonntag family for many years is told in the Foreword to *Tower Sniper: The Terror of America's First Active Shooter on Campus*.[1] That Foreword, "Sanctuary of Time," is available in full in this book's digital archive. I'm now much more conscious of the importance of grieving my loss of Paul and Claudia with others and sharing my experience with those who are interested. I know I must be involved in progressive political action and support candidates who will legislate gun control and other policies to stop or slow down this epidemic of public shootings. In writing my reflections on the Texas tragedy, I returned to the people, memories, and places of fifty years ago in Austin where I grew up. I learned that I wasn't the only one whose internal life had been shadowed by the legacy of that traumatic day. Far from it. It seems only common sense, but if I can stay connected to those who share these horrific experiences with me and listen to the voices of the brave generation of survivors you are about to hear in this book, none of us need pass this way so alone. The fearless narratives in *If I Don't Make It, I Love You* teach us how to endure the trauma of life, and in a certain way, help us find a sense of hope for the future of our country.

ROGER S. FRIEDMAN, PhD
SILVER SPRING, MARYLAND
NOVEMBER 2018

CHAPTER ONE

SANTA FE HIGH SCHOOL

Santa Fe, Texas / May 18, 2018

WE BEGAN COLLECTING narratives and reaching out to survivors in early February 2018. We were already working on this project when we received news of the shooting at Santa Fe. It was quickly reported that there were ten dead and another dozen injured, all at the hands of a seventeen-year-old student. I remember the texts back and forth between Loren and myself, more victims, more trauma, more hurt, more loss, more anger. The weight of this project already felt so heavy, how could we as a nation possibly carry any more heft?

We were careful with the Santa Fe community. At first, we debated on even including the chapter. *They need time to grieve, to mourn, to be alone,* we thought. Then, I noticed a mother being very vocal on Twitter about the shooting and the death of her fourteen-year-old daughter, Kimberly. I followed Rhonda Hart and watched as she mourned her daughter Kim. After a few months, I reached out to Rhonda, and while she was hesitant to write for us, she did agree to let me build a visual story through her Twitter feed.

I spent two solid weeks in October reading five months of tweets. Rhonda had tweeted at least two or three times a day, leaving me with hundreds of options for a story. I knew I had to start with Rhonda's very first tweet posted only two days after the shooting. It read: *Kimberly was murdered on Friday at school. This IS her mother.* I thought about my own twin daughters, twelve years old now, only two years younger than Kimberly. In so many ways, my own story began when I became their mother. And I will never not be their mother. It seemed fitting to start Rhonda's story with her reassertion of motherhood. She still IS Kimberly's mother. She will always be.

I learned so much about Kimberly from her mother's Twitter feed. She was an avid Harry Potter fan, even attending a Harry Potter summer camp. She was a proud Girl Scout and loved her little brother. In every way, she was my daughter, your daughter, our daughter. I knew once I found the beginning that I would have to find the end, and I went about it reluctantly. I didn't want Kimberly's story to end, in any way. But when I found the end, I knew it. In her tweet dated August 16th, three months after the death of her daughter, Rhonda tweeted a picture of a memorial cross with Kimberly's name on it. The makeshift crosses had been decorated to honor the victims; there were ten of them. Under the cross, Rhonda wrote:

REMEMBER THIS WHEN YOU VOTE.

AMYE ARCHER, EDITOR
NOVEMBER 2018

The following students and staff were shot and killed at Santa Fe High School:

Jared Conard Black, 17, student

Shana Fisher, 16, student

Christian Riley Garcia, 15, student

Aaron Kyle McLeod, 15, student

Glenda Anne Perkins, 64, teacher

Angelique Ramirez, 15, student

Sabika Sheikh, 17, exchange student from Pakistan

Christopher Stone, 17, student

Cynthia Tisdale, 63, teacher

Kimberly Vaughan, 14, student

ALWAYS CHOOSE LOVE: A MOTHER'S HEARTBREAK IN TWEETS

by Rhonda Hart and Amye Archer, Editor

Rhonda Hart's fourteen-year-old daughter, Kimberly, was murdered in her art class at Santa Fe High School. The following story was curated from Rhonda's Twitter feed by Amye Archer, editor.

Rhonda Hart 🤟
@KimsMom3

Following

Kimberly was murdered on Friday at school. This IS her mother.

8:09 PM - 20 May 2018

18 Retweets **133** Likes

💬 8   🔁 18   ♡ 133   ✉

Rhonda Hart
@KimsMom3

Following

I have to meet with a pastor today to talk about my daughter's funeral. I shouldn't have to do this. #fightforkim #KJV #onein10 #GunControl @realDonaldTrump how are you going to prevent more school shootings? We want to know?

7:37 AM - 24 May 2018

40 Retweets **219** Likes

💬 14   🔁 40   ♡ 219   ✉

Rhonda Hart
@KimsMom3

Following

My baby should not have a cross this summer. She should have a summer job: A spot at summer camp. @realDonaldTrump what are you going to do about this? #kimberlyjessica #SantaFeStrong #fightforkim

---

Rhonda Hart
@KimsMom3

Following

@tedcruz I wish you could have heard the wails of the families when they announced that our babies had been murdered on May 18th. Maybe then you'd think twice about taking money from the NRA. #ENOUGH #kimberlyjessica #KJV #SantaFeHighSchool

11:22 PM - 2 Jun 2018

10 Retweets **35** Likes

💬 2   🔁 10   ♡ 35   ✉

3:42 PM - 24 May 2018

Rhonda Hart @KimsMom3 · Following

I was in high school when Columbine happened. My own school had to evacuated because of bomb threats. Now 20 YEARS LATER school shootings are still a THING and my daughter is dead. #EnoughIsEnough #kimberlyjessica #GunControlNow

6:12 AM · 11 Jun 2018

8,135 Retweets 28,827 Likes

410 · 8.1K · 29K

Rhonda Hart @KimsMom3 · Following

I read Kim's death certificate today. Cause of death: multiple gun shot wounds. Time of death: 7:45 am. Age at time of death:14. She was ONLY 14. Never got her first kiss, never learned to drive. Never went to prom. #EnoughIsEnough #kimberlyjessica

9:55 PM · 15 Jun 2018

5,361 Retweets 18,345 Likes

740 · 5.4K · 18K

Rhonda Hart @KimsMom3 · Following

This sweet girl will never get to play in the snow again. #kimberlyjessica #EnoughIsEnough #GunControl

10:04 PM · 15 Jun 2018

Rhonda Hart @KimsMom3 · Following

Dropping her off at summer camp a few years ago. This was horse camp. I'm sure camp lasts all summer in heaven and they never run out of s'mores. #EnoughIsEnough #kimberlyjessica #SantaFeSchoolShooting #GunControlNow

8:12 AM · 16 Jun 2018

Rhonda Hart @KimsMom3 · Following

30 days and 3 hours since my baby left this world. Kimberly Vaughan was MURDERED in her art class on May 18, 2018. She passed away from MULTIPLE gun shot wounds at 7:45 AM. This CAN NOT continue to happen. #gunsafetyNOW #kimberlyjessica #KJV #SF10

10:48 AM · 18 Jun 2018

177 Retweets 693 Likes

29 · 177 · 693

Rhonda Hart @KimsMom3 · Following

Part of me thinks she's still at camp. Part of me knows she's gone. #EnoughIsEnough #kimberlyjessica #SantaFeHighSchool End gun violence now.

10:16 PM · 16 Jun 2018

68 Retweets 612 Likes

27 · 68 · 612

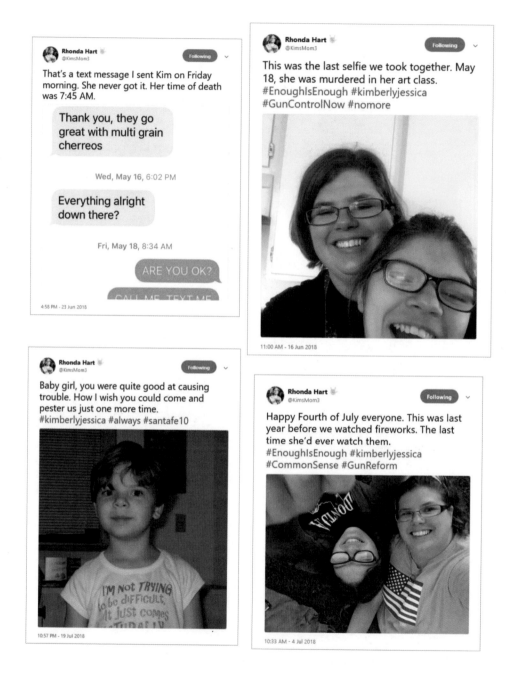

Rhonda Hart
@KimsMom3
Following

That's a text message I sent Kim on Friday morning. She never got it. Her time of death was 7:45 AM.

Thank you, they go great with multi grain cherreos

Wed, May 16, 6:02 PM

Everything alright down there?

Fri, May 18, 8:34 AM

ARE YOU OK?

CALL ME TEXT ME

4:58 PM · 23 Jun 2018

Rhonda Hart
@KimsMom3
Following

This was the last selfie we took together. May 18, she was murdered in her art class. #EnoughIsEnough #kimberlyjessica #GunControlNow #nomore

11:00 AM · 16 Jun 2018

Rhonda Hart
@KimsMom3
Following

Baby girl, you were quite good at causing trouble. How I wish you could come and pester us just one more time. #kimberlyjessica #always #santafe10

I'M NOT TRYING to be difficult, it just comes NATURALLY

10:57 PM · 19 Jul 2018

Rhonda Hart
@KimsMom3
Following

Happy Fourth of July everyone. This was last year before we watched fireworks. The last time she'd ever watch them. #EnoughIsEnough #kimberlyjessica #CommonSense #GunReform

10:33 AM · 4 Jul 2018

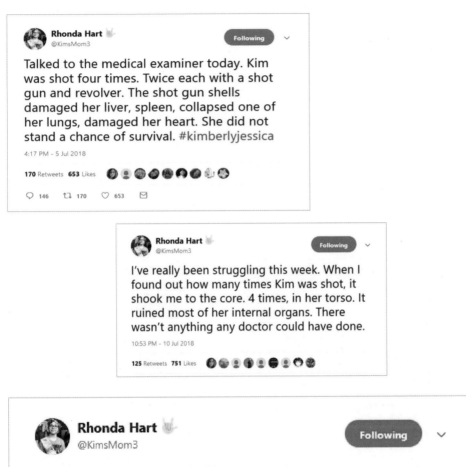

Rhonda Hart
@KimsMom3
Following

Talked to the medical examiner today. Kim was shot four times. Twice each with a shot gun and revolver. The shot gun shells damaged her liver, spleen, collapsed one of her lungs, damaged her heart. She did not stand a chance of survival. #kimberlyjessica

4:17 PM - 5 Jul 2018

170 Retweets 653 Likes

146   170   653

Rhonda Hart
@KimsMom3
Following

I've really been struggling this week. When I found out how many times Kim was shot, it shook me to the core. 4 times, in her torso. It ruined most of her internal organs. There wasn't anything any doctor could have done.

10:53 PM - 10 Jul 2018

125 Retweets 751 Likes

Rhonda Hart
@KimsMom3
Following

And I sit here and think: "it doesn't even take that many shots to kill an animal." That physco ruined my baby's perfect body. He stopped her heart. I could not donate any of her organs, there was nothing left.

10:54 PM - 10 Jul 2018

35 Retweets 216 Likes

Rhonda Hart
@KimsMom3

Following

Today is Kimberly's birthday. She would have been 15. On May 18, 2018 she was in the art class at Santa Fe high school. She was shot four times. She passed away almost instantly.

Please remember Kimberly today and do a good deed. #kimberlyjessica

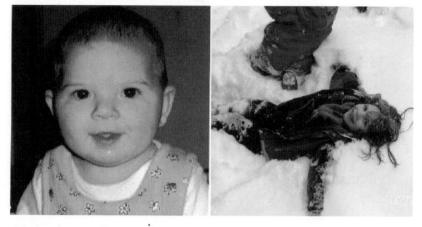

8:38 AM - 12 Aug 2018

Replying to @estababyy

It comes and goes. Yesterday was lots of ugly tears for me. No idea why. Better cry them out than keep them in. 🩶

10:43 PM - 20 Jul 2018

Rhonda Hart
@KimsMom3
Following

REMEMBER THIS WHEN YOU VOTE.

1:52 PM - 16 Aug 2018

JOURNAL IN THREE PARTS
By Bree Butler

Bree Butler was a senior at the time of the Santa Fe shooting.

1.

I hated living in a small town. Never having anything to do on the weekends, the closed-minded and small pool of people to choose friends from once aggravated me. I constantly made fun of the culture and the locals, trashing it and expressing my discontent every chance I got. On May 18, 2018, that changed. I don't feel this way anymore. I want home to remain.

2.

*I would do anything to get the days back: the cheerleaders line dancing to Copperhead Road before the Friday night football game; the dress up days, making myself look like a fool just for the sake of approval of my Student Council teacher. I would do anything to get back knowing everyone's face as I passed them by in the hallway. I don't get **that** anymore. Don't see those familiar faces. I may have spent my whole life disliking Santa Fe, Texas, but that's all changed. This tragedy made me appreciate the everyday Santa Fe I never did.*

3.

Today these thoughts again. I never thought I'd miss this little town, yet here I am, six months later and six hours away in a small car. I'm reminiscing on the small things I never appreciated before. I think about the line dancing again. I think about the faces in the hallway again. I want to go back to my school before the shooting. I want to relive those days somehow.

I wish I could stand beneath the glorious Friday-night lights. But it's all different there. I understand that. I wish I could appreciate the good times before they were taken without any warning.

CHAPTER TWO

GREAT MILLS HIGH SCHOOL

Great Mills, Maryland / March 20, 2018

IN THE WEEKS that followed the shooting in Parkland, Florida, it became clear that something was happening among students in America's high schools. Tired of being shot at, tired of watching their friends die, and tired of being afraid, young people were speaking up and using social media to shine a brighter light on the issue of school shootings. This was also the case at Great Mills High School in St. Mary's County, Maryland, where dozens of students were joining the movement to end gun violence. There was a walkout on the one month anniversary of Parkland, and several students were joining the movement on a national scale. Then, tragically, Great Mills became the site of a school shooting only days later.

This story was slightly different from the others. While it lacked the terrifying designation of "random," it was equally as horrific in its familiarity. A seventeen-year-old student used his father's gun to shoot and kill sixteen-year-old Jaelynn Willey, a young, bright girl who was also the ex-girlfriend of the shooter. When news broke, I panicked. I have two daughters, and I remember thinking *it's hard enough raising girls in this world, now we have to worry about this?* I was also painfully aware of the privilege in that statement, as there are so many communities in which mothers have been worrying about losing children to gun violence for decades.

Still, as a mother of girls, researching twenty school shootings and the boys behind them has taken a toll. When my daughter wanted to break up with her boyfriend a few months back, I was a nervous wreck, I advised her to go easy. *Don't hurt him*, I thought to myself, *he might hurt you back.* She was eleven. Teenagers hurt one another. It's inevitable. Girls break hearts, boys break hearts. How does it end up like *this*?

The new culture of activism was obvious when we started this project. Connecting with those who had lived through some of the earlier shootings

14

had proven difficult, but with Great Mills, we were easily able to connect with Mollie Davis, a student who has become an important voice in the March for Our Lives movement. In Mollie's story, we see the transmutation of the life of the American teenager from carefree and innocent to terrified and hunted. A change I am acutely aware of as I navigate the teen years with my own daughters.

AMYE ARCHER, EDITOR
DECEMBER 2018

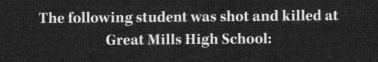

The following student was shot and killed at Great Mills High School:

Jaelynn Willey, 16

A DAY IN THE LIFE OF AN AMERICAN HIGH SCHOOL STUDENT

By Mollie Davis

Mollie Davis was seventeen years old at the time of the shooting.

That day comes in flashes of memory:

A boy runs by my math class so fast he is a blur of a human. I tell myself he's running to get away from a fight. Learning later that he was running for his life, shakes me to my core. I see him in my head everytime I look out the door of my math class.

Two people from my class running into the hall to see what's going on.

My friend texts—they heard someone had a gun and to get in a classroom.

The two students who just left come running back in, saying people are fleeing and something about a gun.

There is some talk of a balloon pop, a sound I realize I had heard, causing mass hysteria. I get a sinking feeling, but I push it aside. I still think this whole thing is a joke or some sort of misunderstanding. I text my parents, angry that someone is causing so much panic as a sick joke. As I do, I hear the voice of a teacher from the hallway yelling at everyone to get in their classes. This normally happens after fights, no biggie.

Then, the urgency.

Two minutes later, the voice of our principal over the intercom informing us there is no immediate threat, but to go on lockdown. I hear a slight panic in his voice. The sinking feeling comes back, and I shove it aside again. This can't happen to us, not my school.

My class does not fully lock down. Many of the classrooms downstairs do, but upstairs is a different story as we're farther away. We lock the door, but leave the lights on and stay at our desks. We talk among ourselves, and I text my group-chat of friends, all of us trying to piece together what we know. One of my friends downstairs says she can hear people yelling about victims and while at this point I knew rationally something had happened, I was in shock and still did not genuinely believe it.

News articles with confirmed police reports start to emerge on social media and we pass them around the classroom, all of us stare at the screen, stunned.

Time is fuzzy, I can't recall exactly how or when things happened, they just seem to happen all at once. Time still hasn't gone back to normal. At some point, before the police get to us, reports are that seven people have been shot dead. While this would later prove untrue, seeing that number makes it all real. I start to cry.

A friend messages me asking if I've seen Jaelynn because her mom hadn't heard from her, I haven't, and little do I know, I never will again.

At some point, I'm in the corner charging my phone when heavy footsteps approach. The police come into our classroom with guns pointed telling us to put our hands up. My warm cell phone in my left hand falls to the floor, I pray it doesn't shatter. They tell us that it's over and that we'll be leaving soon. They leave again.

After some time, they return and tell us that we're evacuating to another high school. My teacher quips with them about wanting to "just go home from here," and asks if we can use the bathroom. They walk us to the bathroom and back and tell us to hold tight because they'll be back for us. After what seems like days of reading news article after news article and texting loved one after loved one telling them I'm alive, the police return for the last time to escort us out.

Before we leave the room, they line us up against the counter to pat us down. I am shaky and have a little trouble following directions, which causes me to laugh out loud. I want to scold myself for laughing in that situation, but I didn't know what else to do. Shock is weird.

We are told to leave everything behind except the valuables we can carry in our hands like our chargers and phones. Just before we go downstairs, I realize I left my glasses behind and my teacher convinces the police to let him get them. We start to make our way downstairs and to the back exit in the cafeteria to the buses.

Down the long hallway to the cafeteria, we pass classrooms doors with ALL CLEAR written on them in big black marker.

Police line the hallways with long guns and block us from seeing where the shooting happened. Now everytime I walk this hallway I feel like a zombie. This happened. Here. At my school. My school isn't safe anymore.

On the bus to the reunification center, I'm crammed against a window in a seat with two other people. I stare out at all the police vehicles, at the people on the streets who've come out of their houses to stare. I want to scream, but I can't do anything but sob.

At the center, there is a sign-in sheet, someone asking me for my name. My hands shake so hard my name is near unreadable. Apparently, this is part of why it took so long for my dad to get to me.

We're shuffled into a conference room full of people and I realize that we are the last bus. There are no survivors coming later. I spot my friend Carolyn and step around people and chairs to get to her as fast as I can. I hug her like my life depends on it. We sit down and I stare into the crowded room. Some people are so chill it's like nothing happened. Some are a total wreck. I see a teacher with tears streaming down his face.

For hours I stare the wall some more, eat pizza, and charge my phone before being picked up by my dad. We walk the equivalent of a city block in the rain back to his truck. I talk to a reporter briefly, and we head home. Halfway home, my chest starts hurting so bad I can't sit up straight and when I get home after I hug my mom, I more or less drag myself upstairs and into the shower. I stare at the wall and almost burn myself with scalding hot water for forty-five minutes before getting out and putting a new outfit on.

When I tried to wear that sweatshirt again over a month later my back broke out in hives, like my body was rejecting it.

In the end, two people were shot at my school that day. Desmond Barnes, only fourteen, was shot in the leg and has survived his injuries. Jaelynn Wiley was only sixteen and is dead. She will never graduate, never have another summer break, never attend college. I didn't know Jaelynn well, but I knew some of her friends and got to know more of her friends and family after the shooting. If love alone could have saved her, I know it would have.

CHAPTER THREE

MARJORY STONEMAN DOUGLAS HIGH SCHOOL

Parkland, Florida / February 14, 2018

ON SEPTEMBER 11, 2018, I left my office to get comfortable in my car. Inside, I made final notes in preparation for my interview with Lori Alhadeff, whose daughter, Alyssa, was killed at the Marjory Stoneman Douglas High School (MSD) shooting on February 14, 2018. Like many interviews I've had with parents whose children were murdered during a school shooting, my anxiety levels reach an all-time high, breaking out in fiery red hives across my chest.

At first, my interview with Lori began with hope. She told me that while Alyssa wasn't looking forward to Valentine's Day, she lit up when Lori gave her a gold bag with a *pair of diamond earrings and a chocolate bar* inside. *I gave Alyssa the present, and she was excited. I told Alyssa I loved her.* But then, the air changes. *That would be the last time I'd ever see Alyssa alive.* I try hard to hold back the tears. And in that moment, I want her story to be about something else like Alyssa's soccer match or her love of the ocean. *I want* Lori to stop me on the phone because Alyssa has interrupted her. Nothing can be *this* true. Nothing can be *this* final. But it is like so many of the Parkland stories we collected.

Lori described, at length, how her daughter looked on the cadaver gurney in the morgue. I cried as she described her daughter's bullet wounds, her long brown hair, and cold skin. *I'm so sorry. I don't know what to say,* I said. *It's okay,* she replied. *You don't have to say anything.*

I called Amye immediately after hanging up with Lori. I told her I wasn't sure I had the stomach to transcribe that interview. I was being ridiculous, maybe. But she reassured me I wasn't *ridiculous at all,* and said she felt the same way after interviewing Susie, a mother whose daughter watched her teacher get killed at Sandy Hook. *Take your time with this,* she said. *Return to it when you're ready. I'm doing the same with Susie. Or I can do it for you, and you can transcribe my interview with Susie.* We knew how to hold one another's pain when the weight of these stories became too much.

About an hour after hanging up with Lori, she sent me photos of Alyssa to use in the book. I stared at Alyssa's soccer picture for two days. Her low pony-tail draped over her shoulder. Her eyes smiling across her face. She is a bright star in this darkness. There was no way she was dead. Later in the week I wonder if she had the chance to try on the diamond earrings her mother gave to her? Or taste the chocolate from inside the gold gift bag?

It was days like these that, like Amye, I yearned for this project's conclusion. I often told her, *as much as I love this book, and as much as I feel this is what I was meant to do, I welcome its ending.* And with this statement came intense guilt. Amye and I recognized the privilege in those statements. For Lori and many of the parents whose children were killed at Parkland, they can't walk away. They have to live without their children for the rest of their lives. And it's not fair.

And while I've never met Alyssa, I miss her. I pray one day when I visit Israel, I meet her on top Masada, the holy rock where she was Bat Mitzvahed. I hope we can stand together, close to God, and that she is happy in Shamayim (םַיָמַשׁ), wearing her diamond earrings and eating her chocolate in the heavens.

LOREN KLEINMAN, EDITOR
JANUARY 2019

The following students and staff were shot and killed at Marjory Stoneman Douglas High School:

Alyssa Alhadeff, 14, student

Scott Beigel, 35, teacher

Martin Duque, 14, student

Nicholas Dworet, 17, student

Aaron Feis, 37, assistant football coach and security guard

Jaime Guttenberg, 14, student

Chris Hixon, 49, athletic director

Luke Hoyer, 15, student

Cara Loughran, 14, student

Gina Montalto, 14, student

Joaquin Oliver, 17, student

Alaina Petty, 14, student

Meadow Pollack, 18, student

Helena Ramsay, 17, student

Alex Schachter, 14, student

Carmen Schentrup, 16, student

Peter Wang, 15, student

HERE'S THE FUNNY THING ABOUT TRAGEDY: IT NEVER REALLY GOES AWAY

By Rachel Bean

Rachel Bean graduated from Marjory Stoneman Douglas High School in Parkland, Florida, in spring 2017, one year before the shooting on February 14, 2018. She was a freshman college student at University of Central Florida at the time of the shooting

On February 14, 2018, I was working in the Digital Services department at the University of Central Florida's (UCF) library. My office was small; there were only five of us that handled the old documents and books that needed to be transferred to computers, a type of job that twists and bends the past and present.

While I was working, my supervisor, Page, told me there was another school shooting at a high school in Parkland, Florida. My heart dropped to my stomach, and a layer of frost crept up spine. I knew it was my high school because there's only one in Parkland, and it was Marjory Stoneman Douglas High School (MSD). I graduated in the spring of 2017, one year before. After I heard the news, I turned to the massive twenty-four-hour news sites as well as local and national news. As I read and watched the news, I remained calm. I'd been trained for an active shooter situation, as had the entire staff at MSD, so they'd know what to do. They also had an armed officer on campus, multiple security guards, and a camera. Everything would be okay, but an hour into the news coverage, I realized I was wrong.

I called one of my closest friends, Olivia Sands. We went through K–12 together and ended up at the same college. She lived across the street from me our entire lives, and her brother was a freshman at MSD. Olivia and I shared vigil at our computer screens. She kept calling and calling her brother who couldn't or wouldn't pick up the phone. I went into overdrive: texted my friends who were still in the school, texted relatives of those friends. I hoped and prayed to hear something, anything. While I waited, I also texted my teachers who I'd grown so close to over my four years at MSD: Teachers who were mentors and who I even considered my surrogate parents were now in danger.

Life stalled. Olivia and I kept hearing the same information over and over again, not getting anything of substance. Watching the news wasn't helping. So, I did the only thing I could think of at the moment: I continued to work. Olivia left our computer vigil to be with her boyfriend, and I kept scanning documents and old books for the next two hours trying to keep my eye off the news reports until my shift was over.

At work, my colleagues expressed their concern for me, but I disregarded their offers to listen or to support me. There was no use getting worked up over something I couldn't do anything about. I was helpless, and that scared me.

After work, I sat on a hard stone bench outside the library and pulled out my phone. I saw the video from inside the school. Bodies on the ground covered in blood. There were sounds of gunshots going off, which were recorded in a classroom that I had spent time in.

Then, I started to cry.

Grief churned from the pit of my stomach and rose through my throat—it was like bile, bitter and harsh. I couldn't make a sound. How could I? A couple of my friends who I had met at university found me on that park bench. They didn't say anything. I didn't say anything. They heard what happened. Nothing they could say would make the shooting better. They helped me back to my dorm because my legs felt too weak to stand.

I called my brothers, who had also attended Douglas with

me. We're triplets, and we all shared the same grade. One picked up the phone. One didn't. Both later admitted they didn't know what they could say that would help. Neither did I.

Back in my dorm room, alone with my thoughts, I felt rage bubble up within me. I grabbed my cell phone, turned on the camera, and started talking. I talked about gun violence. I talked about how someone went to my school and shot my friends and peers. I talked for nearly seven minutes. Without thinking, I posted it and called it "My high school was shot up today."

Within minutes I received thousands of views, and many hateful comments. In fact, I had more negative comments than supportive. People were calling me a traitor, a liar, an actor, paid by the government to lie to support an agenda. I disabled the comments.

I slept for the next two days, unable to attend class or eat. That weekend I got drunk for the first time, hoping to forget. But the next day I woke up, and life was still the same. My first thought was that I needed to go home. I needed to get a bus ticket down to South Florida to be with my family, to be there for my community and my friends, but I couldn't. My parents didn't want me to come home, midterm exams were coming up, and I couldn't afford to miss classes. So, I stayed in Orlando.

The UCF community hosted a vigil. The speeches lasted an hour; I stayed for three, with Olivia at my side, her brother alive and well, but traumatized. They had posted pictures of the victims. People I knew, people I had known: Coach Feis, who always stopped me from making left turns out of the senior parking lot, but sometimes let me out early if I was skipping class; Nicholas Dworet, who I sometimes saw at the local pool, swimming; and Helena Ramsay, who I met in elementary school and played pretend games with; imagining us as superheroes who could defeat any monster we came across on the playground.

I came home for one weekend in March. There were only a few news vans left at that point. And as the media faded, I continued my life in Parkland: went around town running errands, visited local shops I loved as a high schooler. I couldn't drive ten feet without seeing a banner of support, or a decal on someone's car, or red and orange ribbons attached to trees, fluttering in the wind.

Today, the high school looks like a prison. The building where the shooting happened is boarded up, fenced in, and a police car is stationed outside the doors to keep people out. And when I drive on the highway, past the school, no matter whom I'm with (family or friends), words fail me. Silence fills the car, and we reflect on our tragedy.

In some ways, I felt and still feel incredibly guilty for not going home right after I heard the news to be with my friends and family. My guilt even extended to a school project I did in high school. I had always had an interest in school shootings. Call it morbid curiosity. I read books on Sandy Hook and Columbine; I watched documentaries on Virginia Tech and studied the timeline of the Pulse shooting. And in my junior year, I made my documentary on school shootings with my friend Daniel from my film class, for the C-SPAN StudentCam documentary contest. I interviewed the mayor of Parkland, the congressman at the time, and I talked my film teacher Eric Garner, who was later credited for keeping nearly sixty-five students safe and calm during the shooting. I took video of students going about their day in the high school, in the building where the shooting eventually happened. Daniel and I won an honorable mention that year for our documentary, never realizing that one day our own school would be victim to a shooting. I mean what were the chances? I can't help but wonder that maybe, in that documentary, I should've pointed out security flaws. Maybe I should've done more research on safety protocols. I could've done more. I should've done more. I didn't.

I went to the 2018 MSD prom with a friend who invited me, but rather than having fun, I struggled with sadness and remorse. I cried in the bathroom that night. Why was I able to go to such a beautiful event when so many others would never get to go? Life was unfair and cruel.

I even got to attend graduation and watched my surviving friends graduate. But why did I have to refer to them as *surviving friends*?

I wasn't directly involved in the shooting. I wasn't in the classrooms, and I didn't have any family there, so who was I to feel sad? Who was I to flinch at loud noises? I ask myself a lot of those questions now.

I didn't want to be defined by the shooting. I didn't want my town to be defined by the shooting. So, I joined March for Our Lives in D.C. I participated in the die-in at Publix, and I joined the MSD alumni group.

Life is different now. Whenever I go anywhere like the movies or to the store, I look for exits, places to hide, and weapons I can use to fight back with in case of an active shooter. I can't wear my class T-shirt without getting sympathetic looks from strangers on the street. I can't say I went to Stoneman Douglas without someone asking about the shooting. That's what we're known for now, that's what we're all known for, and that's who we are: a town, a city, a family, students, and peers—torn apart by a massacre.

Maybe that's all we'll ever be.

A CONVERSATION WITH LORI ALHADEFF

Lori Alhadeff's daughter, Alyssa, was killed at the Marjory Stoneman Douglas High School (MSD) shooting. Alhadeff is the founder of Make Our Schools Safe and the Dream Team. Learn more about the Dream Team at makeourschoolssafe.org/dream-team. The following is an excerpt of the conversation between Lori and Loren Kleinman, editor, which took place on September 11, 2018.

LORI: The morning started off as Valentine's Day, a day that was supposed to be about love, and I knew that Alyssa was not looking forward to this day, because she's, you know, a typical teenager, she wanted someone to love her as her Valentine. So, I knew that, and I bought Alyssa a present. In a gold bag, I put a pair of diamond earrings, a chocolate bar, and I put it in this gold bag, and that morning, when I drove Alyssa to school about 7:15 in the morning, I gave Alyssa the present, and she was excited.

We drove to pick up another [kid], a boy, that I drove every morning, and I got out of the car, and I put the earrings on Alyssa. Then we proceeded to the school. Then, we stopped at a light, and I opened the door, and Alyssa had got out, and as she got out of the car, I told Alyssa I loved her. That would be the last time I'd ever see Alyssa alive.

My day proceeded, and it was about 2:10 in the afternoon, I received a text message from my friend, and it said, "Shots fired at Stoneman Douglas High School, kids running and jumping the fence." Immediately, when I received that message, I had this overwhelming sense of loss that came over my body. I quickly put my shoes on, and I went into my car, and drove as fast as I could to the school. I was only able to go so far because there was traffic. I parked my car up on a sidewalk, and I started running toward the school. There was this yellow tape going across, and I had to stop. There were all these people standing around, and kind of looking at each other. No one knew what to think.

A couple of minutes later, Alyssa's best friend Abby came up to me, and I remember looking at Abby, and then looking at the space next to her. They were like twins, inseparable.

I looked back at Abby, and said, "[Where's] Alyssa?"

"I don't know," she said.

So, a few minutes later, Abby received a text message, and that's when I found out the worst news of my life. Somebody told Abby that Alyssa was shot. I fell to my knees and started screaming: "Why? No, not Alyssa."

I got up and ran toward the school. I was stopped by a big police officer with a gun in his hand, and he pushed me back. I told him my daughter was shot.

I asked him, "Where would she go? Where would they take her?"

He said, "The hospital."

So, a police officer started running with me. He said he'll take me to the hospital. I started running, and he was running slower than me. I could feel him keeping up with me. He put me in the back of his car, and I can remember feeling like I was the victim. The seats were very cold, and the air was very hot around me. He took me to what was called the Command Center at the Marriott in Parkland. I can remember being the only one there. It wasn't even set up yet.

We run inside, and we tried calling the hospital. Then, I decided to go to one of the hospitals, and I told my parents and my husband to go to one hospital, and I texted, or I put on Facebook, for people to look at Coral Springs Hospital.

I ended up going with a stranger in a car who said he'd take me to the hospital. We ended up getting to the light, but I wanted to get a police escort because I knew it would be faster. I got out of the car, then went into the police car, and he drove to the hospital. When we got there, we went into the ER, and I can remember running into one of the rooms, because I thought I saw Alyssa. There was a girl that looked like her, but it wasn't.

Then, we were speaking to the doctors, and trying to figure out if Alyssa was in one of the rooms. Then they said she could be a Jane Doe in the OR. So, I ended up going back with the police officer. We went back to the Command Center, and this time there were hundreds of people.

They took people that couldn't find their loved ones to a section of the Marriott, and then they took us into a mini room. . . . Nobody knew anything.

I remember going into the bathroom and screaming because I knew my daughter Alyssa. She was the type of kid that would be able to find me in a second. She knows my phone number She would've borrowed someone's phone. I knew time was passing and it wasn't looking good. At 10:00 p.m. our rabbi was there, and I told him he needs to start planning the funeral arrangements for Alyssa, and he said okay.

It was about 2:00 a.m. when someone finally called us into the room, and they told me something bad happened. They didn't want to say it in front of me. They only wanted to tell my husband. I said, "No. Tell me." He said that Alyssa was shot in the face, so she was unrecognizable. It turned out to be a lie. We left there that night and the next morning I went to the Everglades, the closest place I could think to be with God, and asked him why he took Alyssa. As I left, there was a big gleaming light in the sky. The sun was rising. I went to my mother's house, and I got my mom. I told her that we were going to the medical examiner's office which was forty-five minutes away from Parkland. When I got there, I told them I wanted to see my daughter, and they told me that I couldn't see Alyssa. But they brought me back an 8 × 10 color photo of Alyssa's face, and that's when I knew . . . with 100 percent certainty that Alyssa died.

I left there and went with my husband to the funeral home. We spent two hours planning Alyssa's funeral. When we got to see Alyssa, I touched her and tried to warm her with my hands. She was so cold. I was trying to bring Alyssa back to life. I was looking at the places where she was shot. She was shot ten times: in the heart, in the femoral artery, in the head, and in the hand. She was shot in other places, too. I cut a piece of Alyssa's hair off because I didn't want the killer to take everything from me. I wanted to have something to remember Alyssa by.

I told my husband I wanted to go to the park where they were doing the memorial service for the victims. When I got there, I was angry, and I went up to a reporter, and I told her I had something to say. She brushed her hair off, and said, "Well, we're not on the air." So, I went down the line, and there was another reporter there standing with a microphone, and I told them I had something to say. He handed me the microphone and he said, "We're on in five seconds," and that's when I did my speech about Trump, about what he can do.

EDITOR'S NOTE: View the video of Lori Alhadeff's speech to President Donald Trump: youtu.be/-cmaeYG3EIE

So, the next day, we buried Alyssa, because we're Jewish, and in the Jewish religion you bury in the next day. There was hundreds of people there, and I put my hand on Alyssa's casket as it was being lowered into the ground, and I touched it until the last possible second that I could touch it. As a mother, you birthed your child. You raised your child. When your child dies, it's your job to make sure she's buried.

So, we ended up sitting shiva for Alyssa for seven days at my house . . . I knew to honor my daughter and to be a voice of change. I empowered myself to want to run for school board . . . to have a seat at the table. To have a vote and a voice. So, I ran for the school board and was elected.

LOREN: *What are some of your favorite memories of Alyssa?*

LORI: Alyssa loved the beach. She loved the ocean. She loved riding the waves in the ocean, especially in New Jersey. We used to go to Long Beach Island all the time. So, when she came [to Florida], the waves weren't as big as they are in New Jersey. She'd always try to go to the beach, to Deerfield Beach, any second she got. She loved to hang out with her friends, and she loved boys, and she was social. She was beautiful, and very smart. She already had ten high school credit classes, and she was only a freshman. She was taking high-level classes.

Alyssa had such zest for life. She was always doing all these things. One activity from one to the next, which was great. She played soccer since she was three years old. She played competitively. She was the number eight and wore the eight on her soccer jersey. She played the eighth position. So now I say play for 8 or #playfor8, and when you turn the eight sideways it's the infinity symbol, which means forever. I told Alyssa's friends #liveforAlyssa, #playfor8. I try to empower the kids to say, "Hey, I still have a life, and it's really special, and I can live for Alyssa and do all these things for Alyssa because she can't. Her voice was silenced. We miss her a lot.

. . . Alyssa was Bat Mitzvahed on top of Masada in Israel . . . Alyssa got to be in Israel on top of Masada. [Really] close to God. That was really powerful, and the Jewish community has embraced my family since the tragedy . . . [Everybody] from every faith has been so loving and caring. It's helped us with the healing process and empowered me to be positive, to make sure change happens, that Alyssa's death isn't in vain. That no other child or family has to go through this.

ROOM 1216
By Dara Hass

Dara Hass is an English teacher at Marjory Stoneman Douglas High School. Her classroom was one of the first entered by the gunman. Three of her students were shot, and multiple others injured.

PART ONE:
WRITTEN TWO DAYS AFTER THE SHOOTING

On February 16th, I visited the Channel 10 News website and read the timeline for the Marjory Stoneman Douglas shooting for the first time since the horrific events only two days earlier. My heart sank when I saw the numbers, *1216*, staring back at me. This was my classroom. I am classroom 1216. In my classroom, five of my students were shot multiple times. Many others from my class will have shrapnel souvenirs in their arms, legs, and heads to remember this horror. I lost three sweet, beautiful souls in my classroom that day. I just keep saying to myself this cannot be real.

There are two timelines of the Marjory Stoneman Douglas High School massacre on Wednesday, February 14th. One from Broward Sheriff, Scott Israel, and one from someone who lived it. I apologize if it is too real and understand if you don't read it. Maybe I should not write it. I don't know. I am so sorry if I am in the wrong for writing my timeline of the event. My head is still trying to process it all. I honestly just don't know what to do. I just keep telling my story because I cannot believe it. Soon I will believe it and reality will truly sink in and I may not want to share it again.

2:19 P.M.
UBER DRIVER DROPS OFF NIKOLAS CRUZ AT THE SCHOOL AT 5901 NW PINE ISLAND RD., IN PARKLAND.

2:21 P.M.
CRUZ ENTERED THE EAST STAIRWELL WITH A RIFLE INSIDE A BLACK SOFT CASE. HE EXITED THE STAIRWELL AFTER PULLING THE RIFLE OUT OF THE CASE.

I sent a student out to use the restroom. He said he saw the shooter and the young man told him, "Things are going to get bad" and to get out. The brave student reported it to Coach Aaron Feis. Feis took the student off campus. Feis saved this student. This student saved MSD. Feis went into the 1200 building to investigate the report of a student with a gun. He saw Nicholas Cruz and lost his life protecting students entering the building.

2:21:33 P.M.
CRUZ BEGAN SHOOTING AT CLASSROOMS 1215, 1216, AND 1214.

It happened so fast—there was no warning—we all dropped to the floor and hid. I called 911 and texted to my husband that my students have been shot and to call 911. I hugged the students who did their best to hide under and behind my desk. I communicated nonverbally to the students hiding across the room. These students witnessed three of their classmates and friends lose their lives. Injured students were pulled to safety by their fellow classmates. They barricaded themselves under fallen desks. We sat in silence while the 911 operator told us she was with us and help was on the way. I held back tears and panic as I hugged my students. I knew that if I lost control of my emotions then my students would lose hope.

TIME UNKNOWN
CRUZ RETURNED TO CLASSROOMS 1216 AND 1215, AND THEN TO CLASSROOM 1213.

The 911 operator told us to be quiet and the shooter was coming back. The students and I did not move—perhaps we did not even breathe. I texted goodbye to my parents saying I loved them and thanked them for everything they have done for me. They did not know I was in this horrific moment. I did not want them to know. My mom replied to my message thinking it was a Valentine's Day text with an "I love you too." I also texted good-bye to my husband and said I loved him and that I loved our girls. I hugged my students. I prayed for God to protect us all. Then, I heard shouting outside my door. I saw movement out-side the slender rectangular shattered window on my classroom door. Someone pushed through the shattered glass and an arm went through the window to open the door. In ran law enforce-ment to get us out of the building.

My students were escorted out of my room to safety by the police. I stood up making sure the students were all out. They were not all out. I stood in shock as I stared at the bodies still in my room. I was silent, but my thoughts screamed, "This can't be real! These kids must be okay! Maybe they are unconscious from the shock of their injuries, and they will be okay. Perhaps they will never walk again, but they will be alive. I will push their wheelchairs everyday if I have to! They just have to be okay!" I just stood there, wide-eyed at my precious students lying motionless. The officer walked over to me and wrapped his arm around me gently, leading me out of the classroom to safety. I did not want to leave the students. They needed me. They needed me to comfort them. I wanted to just hold their hands and tell them they would be okay. The voice in my head screamed, "They have to be okay!"

Law enforcement got us out and safe in sixteen minutes. They saved us.

2:29 P.M.
CRUZ TAKES A SOUTHBOUND TURN, CROSSES FIELDS, AND RUNS WEST ALONG WITH OTHERS WHO ARE FLEEING AND TRIES TO MIX IN WITH THE GROUP RUNNING AWAY.

Once out of the building, I felt confused, shocked, and just plain helpless. I was frozen crying in front of the building as I watched students and police run in all directions. Another officer ran over, and he quickly walked me to the safety of the sidewalk. He talked to me and calmed me down. The officers were so kind and gentle as they guided me out. The shooter was still on campus and they needed me to get to safety, yet they still showed their hearts with patience.

Once I reached the sidewalk and was at a safe distance from the building, I began to breathe again. The officer let go of me and said I was safe and to head to the police car barricade. I nodded and wiped the remaining tears from my face. I took a deep breath and began to turn toward the barricade, which consisted of crowds of concerned people surrounding police cars and ambulances. As I took my first step, one of my students came to me covered in blood. I looked into his sweet blue eyes pleading for help. His eyes that were so scared and lost. I said that I would take him to the paramedic and asked him where he was hurt. He looked at me with a mix of sadness and confusion and said I don't know if it is me or my friend. I nodded realizing he was sitting next to two of the students who had been shot. I put my arm around him and led him to medical help. Once I was able to get him to the paramedics, I turned and encountered more injured students who needed my help. Students covered in blood and wounded. These are faces I will never forget.

3:41 P.M.
A COCONUT CREEK POLICE DEPARTMENT OFFICER DETAINS CRUZ AT 4700 WYNDHAM LAKES DRIVE. HE IS POSITIVELY IDENTIFIED AND TAKEN INTO CUSTODY.

I am thankful to be alive and home with my family and friends, but I have a huge heartache for all the lives and innocence lost. I tell myself it all happened so fast and there was no warning, but it does not ease the pain in my heart and the tears in my soul.

I can't sleep and my head hurts. My eyes are swollen from tears. The anger is starting to seep in. Why does this evil happen? Why were these precious lives taken? Three students in my class lost their lives. The rest will live with metallic reminders. My friends and fellow staff members are gone. Those sweet young lives taken for no reason.

I just don't understand, and probably never will. I just pray it ends here and no one will ever have to endure another tragedy like this one.

PART TWO:
WRITTEN TWO MONTHS AFTER THE SHOOTING

It took two weeks for the constant anxiety attacks and crying to fade away, I still have those moments, but not as frequent or intense as I did in February. I have begun to live in the "new normal." That is what they call it, the new normal. It is anything but normal.

I have witnessed something horrific. I have endured the fallout of the emotional roller coaster, which occurs after a traumatic event. My life will never be normal. I will always have a sense of fear and look for exits everywhere I go. I startle at the smallest sound, which I brush off with a forced laugh and smile to put others at ease. I focus my thoughts on logic and reality to help guide my way through the pain and confusion of emotions. There will never be a clear answer to why this happened. I will never be the same person I was before this tragic day.

I am weeks away from starting the 2018–2019 school year, and my classroom along with everything inside it is sealed up tight. I don't care because it is just material things that can be replaced. My heart just aches for the innocence lost in that classroom. That is something that can never be replaced.

I will never be the same, but I will push forward. That is all I can do. I will take each day, each moment with my loved ones, each moment with my students as a gift. I will be strong. I will be loving. I will be positive, passionate, and proud to be an Eagle. I will forever be room 1216!

A CONVERSATION WITH MITCHELL DWORET

Mitchell and Annika Dworet's seventeen-year-old son, Nick, was killed in the shooting at Marjory Stoneman Douglas High School on February 14, 2018. Their younger son, Alex, was shot and injured that day. Alex survived. The following is an excerpt of the conversation between Mitchell Dworet and Amye Archer, editor, which took place on October 9, 2018.

AMYE: *Can you share a little bit about Nick and his love of swimming?*

MITCHELL: We joined him up [when he was seven] and he really took to it. He started meeting friends and learned all four strokes. He liked the competition. He learned to win, lose, how to follow directions. He just had fun with it. They'd write on their bodies, "Eat my bubbles." And I would joke with Nick later on, even when he was almost six feet, "Nick, let them eat your bubbles." It was a funny thing, and he'd roll his eyes.

Then, at fifteen years old, Nick quit swimming. It broke my heart and broke my wife's heart. He said "Dad, I'm so bored, the same four strokes." He had reached nationals with Coral Springs Aquatics, and he just was bored.

When high school came around, we had a choice between going to different schools and he picked [Marjory Stoneman] Douglas for the swim team. As we were walking through the school, we said, "Nick, let's just go over to swim team and talk." He was like, "No, I don't wanna go over there." And, as we passed, the coach started talking about water polo with some people. "You don't have to swim. You can do water polo." He was like, "Okay, it's a team thing. Let me try it."

At the same time, he also was struggling academically. But with water polo, he met a lot of kids and made some good friends. Nick was still somewhat fast, he was first to the ball at water polo. But, since he had such poor grades, he couldn't play water polo, either, at that point because of his grades.

So, one of his friends said, "You have to meet the coach that I swim with TS Aquatics in Tamarac, his name's Coach Andre." He went, met Coach Andre, and hit it off. He trained Nick to not only become a great swimmer but instilled important life lessons on becoming a better person.

Soon after, Nick also started going out with Daria, who was a swimmer, but went to a different school. So, Daria came into the picture, his coach at TS Aquatics, and new teammates from many different schools around the area, private and public schools.

That's when he got his GPA up to three-point-something. He was doing really well. His swimming was just extraordinary.

But he learned from that experience. He wrote an essay, which I later found, and the title of the story was, "Never let a stumble on the road be the end of your journey."

Nick also became very big into inspirational things. He has on his board, "When you want to succeed as bad as you want to breathe, then you'll be successful." He was reading a lot of finance books and he would underline a lot of financial stuff and also inspirational stuff that related to finance and life.

Nick was reading his last book and he got up to page 59. He was reading Napoleon Hill, *Think and Grow Rich*. That was the last book he was reading, and he'd underlined a lot of things in it.

AMYE: *What is it like for you to live among Nick's things? Do find that comforting?*

MITCHELL: Sometimes I'm in denial that Nick's gone as we move into our eighth month that this happened. I have a very hard time. Like yesterday, Aalayah Eastmond said she thinks of Nick as a hero. She was the girl that his body fell onto, he stood up in front of her. But she did an interview, and the writer wrote, "his lifeless body was on top of her." It's very hard for me to read, to think of my son's lifeless body on top of someone. Then again, he is a hero, and I cherish Aalayah for all she is doing to honor him.

It's devastating what happened to us, what happened to Nick in relation to being a parent. I'm right here at Nick's empty bedroom. I'm here. This is where he is . . . or was. To look at this, it's surreal still. I talk to people, I'm talking to you, sometimes it's third person for me because I can't believe that this happened. How could this happen, right?

And then when people approach you, "I don't know what to say." I don't know what to say, either. I don't know, it's one step in front of the other, daily. I'm getting stronger about it for us, for my other son, of course. I have a double whammy, my other son Alex was injured, he was in the first room. He has shrapnel under his head, he saw three kids get killed.

AMYE: *How's Alex doing?*

MITCHELL: He's doing okay. He's my hero and he has courage to go back to school there. He has a lot of friends. He's changed in certain aspects, of course. He's got PTSD and all that entails. He's doesn't feel safe in many places, and he definitely looks for escape routes, as an example, wherever he is.

I'm very proud of him, he's a strong boy. He's going to the gym, and he listens to music. He's a normal fifteen-year-old kid. He's come out more about talking about it and also about his brother. He wasn't talking about Nick at first. They were very close.

AMYE: *So, he's grieving plus processing his own trauma.*

MITCHELL: Yes, which we all do as a family. I'm in a situation that no parent would, could ever imagine—as the only parent with two children, one killed, and one wounded by this shooting. I also have to deal with the trauma of the event. The trauma started that day while waiting with my wife, in the parking lot at 2:20 p.m. that day—to finding out what happened to Nick at 3:00 a.m. the next morning in a hotel from the FBI. Alex deals with three issues from that event. Being injured, seeing classmates murdered, and losing his brother. We just can't imagine, this is why he is my hero, my everything.

I'm grieving for Nick. Nick is just . . . he's a presence, man. I just miss him walking through the house with his swim gear and his backpack and his gigantic water bottle.

AMYE: *How has meeting other parents helped?*

MITCHELL: Sandy and Lonnie Phillips, from Aurora [Sandy and Lonnie's daughter, Jessica, was murdered in the Aurora movie theater shooting]—they were coming here anyway, and a mutual friend introduced us. We [had] Sandy and Lonnie over to our house and we sat with them for about three hours. They went over their experience in the past six years and what they experienced immediately after the shooting, what we should look out for. They never invited us to join anything. They came to us as parents. As other parents of mass shootings have come to us.

I'm very close with the other parents through this tragedy. I sit with them, mourn with them, grieve with them, and I honor their children, the husbands, and the coaches. There is a fight to be had, though—

AMYE: *There is.*

MITCHELL: Grief is grief. But this grief, the trauma associated with this grief and the mass shooting and the politics of it.

My son was in a classroom going to school that day. I dropped him off that morning. I told him I loved him. I didn't know that would be the last time I'd see him. I didn't know texting him, waiting for him that day, "I love you, Nick." And I had a bad, dark cloud feeling that day. When I texted him "I love you" twice, I felt it. I've moved on from that point, but I was stuck in that parking lot for a while psychologically.

Looking at gun violence now for what it is, an epidemic in our country. So now I have a voice, I'm getting stronger. I have to tell my story to honor my son, and the sixteen other beautiful people we lost that day senselessly. No other family should experience this, I do not want to visit other parents like Sandy and Lonnie did for me. This is a club you never want to join.

AMYE: *How do you feel about the Parkland kids out there advocating for change?*

MITCHELL: Oh my God. I'm a big supporter. I don't buy into, "They wanna be famous." These are Nick's classmates. Whenever I talk to the ones that are really the face of it, they say "We do this for you, Mitch, we do this for your son." They know Nick, quite a few of them. They're [Nick's friends]. I support them 110 percent. They are the future. I firmly believe that they made a change.

How could I ever say anything bad about these kids? I am totally in awe of what they've done. When people speak bad of them or denigrate what they're doing or have nasty, cruel comments, I think it's despicable. I think it's disgusting.

AMYE: *What would you say to other parents who are going through this? Hopefully there won't be more parents going through this but, unfortunately, after Parkland there have been.*

MITCHELL: Again, I don't ever wanna look at another parent's eyes and cry together. I don't wanna do that. Because I look in eyes six years out now and we're on the same place. There's no secret sauce here. I would stay close to who you've been close to and let go of those people and things that do not serve you. Do not make any major decisions.

Still, you're gonna be in a different place, you change. I am not the same Mitch Dworet I was on the 13th, as I became on the 15th of February. I'm a different person. But there's the aspects of me that I took, using fitness as an example. I just got back to my running, I'm trying to eat right, I don't abuse alcohol or any drugs, I went into therapy very early on. I wanna be here for my wife and my child.

But it's very difficult. You could just curl up and just wanna die. At first, I wanted to just follow Nick, I wanted to just be with him. It's a very heavy thing to say but I can't do that.

AMYE: *I imagine many parents would feel that way.*

MITCHELL: So, I try and find things that serve me and stay strong so I can be strong for those out there. It's funny, people will say, "Oh, you need to be strong for others." In my mind I think I don't need to be fucking strong for anybody. My grief and trauma, I have to deal with that.

I cannot find forgiveness in my heart at this point in my life. There is no forgiveness. I wanna see retribution and I need to see justice done as quickly as possible. I could put this young man to death with my bare hands right now. That's how strongly I feel about it.

And I think death by [lethal] injection is too good for him. So I have no forgiveness in my heart. But I've heard through others who've been through this and there are certain communities that are forgiving, blah, blah, blah, not me. Ain't happening. I see no forgiveness. I don't see God. God wasn't there for seventeen souls that day. But then again, I was blessed to have [Alex] saved that day. This is something that I have to confront and find peace with for the rest of my life.

But I lost Nick. So . . . Where am I?

LEARNING TO TRUST MY INSTINCTS
By Keely Owen

Keely Owen was a fifteen-year-old freshman at the time of the shooting.

I am fifteen years old, and I've already had a very near-death experience inside the place I'm supposed to feel safest: my high school. I've been participating in active shooter drills my entire life, yet nothing prepared me for the real thing. In the moment, I had to make a series of choices, some conscious—some not, and hope they were right.

At the start of fourth period on the day of the shooting, I asked my teacher if I could run over to the freshman building quickly to get a permission form I needed. She told me no. It was 1:10 p.m. and class was starting. I was frustrated, and I could have fought with her, but I listened. As class went on, I heard loud, startling noises, like large boxes dropping. There were workers on campus that day, and I assumed they dropped something very large.

Soon, my teacher gave me permission to get my form, and as I stood up from my desk, the fire alarm started to go off. I almost ignored it since we already had a fire drill that day, but I went with procedure. It soon became obvious that this was no drill. As I walked outside toward the senior parking lot, I saw a lot of smoke. I heard loud screaming. There was complete chaos. Then, for what felt like a whole minute, the air grew silent. Gunshots. Gunshots everywhere. I quickly realized there was a shooter. Someone was shooting at us.

Coach Aaron Feis was by the freshman building yelling and directing kids to go the other way. I listened to him. I ran for

49

my life with a small group of my friends at my side. I didn't know it, but I was one of the last people to see him alive. In his last moments, he saved me, my friends, and countless other students.

No one knew where the shooter was, it was terrifying. I stayed against the outside wall, leading my group of friends all the way to the bus loop. I could hear my heart beating loudly in my ears, and I could hear my families' voices telling me they loved me. I had been late that morning and, in my rush out the door, I forgot to say goodbye to my mother. Would I ever see her again? I felt sick to my stomach. I thought it was the end. I got to the fence where I thought I was safe, and as I began to prepare myself to hop over, I heard someone screaming *RUN, RUN!*

Loud, alarmed voices were screaming at me to run back *into* the school. I hesitated. Outside felt safe, and inside did not. Still, something told me to listen. I ran back into the school and into the leadership room, where I dove into the closet. One of my best friends was there, with at least thirty of my classmates. For over two hours, we hid in the closet sweating with no fresh air. We had no idea where the shooter was, who the shooter was, or if we would be okay. We had no cell service, but I was able to connect to Twitter through Wi-Fi. I couldn't even believe what I was reading. The top trend was a shooting at Marjory Stoneman Douglas High School. This couldn't be real. How could my school in Parkland, Florida, be the site of a school shooting?

We soon heard the SWAT team above us, bursting open doors and moving desks. Their footsteps shook the ceiling. Soon after, banging—loud and furious—on the door of the classroom. When the SWAT team pulled us out, they had huge guns pointed at us, and I was more terrified than ever. I had to run out of my school with my hands up. I ran past the freshman building and saw black body bags, not realizing at that time that some of my friends were inside.

Later, when it was safe to go home, I remember getting into my car and just feeling numb. My mom was terrified and confused. She didn't believe what had happened, and neither could I. I sat on the couch and cried. Everything hurt. Then, my friend's face was on the evening news. Jaime Guttenberg. She was the first one to be confirmed dead. After that it just started to become one after the other. Alyssa, Martin, Luke, Gina, and Alaina, the names seemed endless.

In the days that followed, I realized how lucky I was. Had I gone to the freshman building when I wanted to, I would have been in the middle of the shooting. If I had not run into Coach Feis, I would have run straight into danger. If I had stayed outside instead of listening to those voices, it might have been my face on the news that night.

While I'm lucky to be alive, I have lost several of my friends. That's a loss I will never fully heal from. I miss them. It was hard, and it still is hard. They cross my mind every single day. Every day I wake up I think of them and see them everywhere. Seventeen, my jersey number for volleyball, was also the number of classmates and friends killed that day. How could a number begin to mean so much? It's always been my favorite number, but now it means so much more than that.

One thing I learned through this experience is to trust my instincts. If I didn't trust my instincts on February 14th, I don't know if I would be here. Also, I have learned to live everyday fully. You never know when life will end. I've been given a second chance at life, and with it, I choose to honor my friends, every day.

DADDY, KEEP GOING

By Andrew Pollack

Andrew Pollack's eighteen-year-old daughter Meadow Pollack was killed in the Marjory Stoneman Douglas High School (MSD) shooting. He's a school safety activist credited with helping to pass the Marjory Stoneman Douglas High School Public Safety Act, and coauthor of *Behind the Gun: How Parkland Created Its Killer and Our Schools Became Unsafe* (Post Hill Press, 2019).

Before Valentine's Day 2018, I had a great life.

I provided a good, middle-class upbringing in Coral Springs, Florida, for my three kids, Huck, Hunter, and Meadow. I never went to college. But I'd built a good scrap metal business back in New York where I grew up, and then a good real estate business when I moved to Florida. My youngest, my princess, Meadow, was three months away from graduating high school. She'd head to Lynn University in Boca Raton, and I'd ride off into the sunset. Literally. I was ready to sell the house and drive my truck across the country to join my wife's family in Northern California. Maybe build a little ranch up there.

On Valentine's Day, my wife Julie wanted to take a day trip. We put our bikes in the truck, packed a picnic, and drove out to Shark Valley in the Everglades. There's a nice fifteen-mile bike loop there. We were halfway through the loop when I got a text from my son saying there was a shooting at the school. Maybe someone shot a gun by accident, I thought. But then I got more calls. People said multiple shots fired. An active shooter. But I still didn't think anything of it. It's not me. Not my kid out of the three thousand at that school. We drove through every fucking red light to get back to Parkland.

When we got to the high school, my son, Huck, and his mother (my ex-wife) were there looking for Meadow. They couldn't find her. After an hour or so, Julie and I decided to check the hospitals. Since Julie is an ER doctor, accessing hospital information would be easy. On our way, we ended up behind police cars and an ambulance. When we got to the hospital, Julie went inside. I stayed outside and talked to the officers. They told me the ambulance I followed had Nikolas Cruz in it. I didn't know what that meant then, or who he was when they wheeled him out.

But, again, Julie couldn't find Meadow. Maybe she was at another hospital. When we got back in the truck, a reporter came over to us. I held out my phone and showed a picture of Meadow. While showing the reporter the photo, Julie got a call saying Meadow was in surgery at another hospital. I hoped it wasn't her, but now I wish it had been. We learned it was a false alarm. It was then I realized: *Meadow is dead.*

The families gathered at the Marriott to wait for news. I couldn't go. I knew the detectives would find me. And at 2:15 a.m. they did. Part of me still doesn't believe it. She was my princess. So sweet, but so tough. She could be a supermodel one day and then go fishing and ATV off-roading with the boys the next. She was an all-American girl. Family meant everything to her. She had this boyfriend, Brandon, for three years. He's like another son to me now.

Meadow was the light of the room. Whenever there'd be someone new at school, she'd show them around and introduce them to people she thought they might like. So many people came up to me after she died and told me this. She could be so sweet, but also so fucking tough. You know, her brothers always wanted to protect her. But she'd protect them. Out of all my kids, she was the most like me. So, I had to be careful around her because if she wanted something she'd *always* get it.

Ever since she died, she's been on my shoulder saying *Daddy, keep going*. Because of this I wanted to do something positive in the middle of this negativity. I raised money to build a playground in remembrance of Meadow and the victims. It was somewhere I could go instead of the cemetery. I ended up raising half a million dollars to make it happen. I did a motorcycle ride for it, we got three thousand riders and raised $80,000 in one day.

But a memorial wasn't enough. I had to stop something like this from happening again. A week after I lost Meadow, I attended a White House listening session with President Trump where I asked him to fix this. I said to him, "I'm here because my daughter has no voice. She was murdered last week. She was taken from us. Shot nine times on the third floor. Everyone has to come together as a country, not different parties, and figure out how we protect the schools." He truly listened to what we had to say.

After I gave that speech, President Trump asked to meet with me and my family. A lot of people in the media wanted to weaponize this tragedy to attack him. But he's a great guy, and we talked about what could be done to end school shootings. I told him he should start a commission to look into all aspects of school safety and make recommendations and pass along best practices. That's exactly what he did. He told me there were some laws Congress was debating that could maybe do some good, so I threw my weight behind them and lobbied on Capitol Hill. A couple other dads and I helped them push through the Fix NICS Act to close some loopholes in firearm background checks (even though that wouldn't have done anything in this case), and to pass the STOP School Violence Act to support states in their efforts to make schools safer. Then, I went to Tallahassee to lobby the Florida state legislature to pass the

Marjory Stoneman Douglas High School Public Safety Act. You'd think that, after this awful massacre, it would be easy to get Florida politicians to act on school safety. But it wasn't. Republicans didn't want the bill because it had gun control provisions. Democrats didn't want it because it provided funding to train armed guards. It almost failed. But we pushed hard and got it passed.

But after doing all that, I learned the most important lesson: you can do as many marches on Washington and pass as many laws as you want on the federal and state level, but what matters the most is what happens at the local level. I realized that when the Broward County School Board rejected money from the MSD Public Safety Act to train new armed guardians. They explained it was because they didn't want to "arm teachers." It had nothing to do with arming teachers. That wasn't even possible under the act. But the ideology was so ingrained in the school board and superintendent that it didn't matter.

Everyone wanted to blame the NRA for this. If I thought it was the NRA, I would've gone after them hard. But the shooter didn't buy his gun through a loophole. Stronger background checks would not have stopped his gun purchase, because he had a totally clean record, despite being in trouble with the law many times over. But the ideological approach to just stop arresting kids in schools and in the community for crimes (pioneered by Superintendent Robert Runcie and Broward Sheriff, Scott Israel) meant he never got arrested. Sheriff Scott Israel declared "we measure our success by the amount of kids we keep out of jail." His deputies visited the shooter's house forty-five times and never arrested him, so I guess that by Israel's standard he succeeded with the kid. At least until Valentine's Day. And Superintendent Runcie declared "We are not going to continue to arrest our kids," and launched the PROMISE decriminalization initiative, which lowered arrests by 70 percent in the school, so he never got arrested there, either.

He was also a psychopath who should've never set foot in MSD in the first place. But the school district moved him out of the specialized school where he belonged and then hid all his misbehavior once at the high school. He threatened to kill kids and shoot up the school. He brought in bullets and knives. But none of it mattered because school administrators refused to do anything about it. They were under pressure to underreport and not arrest. The shooter was crying out his entire life for someone to stop him (or to help him) and every public agency, including the police, mental health authorities, and the school, failed him.

This is a story you might not know. It's a story I fought to learn. In part because the school board tried to cover it up. And in part because no one wanted to talk about anything except for the type of gun he used: an AR-15. It didn't matter what type of gun he used. He walked through an open gate that should've been locked. A campus monitor, Andrew Medina, saw him, and thought he had a gun, but wouldn't call a code red. Not even when he heard gunshots. He said he didn't want to get in trouble if it was the wrong call. Medina was a problematic employee who never should've been allowed to stay in his position with the school district. I learned after Meadow died, she and another girl lodged formal complaints against him for sexual harassment and inappropriate behavior. But again, the administration didn't take responsibility, and Medina remained at the school. Adding to the school's incompetence, Scot Peterson, the School Resource Officer, took cover outside and hid, instead of helping the kids. He even prevented more help from coming in.

This was the most preventable mass shooting in American history. It wasn't the laws that failed. The laws should've worked because they say criminal psychopaths shouldn't legally buy guns. But people failed here. When he went to buy his gun—and when the police and the FBI were called to be warned that he'd use it—the kid had a totally clean record because no one was ever willing to make one responsible decision about him. I guess they figured "what's the worst that could happen?" Well, the worst happened. And even then, it didn't matter for them. No one was going to be held accountable if I hadn't made it my mission. So, I am going to keep fighting to #fixit.

CHAPTER FOUR

MARSHALL COUNTY HIGH SCHOOL

Draffenville, Kentucky / January 23, 2018

I CONNECT WITH Heather Adams through her advocacy work, which she began after a fifteen-year-old boy walked into Marshall County High School and fatally shot two of his classmates, injuring fourteen others. Heather's son, Seth, was in that school. Her voice beams with pride as she tells me how Seth emerged as a natural leader during the panic of the shooting. He was calm and was able to help many of his classmates who were panicked.

As Heather tells me her story of the shooting, her panic, her rush to the school, the unreturned texts, she lands on the waiting. The waiting to hear, the waiting for names, the waiting for what comes next. This is a theme I've found prevalent in this work—the waiting. Parents sending texts and desperately needing to see that read receipt, or to feel the vibration of a returned text in their palm. But Heather's story is not of her own waiting, it's of someone else's.

Heather spent the better part of that terrible day comforting a woman whom she would later discover was the shooter's mother. *The sins of the parent. The sins of the child.* This woman had no idea her son was the shooter, she simply showed up at the school as afraid as the others who had gathered and prayed that her son was safe. Even after the connection was discovered, Heather treated her with kindness.

There are so many parents devastated by mass shootings, there is enough pain and loss and sorrow to go around the world five times. But Heather's story made me think of the parents not represented in that collective grief. Theirs are the stories left untold. Theirs are the deaths often not counted among the dead. Judgments are made: this parent is responsible, this one isn't. This one was careless, this one too indulgent. As a mother, I have made a hundred bad decisions, how do I know where any of them will lead? Will I be judged for those mistakes? Who decides?

AMYE ARCHER, EDITOR
JANUARY 2019

**The following students were shot and killed at
Marshall County High School:**

Preston Ryan Cope, 15
Bailey Nicole Holt, 15

LIKE ANY OTHER DAY

By Cloi Henke

Cloi Henke was a freshman at Marshall County High School when the shooting took place.

My best friend, Hailey Case, and I were leaving the school cafeteria on January 23, when shots rang out. My smile disappeared, and without hesitation, I took off running. I didn't know what was happening. But I knew I had to *run*.

I ran with my classmates. I could feel my heartbeat pounding in my ears. I couldn't breathe. I couldn't hear the screams.

I got about fifteen steps away from the door and stopped. I panicked. I didn't see Hailey. I headed back in. She meant and still means everything to me. Even though I was confused and didn't know the details of the danger, I had to find her. I barely stepped back inside when I heard Hailey call my name. After we met, we held each other close, and started walking, surprisingly calm considering the shooting.

Outside, we ran into a friend of ours who was having a panic attack. He was facing the commons and saw everything. That was the first time I had to help someone through a panic attack, and it was upsetting.

When he regained his breath, we started walking again, talked about what *just* happened.

"Is this some kind of sick joke? Is this really happening?" I asked.

We walked to town. The road was full of us kids wandering after running or walking as far as we could from school. Drivers stopped their cars and asked us what happened, but instead of staying on the road, Hailey and my other friends, went to a golf cart store. I sat down. I hadn't thought about calling my mom until a friend offered me her phone. I called twelve times before she finally answered. I attempted calm, but when my mom answered and I heard her voice, I broke down sobbing. I told her everything that happened, all of it releasing from me. Her own panic was obvious, she struggled to breathe as she repeated what I told her to my father.

When I got home, my phone was blowing up. Everyone at Marshall was calling and texting each other, asking if everyone they knew was okay. My parents had the local news on. The shooting was plastered on almost every channel. It was unreal. It still didn't feel like I was there.

The day after, there was an odd quiet in the atmosphere. It looked dark outside. Time slowed. And then began the waiting.

WAITING TO FIGURE KNOW WHO PULLED THE GUN.

WAITING TO KNOW WHOSE LIVES WERE LOST.

WAITING TO KNOW WHO WAS INJURED.

WAITING AND PRAYING.

PRAYING AND WAITING.

HOPING I DIDN'T KNOW THE SHOOTER OR THEIR VICTIMS.

I wasn't prepared for a shooting at my high school. The closest Marshall ever came to preparing us for a shooter was by lockdown drill, which consisted of us locking our classroom doors and turning off the lights. The training also allowed us to ask our teachers questions.

"What would we do if a kid was at the door needing in?" one student asked.

"We wouldn't be able to open the door for them, it's either them or a classroom full," the teacher responded.

That line of questioning haunted me, but still I didn't think that one day, we'd have to make those decisions.

In all honesty, I don't think we are preparing kids properly for a shooting. But perhaps this is because there is no *true* way to prepare for trauma, for tragedy. I often question why someone would do something so horrific, and why youth must suffer these actions and consequences. It's all so frightening. And something's gotta change. Something's gotta give. I never want to experience a shooting again. I don't want anyone else to have to experience it, either.

FEELING SAFE
By Hailey Case

Hailey Case was a freshman at Marshall County High School when the shooting took place.

DO YOU KNOW WHAT IT'S LIKE
TO BE SHOT AT?

It's terrifying. You see it on TV and hear about in the news, but you never realize how scary it actually is. You never think it can happen to you, until it does. And you're never prepared for it. It's panicking and freezing. It's running, even before you know what's going on, because everyone else is. It's hearing screaming. It's not knowing if you're okay, if you're hurt, or even shot. It's watching people get shoved to the ground and trampled. It's stepping over them and not stopping because you can't stop running. It's not being able to focus on anything except getting away as fast as you can.

DO YOU KNOW WHAT IT'S LIKE
TO BE SHOT AT IN YOUR SCHOOL?

It's laughing with your friends before hearing gunshots and not realizing what they are until it's almost too late. It's watching your friends run for their lives. It's stepping over people you've gone to school with your entire life, not knowing if they're dead, alive, injured, or in need of help. It's knowing you wouldn't be able to stop even if they were. It's running through the halls of your school with panic and fear at your heels. It's a rescue. It's calling everyone you know, trying to get someone to answer. It's a body count.

I know what a school shooting looks like because I was in one. I was a freshman at Marshall County High School on January 23, 2018, when a fellow student came into my high school with a gun. Shortly before first block, he opened fire and ended up killing two students and wounding fourteen others.

DO YOU KNOW WHAT IT'S LIKE
TO BE A SCHOOL SHOOTING SURVIVOR?

It's running and jumping into your dad's arms when he comes to pick you up. It's him squeezing you so hard that you feel like you can't breathe. It's riding in the back seat, holding your best friend's hand because neither of you can stop shaking. It's being terrified to drop her off because you don't understand that neither of you are in danger anymore.

It's getting your little brother and cousins from school because if it can happen at your school, then it can happen at theirs. It's picking your mom up from work and having her climb into the back seat with you as you sob into one another. It's nightmares and panic attacks. It's therapy session after therapy session, just trying to feel normal again. It's being too numb to cry for days and then sobbing in your mother's arms, asking her why it had to be them and not you. It's wondering what made you so special, that you get to live and they don't? It's your family telling you that you did everything right, but you dig your nails into your arm so that you don't tell them what you're really feeling: that you'd rather have gotten shot trying to help someone than to feel like a coward right now. That the guilt that you got out unharmed is bearing down on your chest until you can't breathe.

It's jumping at every loud noise. It's locating the closest exit every time you go somewhere. It's worrying you will never, ever again feel safe.

THE TIMELINE OF TRAUMA
By Heather Adams

Heather Adam's son, Seth, was a fifteen-year-old freshman at Marshall County High School.

It was an otherwise uneventful morning, with normal rushing around the house, making sure the kids had their backpacks and lunchboxes, checking that their bed head wasn't too bad. I drove my blue mom-van into the sun on the way to drop my fifteen-year-old son at the bus, and my ten-year-old son at Benton Elementary School. It was a bright and warm-enough January day to wear a hoodie instead of a winter coat. Then, it began.

8:11 A.M.

My mother called. She was hysterical. I could hardly understand what she was saying. Maybe I didn't want to. **"There have been shots fired at the high school,"** she yelled. I screamed into the phone incoherently, fearing for my son, Seth. **"Oh my God, Seth! Fuck, no. Oh my God. I gotta go."** I was almost sure that Seth had been targeted because of an issue we had earlier in the school year. I imagined a black semiautomatic handgun, but an AR-type soon replaced it.

I was scared, but not surprised there had been a school shooting here. I had been waiting for this day to come ever since the Valentine's Day, 2008, Northern Illinois University shooting. In my hometown, a shooter armed with a shotgun and three pistols killed five and injured seventeen students. I had family and friends on the campus that day, and it took us two hours to get in touch with some of them because all the cell towers went down.

I texted Seth. No response. I messaged again. Nothing. I called. He answered and whispered, **"I'm okay. We're safe in a classroom, but I can't talk."**

8:13 A.M.

Seth texted. **"We're ok. Everyone is safe,"** he wrote.

"Omg I'm coming for you," I replied, already en route to the school.

"No, they won't let you on campus. Mom, trust me. We are safe in a room. Don't put yourself in danger. Please. We are all okay. The shooter stopped. Listen to me. Don't come here. We are okay. Mom, I am okay. Nobody is being hurt right now."

8:14 A.M.

I left to pick up my mom and rush to the school. While driving, I called my husband at work. He just received a text that something was happening at the high school. I told him, **"Seth is safe, but there's been a shooting at the high school. I'm on my way there now. I'll be in touch."** He simply told me, **"You need to slow down and be safe. Call me when you get there."**

8:25 A.M.

I arrived to pick up my mom. She looked devastated. We hugged and jumped in my van. We arrived at the school but couldn't get very close. I parked in a no-parking zone by the high school, confident the police were too busy to ticket me. I remember it smelled like wet earth because it had rained the day or night before. Helicopters roared overhead, some for Life Flight, others for news. It felt like a war zone.

8:28 A.M.

Seth texted again, **"The police are here. The shooting is over."** I called the elementary school to find out if the students there knew about the shooting. The office said the children were still blissfully unaware. I asked that if word got out, would they please find my son, Miles, and let him know his brother is okay.

8:30 A.M. AND BEYOND

Adrenaline flooded my system. I was thirsty and my lips were dry. I tried to stay calm. I called one of my best friends, Jan, in Nebraska, a fierce gun violence prevention advocate. I needed to tell her before she saw it on the news. She was at once sorry, supportive, and angry. I didn't cry, knowing I had to keep my cool. It felt good to know that Jan was there for me.

At the high school, more people arrived. I was relieved to see another mom I know, whose son was safe with Seth. With nothing left to do but wait, I turned to see if could help other parents, some of whom looked distraught. I approached them to ask if they have heard from their child. I started texting Seth names of students whose parents still hadn't heard from them because he was in a room with a lot of other kids.

I approached another mom, with sandy-blonde hair, a dark sweater, and a sparkly, yellow-gold scarf. Her name was Mary. She looked scared. She said she had heard from her son early on, and that he was out by the stadium, but she hadn't heard from him since. I explained to her that the shooting happened in the commons, so if he was out by the stadium, then he's probably safe. Maybe he dropped his phone while running. Many of the kids had.

I asked Mary her son's name and I messaged Seth, **"Gabe Parker, safe?"** Seth knew Gabe because they were in marching band together.

He messaged back, **"Don't know where Parker is."**

Mary's knees buckled. I held my arm around her as she vomited, holding back her hair and scarf. I tried to reassure her. I reminded her to breathe.

I started asking some of the officials if they had any information about Gabe Parker, but they didn't know anything. Mary became less steady on her feet. I kept talking to her, reassuring her that I would help her reach her son, speculating that maybe he had run and lost his phone. Soon, she was shaking and crying. Again, I reminded her to breathe.

Suddenly, Mary's phone rang. The call was short. She was screaming into the phone, **"Why are the police at my house? Why would they be at my house?"**

I could no longer console her. I asked the police officer posted nearby for an ambulance because she needed help I couldn't give her. He said he would try, but they were busy tending to the fourteen wounded teenagers.

We stayed with her while she cried. She said she needed her husband, and that she was waiting for him to call her back. She was leaning on me when her phone rang again. It was her husband returning her call. She was shaking so much that we had to help her answer her phone. She began to sob hysterically. Whatever was said in that phone call, one thing was clear: her son was the shooter.

I tried to support Mary the best I could. I tried to get her medical help. I held her up, and held her hand while she wept, knowing that in some way, she was grieving her son, too. Someone nearby tried to comfort her by telling her it would be okay. **"No, it won't,"** Mary replied.

I tried to be with Mary in that moment without giving her false hope. **"You're right,"** I said, **"this is not okay, it won't ever be okay."** I held her until Seth messaged saying that he was on a bus and on his way to North Marshall Middle School for pickup. I turned over Mary's care to a very nice man from the rescue squad. After I stood up, I stopped, took her hands in mine, looked her in the eye, and told her that I'd be thinking about her. And, I have been. I often think about reaching out to her, but I don't know how. Even though I'm mad as hell that she had an unsecured gun in her home, she suffered a trauma that day, too. All I can do now is hope I helped soften the blow of her pain. She has suffered death threats so bad she was unable to leave her home, and she actually moved away in the months following the shooting.

When I picked up Seth and his girlfriend, Lela, I hugged them both. I dropped my mother off at her car, and then went to get my youngest, Miles, from his elementary school. The school was eerily quiet, somber. I went into the office and had them page Miles up from his classroom. The sign-out sheet was long. A lot of parents had already come to pick up their kids. When Miles rounded the corner, I could tell that he knew something had happened. His eyes were wide, and his face was pale. I later learned that Miles found out about the shooting hours before I picked him up, but the teachers were unaware that the students knew. So he spent hours worrying about and not knowing his brother's condition.

I took Lela home so she could spend some time with her parents, but she came back over around 6:00 p.m. It was just me and the boys when their dad got home from work. He hugged the children. Then we shared our stories.

Seth told us that he and his friends had been in the cafeteria. They had finished breakfast but were hanging out waiting for the bell. He was getting ready for an Algebra II exam he would have that morning when he heard the first shot. He had thought it was someone banging a lunch tray on the table. Then he heard the second shot, and knew it was gunfire. He yelled at his friends that those were gunshots, and said, **"Let's go!"** He threw his backpack two tables over and ran in the opposite direction. He shepherded his friends out the back door of the cafeteria. They were only twenty yards from the gunman. They saw students fall. They ran to exit the back of the cafeteria and dove into a classroom across the hall.

There was a teacher escorting them into the classroom and he had them hide in a corner behind some filing cabinets. The teacher turned off the lights, locked the door, and periodically looked out the long thin glass window in the door. Lela went into shock, rocking back and forth, unable to string words together. She remained that way until she spoke with a crisis counselor at North Marshall Middle School.

They had stayed in the classroom until the SWAT team arrived with their rifles. They had to exit the room with their hands locked behind their hands. The police escorted them to the Tech Center like that.

It's now nine months later. Things that should scare me, don't anymore. Like tornadoes. My heart races from helicopter sounds and gunfire. After every new shooting in the news, the memories flood back in. I feel like I must be crazy sending my kids to school every morning, and I have to remind myself that this is what we do in a civilized society. We go to movies. We go to concerts. We go to church. And we definitely go to school.

THOUGHTS AND PRAYERS
By R. Sterling Haring, D.O., MPH

Sterling Haring was a first-year resident physician at Vanderbilt University Medical Center in Nashville, Tennessee, when victims from the Marshall County High School shooting were brought in.

THE EMERGENCY DEPARTMENT
NEVER SLEEPS.

At a major academic medical center like Vanderbilt, injuries and illness bring patients from hundreds of miles away seeking the best medical care available. Most come through the emergency department, contributing to a constant churn and flow unique to this part of the hospital.

In January 2018, I was toward the end of a one-month stint in the ED, part of the first year of my medical residency at Vanderbilt. As an "off-service" resident, my role was to examine patients, conduct appropriate testing, and discuss my diagnosis and treatment plan with the attending physician on duty. In the event of a trauma case, I was to stand in a designated spot in the trauma bay to observe and assist as needed.

As I arrived for my shift on the morning of January 23, something seemed different. I still can't pinpoint exactly what it was that tipped me off, but as soon as I walked in the door, I could tell that something was wrong. I asked a nearby nurse what was happening, and she told me the news. There had been a shooting at a high school nearby, with an unknown number of injuries. Some had already arrived via helicopter and had been rushed to the OR for emergency surgery. Others were en route. I dropped my bag and hurried to the trauma bays.

For weeks, my wife and I had discussed schooling options for our five-year-old son. When he was three, we had spent a year living in Switzerland while I worked as a research fellow. Under the Swiss system, he attended kindergarten at a nearby elementary school and had done well, despite having to learn Italian to interact with his teachers and friends. Now that we had returned to the U.S., we worried about how he might adjust to a new type of school. As we discussed the pros and cons of the local public-school options, we had several competing priorities. How many children would there be in his class? Were there particular subject emphases or teaching styles? Would the student body be sufficiently diverse? What about safety? Is there a dress code? How far is the commute? We decided that on my next day off, we'd go see local schools and gather as much information as possible.

As we visited each school, one priority became increasingly obvious: safety. At some schools, we could walk in through the front door with little trouble. At others, doors were locked and we had to identify ourselves via speakerphone for entry. Still others had a security window where a school employee approved each visitor. It became clear the world had changed since I was in kindergarten, and the risk of a gun-wielding visitor or student was very real. The thought was terrifying.

We ended the day with a short list and only a few days to make a decision about where he would attend. As I left for the Emergency Department (ED) the next morning, I reviewed the options in my head, determined to have a school preference by the end of my shift.

The trauma bay was already abuzz when I arrived, and I was relieved to see that a friend and colleague was already there. We talked as we put on the blue plastic gowns, gloves, and surgical caps required in the trauma bay. I learned that some of the students had already come through had potentially fatal injuries, and rumors were circulating about a possible fatality. No word on how many more were coming, or how many had been declared dead on the scene. Someone said they thought the school was in Kentucky, but they weren't sure.

We stood in the trauma bay, gowned in blue from head to toe, with a silent energy that toed the line between excitement and fear of what we might see. Not because the team wouldn't be able to handle the injury, but a very human fear that didn't want to see a child with devastating injuries. Somewhere in the reverent silence, I thought about the parents of these children, and the anxiety they must be feeling as they wait somewhere, frantically searching, praying, hoping against hope to find their child around the next corner.

After my third year of medical school, while my colleagues prepared to apply for residency, I had decided to spend a year studying public health at Johns Hopkins University in Baltimore. There, I found myself drawn to the study of injuries and the policies that can prevent them. Injuries, like an infectious epidemic, can often be tracked, predicted, and stopped. Variations in laws between states and across time often created natural experiments that allowed experienced epidemiologists and policy analysts to evaluate the effects of specific policy interventions on rates of injury and death. Such an approach, pioneered by storied scientists such as Susan Baker, Bill Haddon, and others, had led to the implementation of seat belts, air bags, and countless major and minor interventions and regulations that have saved millions of lives over decades of work.

Today, these efforts are led by a coordinated effort between the National Center for Injury Prevention and Control at the Centers for Disease Control and Prevention (CDC) and university- and organization-based researchers around the globe, who continue to search for effective and implementable solutions to issues ranging from traumatic brain injury to the opioid epidemic.

Due in part to a piece of legislation known as the Dickey Amendment, however, the CDC is specifically prohibited from using congressionally appropriated funds for any type of research that could be perceived as promoting so-called "gun control." In practice, this often prevented the CDC and, sometimes, partner organizations from tracking gun-related deaths and measuring the impact of a variety of state laws on reducing those deaths. In short, the agency in charge of reducing death and injury across the nation was explicitly forbidden from investigating one of the key contributors to death in the United States.

I worked closely with the Injury Center for the remainder of my degree program at Johns Hopkins, and after its completion, spent time studying injury policy at CDC and later as a research fellow at Harvard. Our work, which has found its way to the pages of the *New York Times* and *TIME Magazine* as well as network television, focuses on how and why injuries occur, and exactly what types of policies might prevent them.

I heard a commotion down the hall, and people standing in the hallway outside the trauma bay started to step back to make room for an approaching gurney. Paramedics rolled in a young man with a gruesome gunshot wound, and, for just a moment, I stood in shock. Not at the wound itself—in my few weeks in the ED I'd seen many so-called "GSWs" (gunshot wound)—but at the victim. He looked and dressed like I looked and dressed in high school. In that moment, I recognized the biting reality that this young man, in all his humanity, *was* me. He was my brother, my neighbor, my friends, and my family. *And he was my son.* Lying on a gurney, bleeding from a bullet wound from a war he wasn't supposed to be fighting.

The trauma team seemed to jump into action before the gurney had even fully entered the room. I watched as they ran through the well-rehearsed trauma protocol with a speed and efficiency that can only come from years of devastating experience. The decision was made to remove the plastic collar around the young man's neck, but after receiving further information from the paramedics, it was decided that it was best left in place until further imaging could be reviewed. I grabbed a plastic cervical collar from the shelf behind me and my colleague gingerly slid it into place, bracing the fragile nerves of the spinal cord in case a stray bullet fragment had compromised the strength of the bones that surround it.

As the second phase of examination began, I wondered how this had happened. Where had this young man been when he was shot? It was early—maybe homeroom, or an early math class? Had he been sitting at a desk? Hiding in a corner? Running? What had raced through his mind when the shooting began, or did it happen too soon to register?

The trauma team's assessment phase began to wrap up, and my thoughts turned to the next steps of this young man's care. He would be rolled down the hall for a so-called "CT traumagram," which would take a detailed X-ray-like image of every inch from head to mid-thigh. A radiologist would pore over the images, looking for evidence of potentially life-threatening abnormalities such as internal bleeding, ruptured internal organs, or fragments of metal. The big decisions—such as whether he would need emergent surgery—would follow.

I reviewed these steps in my mind and felt a flicker of gratitude that, for the moment, it appeared this young man may have escaped a fatal injury. I took a deep breath. Looking back at the young man, I thought briefly of the impact this tragedy would doubtless have on school safety. The images of children being rushed from a building, bullet wounds packed with gauze, ambulance helicopters landing on a high school lawn before whisking young people off to undergo emergency surgery in the next state over—these images would devastate America, right? Surely lawmakers—many of them mothers and fathers themselves—would be tripping over one another to introduce legislation aimed at preventing another school shooting? Then it hit me. Without warning, like a punch in the gut, I could almost feel the wind being knocked out of my lungs as the all-too-familiar phrase raced across my mind: *thoughts and prayers.*

Another school, another victim.
THOUGHTS AND PRAYERS.

Another teenager with a bullet hole.
THOUGHTS AND PRAYERS.

Another ED, another OR, filled with young people who were bleeding internally and externally. Families panicking. Lives ruined. Lives lost.
THOUGHTS AND PRAYERS.

Press conferences, statements prepared by PR teams.
THOUGHTS AND PRAYERS.

No time for questions, break for coffee after another successful presser.

The thought was suddenly nauseating. I looked for a biohazard bin and wondered if I would make it in time. Realizing that I was gowned and masked and far from the main bin, I rested a hand on a supply cart to my left and took deep breaths while the young man was wheeled out of the room toward the CT scanner. As I tore off my gown and walked out of the trauma bay, I looked at the bay to my left and realized they were getting another shooting victim, but I needed to sit down. I went to a small workroom and took a minute to sit and breathe. The nausea passed, but the disgust stayed. I needed to process the events of the day, but told myself that now was not the time or the place. There were patients that needed to be seen, and the quicker I got to work, the faster I'd be able to put all of this into my pocket to unpack later.

My shift wrapped up that evening, and I walked from the ED to my car on the roof of a nearby parking garage. The cold night air had coated the windshield with a thin layer of frost, and for a brief moment, I was alone and invisible. I turned on the car and sobbed. Big, sad, desperate, devastated sobs. I cried for the children who had been shot; particularly for those who died, but also for those who had survived, I cried for their parents. And I cried for a society that would do nothing about it. I cried that reelection and campaign contributions would outweigh a young man on a cold hospital table with a hole in his flesh, unsure if he would live or die.

I gathered my composure and sent a quick note to the few hundred injury policy colleagues with whom I interacted on Twitter. Surely, if anyone could understand my frustration, it would be these few.

I drove home, walked into our small home, our two young children fast asleep, and sat down next to my wife. As my wife wrapped her arms around my shoulders, I cried again. Harder, sadder, deeper this time. I cried, this time, however selfishly, for me. I cried as a doctor who had seen what no doctor should have to see, especially while still in training. I cried as a human, devastated to be experiencing the result of our collective apathy. But more than anything, I cried as a father. I cried for my young son, eager to start kindergarten in a school not unlike the one in Marshall County, Kentucky, that lie reeling that night from violent death, the blood of its students still staining the pages of textbooks and homework. I cried for him, and for me, and for us.

My wife, to her everlasting credit, wept with me.

CHAPTER FIVE

UMPQUA
COMMUNITY COLLEGE

Roseburg, Oregon / October 1, 2015

ON THURSDAY, MAY 10, 2018, 7:57 a.m. I sent an email to Melinda Benton, one of the professors present at the time of the Umpqua Community College (UCC) shooting. Connecting with survivors at UCC was challenging. Out of the twenty individuals I reached out to (some of which were vocal on social media) most never returned my queries. But it was when I connected with Lori Shontz, a journalism instructor in the School of Journalism and Communication at the University of Oregon and coproducer of the project Reporting Roseburg, that I was able to make contact with the first UCC survivor, Melinda Benton.

Melinda and I exchanged a few emails before we set a date and time to talk. Over the phone, Melinda told me *she got her new office was because her colleague was shot and killed.* She talked about how Snyder Hall was torn down, and its place, a new building, similar to the original hall was built. *People don't realize that after a shooting the buildings come down. They don't realize how hard it is to go back to those buildings even after they've been rebuilt.* My stomach dropped. Is it like going to school on a gravesite?

The sadness is perpetual. Melinda **confirms this** in her essay, *Then I see a mother, my word how the memory of her still makes me cry, who quietly slips under the ribbon meant to keep out everyone but staff and students, and she is dressed as if for Sunday church.*

Like Melinda, Kindra, a student present at the time of the UCC shooting, echoes the ripple effect of memory. I first connected with Kindra after reading her illustrated comic about grief after a school shooting. I was moved by the images, a self-portrait of how one heals in the aftermath of such trauma. She draws a young girl, herself, next to the ticking clock. A metaphor for pain. I message her through Facebook asking if she'd be interested in talking about expanding on her comic for our book. A few days goes by. I anxiously wait for her to respond. When she does, my response is reflex.

Over the phone she tells me how gunfire broke the quietness of the campus. Later in her essay she would describe the noise *like a plank of wood clattering to the ground.* Her voice changes. She's out of breath. And suddenly I'm running with her down the nature path where her friends were going to seek safety from the shooting. She says she *ran with them for a minute, picking my way through the tall, dried grass and sliding haphazardly down the steep incline. If we made it a solid twenty feet down, we'd be right on the natural platform where I had sat for my Illustrating Nature class the previous spring.* But then she slows down. I slow down. *I couldn't do it, I realized.* And she decided to head back up the incline.

I was frustrated, she told me. When she got back up the incline some students thought it was joke. They didn't know at the time how many students had died. Suddenly *everyone was ushered inside my sociology classroom.* Inside, people she never saw before. Some were making jokes about *how terrible the emergency plan for the school was.* Then sirens sounded. She says, *I was still trying to catch my breath.* At that time the students in that classroom were unaware that the assistant English teacher, Lawrence Levin, was dead, as were many others. Some of which the shooter made beg for their lives. Or how six minutes after the initial 911 call, the Roseburg Police Department engaged in a short shoot-out with the shooter, who subsequently committed suicide.

In six minutes, this small town of Roseburg, Oregon, became national news. She says, a friend had a major news network message him on Facebook as the shooting was unfolding and asked for a statement. *The audacity.* And still media was trying to access survivors during vigils held after the shooting. *We're trying to grieve here,* he said.

Before we end our call, Kindra says, *I wish I could say it ended there.* She continued to explore this theme of memory and recovery in her graphic novel piece. She writes, *sometimes I can't get a moment of quiet, only when I can't take it anymore. But then another minute ticks by. And I know. The nightmare is perpetual.*

Today I hold their nightmare. Kindra and Melinda are with me as I travel across country to vacation with my in-laws in Washington. Their home, a few hours from Roseburg. A part of me wants to drive to the small, wooded campus and meet Melinda. Or visit the spots on campus where Kindra would draw. But I'm worried that if I met them, my heartache might overflow. I wouldn't want them to have to hold any more pain.

Loren Kleinman, Editor
November 2018

The following students and staff were shot and killed at Umpqua Community College:

Lucero Alcaraz, 19, student

Treven Taylor Anspach, 20, student

Rebecka Ann Carnes, 18, student

Quinn Glen Cooper, 18, student

Kim Saltmarsh Dietz, 59, student

Lucas Eibel, 18, student

Jason Dale Johnson, 34, student

Lawrence Levin, 67, assistant professor

Sarena Dawn Moore, 44, student

MELINDA BENTON

Melinda Benton is an associate professor teaching in Humanities and Social Science and an adviser for student media at Umpqua Community College (UCC). She was fifty-six at the time of the UCC school shooting.

IN MEMORY OF

Lawrence Levin

Lucero Alcaraz

Rebecka Carnes

Quinn Cooper

Lucas Eibel

Jason Johnson

Treven Anspach

Kim Saltmarsh Dietz

Sarena Moore

WHY NOW?

Before writing this, I had to ask myself, "Why?" and "Why, again?" After all, I've retold whatever little I know to FBI officers, to family, to friends, to doctors, to researchers, to journalists, to students, until I'm sick of the weight of each word. By this time, I am afraid that revisiting the events of the October 1, 2015, mass school shooting at my workplace could be counterproductive, especially since most of us in my small town seem to want to forget. To move on. Returning to those memories of October 1st can feel almost shameful, hurtful, exploitative. So, why me? and why now?

Because school shootings keep happening. Because two and a half years later, people here still hurt. Or feel numb. Or feel helpless. And those feelings matter more than you may suspect. Because erroneous, highly erroneous, public arguments are being made that school shootings, in perspective, aren't monumental enough to justify change. Because I realized that I need to learn more.

Even though I've been inundated with information about school shootings, especially about my own school's shooting, I realized that I didn't know nearly enough about how exposure to this type of trauma affects the whole human body, and I suspected that others didn't, either. And I wanted to know why some of my students are still having such a hard time, why some cannot return to school while others can, and why delayed reactions to school shootings are so common. I also wanted to understand some of my own feelings from a scientific, health perspective, especially since mainstream public media in America has not yet definitely reviewed the health costs of school shootings.

OCTOBER 1, 2015

On Mondays, Wednesdays, and Fridays, I would teach in the Snyder Hall classroom 15 and the Snyder Hall 16 lab from 9:30 a.m. until 12:15 p.m. But October 1 is Thursday, the first Thursday of the first term of the school year, so this morning I am preparing lecture notes and packing up handouts to go to class at the other end of the campus. Just as I am going out of the door, a student on the newspaper staff that I advise calls me. He first asks me where I am—an odd question. He then asks me if I'd heard, an unnecessary bit of tease, I feel, even for a journalism student. And then he quietly, with slow heaviness, tells me the school is in lockdown. I wait for more details, confused. He tells me a shooter is on campus. Deaths have occurred. In Snyder Hall. In rooms 15 and 16.

My close-knit department has always almost exclusively taught in Snyder Hall. I have spent more time there than in my own home. I have known every person who works out of that building for decades, so I am instantly desperate to get more information. The air whooshes out of the room, out of my lungs. I remember the overwhelming buzzing in my head, in my blood, in my bones. I want off the phone immediately, but in teacher mode I tell the student to keep in contact with his friend inside and call me back with reports as soon as he knows anything. He never calls.

I call my mother in Washington State to let her know I'm okay. I answer a frantic call from my daughter in Roseburg. I wail. I try to get in touch with the student editor. I call my son in Colorado who's been notified by a friend. I get on Facebook, start posting warnings and police radio announcements, join the desperate social media mob trying to get information on who's hurt and who's not, keep jamming the college website trying to see when, if, it will finally open, keep frantically messaging and texting my colleagues to see if they are okay. My mind races because I can't find any information on our secretary, a dear friend, or several coworkers. I hear the police radio calls for ambulances. The radio codes for acute trauma. Hear the police radio directions for hospital deliveries. Hear the police radio codes repeating and repeating and repeating requests for ambulance assistance. Hear the codes, again, and again, and again, changing ambulance orders because patients are deceased. I scour websites and phone directories and messages for contact information, answering the phone so many, many times, neighbors, the *New York Times*, too many media outlets to count, my husband, school retirees, a telemarketer with exceptionally bad timing, my mother again, former students from all over the nation. I find the editor, give her directions. She doesn't seem okay, but I don't know what to do other than what we've always done. I answer the front door, another neighbor with my former phone number has received over one hundred calls asking for me. She wants to know if I'm okay. I get in my car and my daughter drives me to the end of College Road for a news conference to be held at the fire station. She won't let me drive. I stand in the fire station parking lot while my friend texts me that it was Larry. It was Larry in Snyder 15. It was students in Snyder 15 and 16. Lots of blood. I'm amazed at how my friend sounds so matter of fact. I stand in the fire station garage while newscasters put their tripods on my feet, elbow me out of the way. I film. I advise and direct media students. They are afraid. They don't want to go back to the place they've escaped. I understand. I answer my phone again, on my phone for about twenty-four hours straight now. A little sleep, then on the phone again with students, with reporters, with my own newspaper staff journalists, with family, friends, pastor, fellow teachers, former colleagues, with the university up the road. So much talking. So much crying.

I won't talk about the crying.
But the faces.
I want to tell you about the faces.

It's October 9, and the campus is open now, supposedly just for staff first and then students so that we can each in our small groups in our own ways address this new thing. But, truly, it's just everyone everywhere. I remember and then forget that this is my husband's birthday. Reporters stand across the street on the road's miniscule shoulder, their toes just in the gravel, as they balance massive camera lenses. A former student, one I taught and liked, has scrunched her face into a knot as she hurries back and forth on the adjoining campus sidewalk, yelling profanities at these journalists who with their dead faces ignore her. So many journalists. So many people everywhere hating journalists. I'm a journalist. My heart can't get any sadder; it just registers the spectacle. Everywhere spectacle.

I walk back and forth across the campus lawn's expanse on the same path for seven hours that I honestly thought were only about seven minutes, and I register odd details: that teacher's green remembrance ribbon is upside down; those people who are not students aren't supposed to be here; a group of strangers are comparing new tattoos with that horrible October 1 date emblazoned over their faces, hands, arms, backs; a group of staff are holding hands in a circle with their heads down reverently and someone, without permission, photographs them; someone else is trying to give away odd, plastic cartoon figures; someone is laughing, but I don't understand how; a veterinary teacher says she is marking her territory by revisiting all of her favorite campus places and reclaiming them; the college president and entourage stride purposely across the quad, but my supervisor trails behind woodenly, and I can tell from here that she knows she will never in any way catch up and that frightens me; a line forms around the beautiful comfort dogs. Then I see a mother, my word how the memory of her still makes me cry, who quietly slips under the ribbon meant to keep out everyone but staff and students, and she is dressed as if for Sunday church. And her son, her beautiful twentyish-year-old son, is holding her hand the way little five-year-old boys hold their mothers' hands. And I sit down, holding on to the bench to keep from falling. And, with tears I can't feel slipping down my face, I thank God she still has her boy; I thank God her son still has his future.

And I look, and I see how everyone looks different, in both senses of the word. They are looking differently at the world. But their faces also look, appear, so different. So different that I can't mentally register how the bones of their faces seem to have rearranged. I've never seen so many faces reconfigure like this, but this is real, this is happening. A vice president's face is an odd mask that says don't look at me because I'm not okay and I don't know what to do. The mouth is lower than where it was, the forehead higher. The security guard, his body forced over onto his toes, follows behind his supervisor, and his face is not his, either. It's flatter, carved out of wood which later, he tells me, was just anger. A recently hired staff member stands tall and alone under an old campus oak tree looking like someone's canonized saint, and his face seems painted on, unreal. A student who works for me walks by, clutched by his girlfriend, and their faces are oddly pulled back, warning me, I think, to just leave them alone. A coworker literally stumbles over something I can't see on the sidewalk, and his whole body has gone so thin that I am shocked enough to take his hand. I genuinely think he will fall if I don't, and his face is just lumps of muscle pulled around.

So many people look ancient. I see their future faces. Red splotches have shown up on cheeks, collarbones, arms. The skin, especially around the eyes, is wrinkled, darkened. Some faces have changed color. And I'm surprised to see more than a few people decades out of their teens with acne again. But really, it's the shape of the faces that scares me. The shapes are just different, wrong, and I can more easily recognize people by their familiar clothing than by any familiar expression.

This, truthfully, is the face of trauma.
Stress disfigures.

BEHIND THE STORY: JOURNALISTIC RESPONSIBILITY WHEN REPORTING A SCHOOL SHOOTING

By Lori Shontz

Lori Shontz is a journalism instructor in the School of Journalism and Communication at the University of Oregon. Shontz is the coproducer of the project Reporting Roseburg, which covers the experiences of the journalists who covered the UCC shooting.

Every time I teach reporting at the University of Oregon, I pick a day to walk into my classes and ask this question: "If there were a shooting right now, on campus, what would you do to report it? *Right now.*"

I hate that I have to do this. But I must.

Because when a mass shooting happened at Umpqua Community College (UCC) in Roseburg, Oregon, on October 1, 2015, this is what some of the state's journalists were doing when they got called to cover it:

A sports reporter from the *Oregonian*, the largest newspaper in the state, was at the University of Oregon interviewing the football coach. He was two hours closer to the scene than anyone else on the staff, so he cut the interview short.

A news reporter from Portland was walking out of a marijuana dispensary, where he'd been covering the first day that recreational pot was legal in Oregon. The *New York*

Times called him because they happened to have his number. He'd previously written some freelance pieces.

A journalism student at the University of Oregon was lying in bed, scrolling through Twitter, when he got a call from *The Washington Post.* He'd signed up for the newspaper's student talent network six months earlier and hadn't heard a thing until the news broke. Before he left, he scrambled to find his only clean button-down shirt. And then, because he was nervous, he called his mom.

The police reporter for *The News Review*, the local newspaper in Roseburg, was half listening to the scanner as he was putting together briefs for the afternoon edition, which was being published in a couple of hours. He'd been on the job—his first journalism job—for six months. He wasn't even sure exactly what it meant when he heard a police dispatcher say there was an "active shooter."

None of them were prepared.

This isn't unusual. News happens, as we say, and part of being a journalist is dropping whatever you're doing and heading to the scene as soon as you can. Most of us thrive on the adrenaline rush, and we get the job done because muscle memory kicks in. Journalism isn't really learned in a classroom. We learn it by doing it.

But what I've learned, after spending three years researching how the UCC shooting was reported and how the community responded to the news media's efforts, is that covering a mass shooting isn't like covering anything else. Particularly, journalists need a sophisticated understanding of trauma—both how it affects the survivors whom journalists are interviewing and how it affects the journalists themselves.

I want my students to be prepared to cover a mass shooting in the same way that I want them to be able to request public records and craft a compelling news hook and put commas in the right places. These are skills that my industry, my craft, demand.

But journalists are not routinely trained in the specific requirements of covering a mass shooting.

The Dart Center for Trauma and Journalism has rich resources, including how to approach and interview children, characteristics of mass killers and how to refer to them, and explainers about trauma. But its website and training programs are mostly sought out by journalists *after* they have reported on a traumatic situation. My colleagues at a number of journalism schools are teaching classes dedicated to trauma journalism. But not all schools have them, and even at those schools, not all students take them. Plus, majoring in journalism is not a requirement to be a journalist. (I didn't.)

The UCC shooting felt close to me. I'm one degree of separation from so many people who were affected, from a student who was hiding in the library to a reporter who had to sit outside the home of a victim, mustering the courage to ask the dead student's family for an interview. I had to do something.

My colleague Nicole Dahmen and I began our exploration of the UCC shooting coverage because so many of our students and our program's young alumni had covered it, and because President Barack Obama had lamented aloud that mass shootings were happening often enough that everyone, from himself to journalists, knew how to respond. "Somehow this has become routine," he said, punctuating each word by pounding his hand on the podium.

We then tracked down nineteen of the Oregon-area reporters who covered the shooting, and we interviewed them for a project called Reporting Roseburg. In nearly forty hours of interviews, we learned a lot. But what struck me most—and what spurred me to add "mass shooting coverage prep" to my basic reporting classes—are these three things:

FIRST AND FOREMOST: Sixteen of the nineteen journalists had never covered a mass tragedy before. They learned on the job, and they wish they'd known more. That's why I cover the basics of trauma—fragmented memories, the danger of recounting and therefore reliving a story over and over, how no two people react the same—and give students some time to decide, before they are in the thick of things, how they'd like to conduct themselves.

SECOND: More than half of the journalists were uncomfortable asking questions they knew they were required to ask.

Joseph Hoyt, the University of Oregon student who was working for *The Washington Post*, was assigned to interview students getting off buses at the country fairground, where they could meet their families. And some of those students got mad at him, asking or yelling, "What are you doing here?" or "Get out of here!" or "Can't you see we're grieving?"

"You know," he said, "the thing is, I completely understand that. I couldn't imagine talking to some person I'd never met before after my son, daughter, brother, sister was involved in a mass shooting."

Hilary Lake, a reporter for KATU, the ABC affiliate in Portland, covered a community vigil the night of the shooting. "And part of me didn't want to go up to people to talk to them, to interview them," she said. "Because I put myself in their position. Would I want somebody coming up to me? And I don't know if I could answer that question.

"But the only thing that helped me get through that as a reporter was, what if there was one person who wanted their story told? Who wanted the world to know what they thought about what happened or to remember somebody who had died? To give them that opportunity, that's what we do in these situations."

That's something I'd like journalism to grapple better with. Can we make a process that empowers survivors to speak on their own terms and still meet the information needs of the community? I hope so.

THIRD: None of the journalists had been formally debriefed after their reporting, which stands in direct contrast to other first responders. Nicole and I hadn't realized until we finished that simply by listening to the journalists, we were giving them a chance to come to grips with their secondhand trauma.

"I was pretty conflicted driving down and going to this press conference, everything," said Scott Greenstone, a student journalist. He had interned in Roseburg over the summer and returned to help with the biggest story that had hit the town in fifty years. "It's weird because there was like this adrenaline shooting into my veins, and then at the same time this deep disgust with what had happened. So, my body is telling me that I should be excited, and my brain is telling me, 'Whoa, this is horrible.'"

Rachael MacDonald of KLCC, a public radio station in Eugene, hasn't been able to forget being part of a scrum of reporters who surrounded a student who was willing to recount her experiences in the next classroom. Or the stories she heard not only from that woman, but from the other students and family members who agreed to talk.

"I had just felt really sad," she said. "I felt like it was such a horrible event and, you know, people had come to class that morning thinking they were going to their writing class. And to have that day end up being tragic and an end of life for so many people, and for other people, you know, still coping with the physical and emotional fallout. It just was very sad, it was very, you know . . . heartbreaking.

"And to be a reporter, I felt the privilege of being able to be a witness of it. But at the same time, it was emotionally exhausting."

This is important, too: Every one of the journalists we interviewed went to Roseburg for the right reasons. They wanted to tell the stories of the victims, to make sure they weren't forgotten. They wanted to celebrate the heroes—and there are always heroes. They wanted to hold public officials accountable, if necessary. And they wanted—we heard this phrase repeatedly—to "help the community heal."

By most accounts, however, the mass of media assembled in Roseburg didn't achieve any of those aims. There's a reason one of the UCC students said during a town hall meeting a month after the shooting, "There was honestly a lot of harassment from media to tell our stories. . . . It was rude, honestly—it wasn't polite. Honestly, the media was probably the second trauma, almost, for us."

After interviewing the journalists, I realized I had only half of the story. I went in search of other people to listen to—community members, pastors, government officials, victim advocates. I spent three days at a conference called Leave No Victim Behind, which was devoted to the victims and survivors of mass trauma.

I got an education in the specifics of trauma-informed care, which I'm incorporating into my lessons. I heard heart-wrenching stories of people who still live every day with the horror they experienced seven months ago, a couple of years ago, even a couple of decades ago. And I got to meet people who weren't ready to speak to the news media right after the tragedy, but who would have eventually appreciated the chance to tell their stories.

The idea I'm holding on to is how the American Red Cross has learned that the needs of families and survivors change as time passes. There's an immediate response. Then there's a Family Assistance Center, which serves a specific purpose. And 10 to 14 days after the incident, after most of the TV cameras and news vans and reporters have left the area, there's another deliberate and important change. The FAC becomes a Family Resilience Center.

Resilience. That's something the news media can cover better, by backing off the breaking news and taking the long view. Acknowledging what went wrong. Respecting what so many people have endured. Working toward something better. Combine those things, and it's practically a definition of journalism's highest calling. We're working to live up to it.

PERPETUAL
By Kindra Neely

Kindra Neely was a student at Umpqua Community College (UCC) at the time of the shooting. The following comic, *Perpetual*, on pages 101–105, explores the grief process in the aftermath of her school shooting at UCC.

CHAPTER SIX

UNIVERSITY OF CALIFORNIA, SANTA BARBARA

Isla Vista, California / May 23, 2014

IT'S NOT THE same thing, a father of a daughter killed at Isla Vista told Amye and I when we associated losing a child in a shooting to that of losing a child in war. *At least when you send your kid off to war you have the understanding that they might not come home. No one should have to send their kid off to school and then get a call in the middle of the night that they're dead.*

Although early, at seven weeks pregnant, I fear I might think the same way when I drop my own son or daughter off at school. Can I trust the school? The students? The boyfriends? Girlfriends? I don't want to entertain such horror, but I carry it with me even when I park my car at my own university where I teach. And in meetings where my colleagues and I review case files of troubled students, I wonder *is this the student?*

That conversation changed me, and reminded me of another conversation I had with a mom whose daughter was shot at Virginia Tech. I made the mistake of using the word "lost." *If someone uses the word "lost" again I'm going to strangle them.* The murdered are not *lost,* right? There is no chance at finding them again? Of them turning up somewhere like a pair of keys or cell phone. They were shot and killed. Call *it* by its name.

And he did. Elliot Rodger's father, Peter, told Barbara Walters in a 2014 interview *that my son is a mass murderer.* He continues in the interview to address Walters's question about how he couldn't have known about who his son was. *On the outside is one thing and on the inside is something completely different,* he tells her. And I wonder how much clearer the signs of suffering must be: obsession with looks, sex, a cyber reality of *World of Warcraft,* bullied by his peers, and a tenuous relationship with his father. It seems there was minimal interest in the *signs.*

I don't want to be the parent who misses the signs. Who refuses to see the signs.

In five weeks, I will have my first ultrasound. I will see the baby's small, fluttering heartbeat in black and white. I imagine there will be nothing like seeing my baby for the first time, and I know that sight of him or her will change me forever. Ironically, this is a similar feeling I share with many of the parents and students that have experienced the shooting at Isla Vista. A single moment, that changed their lives forever.

When I got off the phone with the father whose daughter was killed, he seemed excited about participating in the project, about sharing his and his family's experience about what their lives have been like in the aftermath of the shooting. But months later, he wrote back saying he didn't want to put his family through anymore. I think he was referring to what he mentioned over the phone that his *family wasn't too supportive of my activism*. For some, reliving the events of that night don't make recovery any easier.

This father would be the first of many who would want to tell their story, but later decided they couldn't move forward. I learned this push and pull is a component of their own healing path. They speak when they need to. At their own pace and in their own time. My role was to be there to listen, a role I want to continue when I finally do become a parent.

Loren Kleinman, Editor
November 2018

The following students were stabbed and killed at University of California, Santa Barbara:

George Chen, 19

Cheng Yuan "James" Hong, 20

Weihan "David" Wang, 20

The following students were shot and killed at University of California, Santa Barbara:

Katherine Breann Cooper, 22

Christopher Ross Michaels-Martinez, 20

Veronika Elizabeth Weiss, 19

BEARING THE UNBEARABLE

By Andrea Slominski, PhD

Dr. Andrea Slominski's daughter lived one block from the sorority at the time of the shooting.

I didn't know that my daughter had survived a mass shooting until nearly twelve hours later when my brother called the next morning from Rhode Island to ask me if she was okay. What was he talking about? What mass school shooting? He had seen it on the news. Having my brother tell me the details about the mass shooting at my daughter's school, from across the country, made me feel like a terrible mother. It happened on a Friday night at about 9:30 p.m. I wasn't watching the news. I always watch the news. Why wasn't I watching the news on that Friday night, May 23, 2014, at 9:30 p.m.?

I still carry guilt for not knowing that a deeply disturbed young man had been freewheeling through the campus and the town, murdering and injuring along the way. I still carry guilt for not calling my daughter while it was happening, to let her know how important she is to me, how much I love her, and how much our entire family loves her. I still carry guilt because somehow, I thought that knowing about it, in the moment, even if I was helpless to change it, would have made me feel more connected to my daughter, more in touch, or strangely, more in control, when she was in grave danger. Six people were murdered and fourteen were injured that night. We were lucky our daughter wasn't one of them. Despite her escaping harm, she carries the internal scars of trauma and will carry them her entire life.

Some life events profoundly change you.

I called her the next morning in a guilty panic and my daughter, a senior about to graduate from UCSB, told me she was fine and not to worry. Despite her admonitions, I worried as I watched the horrors unfold on the news and learned the grisly details about the mass shooting in Isla Vista, California. I heard details that my daughter didn't want to share, that she didn't want to speak aloud, and that she still hesitates to discuss to this day. I was in the midst of getting my M.A. in Mythology and Psychology and like the surgeon who cannot operate on their family, but knows the risks, I knew that this event would have a far-reaching effect on her psyche and her life.

I called, trying to tease out of her how she was coping. She told me there were *IVStrong* unity rallies, candlelight vigils, tributes, and events happening on campus and in town. She was spending time with her friends and she was all right. "Okay," I thought, "events, people, and relationships to process the trauma with, good." At least she had a support system that she was gravitating to, in order to begin to work through the horrific events, albeit without my help.

Graduation was coming up and we bade our minds to focus on happier occasions. I had no recollection of her address relative to the multiple locations of the rampage, having only picked her up at her apartment a couple of times to take her to lunch during the school year. On June 14, 2014, graduation day, we parked near my daughter's apartment and began to walk together as a family toward the commencement area. Suddenly, I was overwhelmed with fear, grief, and a deep sense of personal failure, as I realized that her apartment was one short block from where three young girls were gunned down in front of their sorority house. The lawn, the street, and the sidewalks were all covered with memorial flowers, notes, and remembrances. None from me.

I turned to my daughter, "Why didn't you tell me that this happened right across the street from your front door?"

"I didn't want to worry you," she replied.

Questions and self-accusations flooded my mind and heart. Why didn't I hear or see what was happening on the news, Facebook, or Twitter that night? Why didn't she call me that night? Did she think I didn't care when I didn't call? Was she frightened? Should I have picked her up and brought her home? Was it better for her, her sense of independence, self, strength, power, and adulthood to decide how to process this? I had no experience with this kind of trauma. Very few do. No one should.

Now what? That is the question. How do we heal, or just carry on, from this kind of violence as friends, lovers, siblings, family members, parents, or spouses of those killed in a mass shooting? Sudden death is terrible in any circumstance. Sudden death in a senseless mass shooting by a madman seems a bridge too far for anyone. What I would like to offer for those willing to follow is a potential path forward for the survivors, for all of those affected by such tragic and horrifying events.

Some life events profoundly change you.
Some we choose, some are forced upon us.

In our lives, we go through stages of development and change. Some of these big events that fundamentally change us are rites of passage. A rite of passage can be described as an event that happens to you and within you, that clearly marks a place in time. There is a "you" before the event. There is the "you" afterward. Arnold van Gennep first defined the three phases of a rite of passage as *separation, liminality,* and *incorporation.* Often rites of passage are thought of as cultural and religious ceremonies that move a person from one group, to another, leaving the old identity behind. The result is a new identity and larger responsibility among the community. A rite of passage can be a profound experience. However, when glossed over, it can become simply a ceremony or celebration without deeper meaning.

I suggest that a mass shooting and the trauma that follows it are rites of passage. These are rites of passage that are triggered by death; the fear of death, the sudden realization of one's own mortality; raw fear itself, and the endless depths of personal loss. I argue that these mass shootings are a forced rite of passage to those who experience them. They are a kind of rape of the psyche, a violent act perpetrated upon individuals and communities against their will, wounding them deeply and changing them forever.

So much is stripped from the victims of mass shootings with no preparation or consent in the *separation* phase. Their former life is gone. Loved ones are lost and all the hopes and dreams that were associated with those lives. There might be a loss of family wholeness and friendships, or the loss of meaning in the world. There is no way to make sense of the senseless. Survivors may lose their sense of safety and security. They may live with fear and anxiety, not knowing if a random person may start shooting at them, in the street, the mall, their classroom, or their church. Survivors may become hyper-vigilant, depressed, or withdrawn. The fear that you could die, violently, at any moment can shred to tatters the meaning of plans and life goals.

The next phase is *liminality* or the transformation stage, which is described as a threshold, a no-man's-land of time and space, like the boundary between two places, or the edge of the sea, always shifting, not all sea and not all beach. In this liminal space, time stops. It is not inside, not outside, not sea, not shore, not in, not out, but an in-between space, that exists in our inner eye, our soul. It is the place where we change, where both growth and death happen. It is a space that can flash by in an instant or drag on for years. The question is, how do we navigate this space in order to reach the third phase of *incorporation*? How do we find our way out of the maze, regroup, carry on, and reintegrate ourselves back into the community as our newly changed selves?

There is one reliable guide in the liminal world of in-between that can help you find your way back to meaning and purpose. It is at the heart of all effective and meaningful rites of passage, it is the rites performed themselves. A funeral is a rite of passage that often is presented as a ceremony that honors the dead. The rites performed differ widely from culture to culture and may include music, readings, prayer, liturgy, song, dance, and more. Funerals give the living a chance to express their love and grief, while at the same time, bringing a certainty to the ending of life, and the beginning of life without them. It is a moment of in-between.

Ritual, one of the oldest forms of human expression, is another powerful way to move through these *liminal* spaces. It fills our need for connection to the world, it acknowledges the interdependency of all life, it affirms our place in life's grand story, and renews the deep connections of love, community, and soul. Ritual can tap into the deepest parts of our psyche, our imagination, creativity, and our meaning making abilities. Truly effective ritual works to move your psyche from here to there, through a transformation. It must be deep, meaningful, and unforgettable. It must touch the deepest and most vulnerable recesses of our souls. An effective ritual makes it impossible to return to where you began.

We can and should create new, healing and transformational rituals for individuals, families, groups, and communities. These rituals can act as a portal for the releasing of anger, grief, frustration, sorrow, and denial, thereby creating empty space, now available to fill with compassion, forgiveness, healing, future plans, and dreams, a space to fill with new life. The creation of rituals that are effective, that move us out of *liminality* and into *incorporation,* back into the world of the living, is needed now more than ever. With the guidance of depth psychologists, mythologists, indigenous ritual practitioners, ritual scholars, and the survivors of mass shootings themselves, we can create and facilitate rituals to help heal our suffering. These rituals can and should be performed again and again, on the anniversaries of the tragedies, on birthdays, and significant dates until the sorrow and pain are transformed. The power and ability to create these rituals is within our grasp. Let's get busy chanting, crying, screaming, burning, drumming, tearing, dancing, singing, writing, speaking, performing, and releasing so we can get busy healing and living.

A CONVERSATION WITH CARINA SARABIA

Carina Sarabia was a twenty-one-year-old junior at the time of the shooting. The following is an excerpt of a conversation between Carina and editor Loren Kleinman from August 29, 2018.

LOREN: *Can you talk about the night of the shooting? What were you doing on campus? What was the setting?*

CARINA: It was a regular Friday, and I'm sure I had gone to classes, and came back. Me and my roommates were going to go out that night and meet some other friends. And so we were all getting ready to do that. But as we were heading out, my roommate, Kate, started cooking dinner. She was a student from South Korea. So, she was starting to cook a Korean dinner. I asked, "What are you doing? You know, we're getting ready to leave. We really have to go right now. You know, we can eat on our way there." I was trying to tell her that we were going to stop at the deli. And I asked, "Why don't we just get something at the deli?" And she said, "No. I'm really hungry right now, so I'm gonna cook." So, I said, "Okay." And I just sat on the couch and waited.

Then we left the house finally. We saw a bunch of police cars blaring their sirens and driving so fast down the street. And I thought it was weird because Isla Vista is generally a pretty loud town. You know, there's a lot of kids going out and partying, especially on a Friday. But that was weird to see that. So, I thought, "Wow. Either somebody got into some real big trouble or something big is happening." But I didn't really think too much about it, just because Isla Vista was just kind of crazy. You know, crazy town back then.

LOREN: *What do you mean by "crazy"?*

CARINA: I don't know if you had heard, but at the school we have this party every year called Deltopia. And in 2013 when I was first getting there, there were police riots. People were burning mattresses and pulling stop signs out of the ground. For this party, there's a lot of out-of-towners that would go in and stay there with people who live in Isla Vista. And so many of the out-of-towners destroyed the town.

Isla Vista generally has a vibe of carelessness and a cool fun town, and people took advantage of that. It just has a history of a lot of free spirits I guess you could say.

LOREN: *I never knew that about Isla Vista. What did you do after you heard sirens?*

CARINA: I didn't really think much of the sirens from the police cars that were speeding by us. And thinking back now, that's really naive of me, just not really thinking anything of it. And so, we kept walking and we stopped as soon as we got onto Pardall Road. And there was chaos in front of us. Like all four of us girls just stopped dead in our tracks. And I remember seeing this guy with his hands up in the air and he was running for his life. And I remember seeing someone on the ground. And just ambulances and police cars. And just for that quick second, that's all I really remember. I probably stood there for like ten seconds.

I didn't know what was happening. But obviously something was wrong.

So, then my roommate said, "Come on. We gotta go. It's not safe here." And we kind of snapped out of it. And we ran somewhere, to a mutual friend's house. I didn't know this person, but it was somebody's house.

LOREN: *That sounds incredibly frightening. I couldn't imagine running like that. You always talk about what you'd do in an emergency, but you never know. Did you learn anything about the shooter after you settled into the house you ran into?*

CARINA: We later found out about [the shooter's] motives. And usually, I don't think it's appropriate to talk about the shooter, but in this case, now I've changed my mind about it because there's a lot of intersectionalities.

He had posted a whole manifesto. And it was a very long video about how he was a self-proclaimed nice guy and his dad had always taught him that if he was nice to girls, girls would, you know, like eventually they would like him and eventually hook up with him.

LOREN: *I had a chance to watch the video and it was chilling. He talked about being lonely and sexually frustrated. He talked about annihilating those that didn't pay attention, give him what he wanted.*

CARINA: He was mad that he never got the college experience that other guys had. He was jealous of every man who had ever had intercourse. And he was angry at every single girl who had never given that to him. So, it was just fueled by a lot of hate and a lot of rage. And he was able to access guns through his father.

LOREN: *Seems like there was a disconnect between him and his father though. I understand his parents split up when he was very young, and in a Barbara Walters interview his father Peter Rodger said he was envious of men better looking than him, especially his father. Do you think his parents knew about his behavior? Struggles?*

CARINA: [H]is parents actually called the police at one point and said, "You need to check on my son. There's something not right. We think something is wrong. Please go check on him." And in the end, the police actually ended up saying, "Oh, he's okay." You know, they ended up talking to him and, "He's totally fine. You know, we had a few laughs. We de-escalated the situation and he's okay."

LOREN: *What was your feeling after the shooting? Did that affect your time at school?*

CARINA: I finished up that school year. And that summer Kate went back to South Korea, so I moved in with other friends for fall. Professors for many classes had to pass us during the final exam because students were not in a place to study. It definitely affected my ability to focus because I was still stunned from what happened. Also, from time to time residents in I.V. [Isla Vista] would set off firecrackers and because we were still suffering from PTSD we would fall to the floor and protect ourselves. So obviously, people were not very considerate of others during this time.

[Carina crying] You know, looking back, I'm really sad about how it turned out because I really missed the part of my life and I feel like it gets a little emotional.

LOREN: *It's okay.*

CARINA: So, coming from a low socioeconomic status, I'm a first generation Mexican American here in the U.S., I expected so much from the university. And going to school. I wanted to make my parents proud, and I wanted to set an example for my brothers. And when this happened, it really stunted me emotionally. And I became so irritable. And I lost some friends because of it. When I did go out and party, it wouldn't end well for me. You know?

Even in class. I remember sitting in my Chicano Studies class, and I was so unfocused and just so, well I didn't know what it was, but it hit me in that class that I was feeling depressed.

I'm like, *why do I feel so numb? . . .* Then I realized, *Oh, okay. I must be having some depression and that's what I'm feeling. That's what it must be. And there's probably more.* Every time I would go to sleep, I would wake up having night terrors. I would wake up screaming.

But I finally finished [school] . . . the closer it got to graduating, the more I cried, the more I wanted to be done.

LOREN: *I'm sorry. I know, though, that now you've turned to activism, to sharing your story with others who've experienced gun violence. Could you talk about that more?*

CARINA: . . . [For] some reason it happened to me. And it happened to me because I'm supposed to do something about it, but it doesn't stop me from doing what I feel like I should do. Because six people were murdered. And I didn't know them, but it doesn't matter. They were young and they were students, and they were trying to live their lives just like me. . . . And they were killed for no reason. And just because I didn't know them doesn't mean that it didn't hurt me. It hurt. It hurts a lot. Because their lives mattered.

LOREN: *Thank you, Carina. I know you will help a lot of people. I appreciate you sharing your story with me today.*

THE SEEDS THAT GREW IN ISLA VISTA

By Sky Serge

Sky Serge was a student at Santa Barbara City College, living in Isla Vista at the time of the shooting.

I remember when loud noises didn't make me so nervous. With every *BAM* of a spontaneous firework, I'm helpless, eerily overwhelmed with emotion. The lights that fill the sky are no longer a burst of creative and random energy, but a quick and visceral reminder of my most repressed memory born on a late summer afternoon in Isla Vista, California. But this year, 2018, I understand the correlation between both sounds: a wild crack then explosion, alarming listeners within audible reach. And then I push my mind to remember the flashes, close my eyes, and take a deep breath, attempt to put the pieces back in order. But all that comes through are frames, as if from dirty film.

Sometimes the day of the shooting feels disconnected and unrelated to my daily life as I was a spectator for the last few minutes of the shooter's rampage. I didn't know three girls were dead on the front yard of their sorority house, a short walk from my door. I didn't know young men were stabbed to death and were lying like that for hours in the shooter's apartment. Those last few minutes felt like half an hour, fragmented, yet vivid pieces of memory.

It was a late, quiet afternoon. With the school year just closing, the residents of Isla Vista were beginning to go home, and the parking situation became an ease for those who liked to stay through the summer, I was quite happy to be one of those people. I was so ready to enjoy this place, a haven I created for myself after relocating from my miserable teenage life in Scottsdale, Arizona. It was magic. Isla Vista felt like a snow globe, found off a highway exit heading north on the 101 from Los Angeles. And if you followed the trail, it would take you right through the picturesque town full of beautiful beach houses, sororities, organic cafés, and the ocean. It was the place to become someone new, to flourish, be free for the first time in so many of our lives. When my friends came to town they were enamored. But after May 23, 2014, I don't think of Isla Vista like that anymore. I hate going back.

I lived behind a 7-Eleven, and the only thing separating my living room from their walls were two huge garbage containers. Mid-nap I heard one container slam shut. I imagined it was the clerk I had seen so many times when buying snacks at 2:00 a.m. taking his *I-wish-I-wasn't-at-work-anymore* sentiment out on the large dumpsters. But I heard it again. So, I looked out my window to confirm the noise, and didn't see anyone, not even the worker. Even the dumpster lid was standing up, leaning against the cement wall.

I walked outside and my roommate, who could also hear everything from her bedroom, yelled at me to come back inside. She grabbed me, and we ducked under the desk in my room, sitting on our knees. The desk faced the front of the street looking out toward the ocean, with a perfect view of the sidewalk. We saw a tall girl with blonde hair just outside. She flinched as if an imaginary punch hit her face. As she walked toward us, a car at the same moment peeled past her, headed the opposite way, toward the ocean making a sketchy right turn before completely leaving our sight. Several bangs and what sounded like a car crash followed. We later learned that the shooter was driving that car.

We saw another girl. She had fallen off her bike, which lay across the ground surrounded by her belongings scattered on the sidewalk. A 7-Eleven clerk ran out to her. He tied a tourniquet around her leg without speaking, and we all realized she'd been shot. We yelled from the living room window, offering her water, but before we could deliver, an ambulance came. The scene quickly turned into a yellow-taped maze. Even the cop who placed the barrier seemed confused.

Those next moments, after the tape was set and secure, and my apartment within the seclusion, are ones I hardly remember. Our phones rang and pinged into the atmosphere. I texted everyone back in a blurry exchange.

"I'm fine," I wrote, "I don't know anything yet."

I was annoyed having to respond to so many people. I had no information to report, but slowly details started to emerge. A manifesto was published, the cringing YouTube video I watched once, but will never again. The shooter's video, filmed in his car, with the Mesa beach of Santa Barbara encapsulating the entire background and the palm trees in perfect alignment, showed a young, angry person who spoke of his hatred of women and how he would win in the end. It was filmed in the parking lot of my school.

Seven lives ended that day, including the perpetrator, who killed himself by a self-inflicted gunshot once he made that right turn down Del Playa.

The community that came together in the aftermath of this atrocity was incredible. We all silently (and some loudly) planted these tiny seeds in the shock that consumed our minds, and they were starting to sprout, quickly. People began to organize. Silent vigils were held, walks through the town, protests against guns—more can be said about this. But truly, it was inspiring, and my heart felt something it never had before. I still think about the father who lost his only son. A son whose friends spoke so highly of him. His father now a crusader for mental health support and gun reform. A seed planted.

My memories of Isla Vista are forever ingrained in my heart and mind:

Everytime I hear of another school shooting,
I'M REMINDED OF MAY 23.

Everytime I hear of young people dying by gun violence,
I'M REMINDED OF MAY 23.

Everytime I hear a firework,
I'M REMINDED OF MAY 23.

This is my story, one written and heard like thousands and thousands of others, a multitude of creative energy bursting through from tragedy. The way it feels to be a part of something like this while knowing there's a way to eliminate its cause is yet another layer of my heartbreak. Both demand action, their seeds rooted deep in the dirt, a growing garden.

CHAPTER SEVEN

NEW RIVER COMMUNITY COLLEGE AT THE NEW RIVER VALLEY MALL

Christiansburg, Virginia / April 12, 2013

I FIRST LEARNED about the New River Community College shooting when Megan Doney, an English professor who worked at the New River Valley Mall campus at the time of the shooting, submitted a letter for publication to the book through an open call. In this letter she writes to teachers about living in the aftermath of the Santa Fe High School shooting, she writes *This experience is lonely and isolating. It halts conversations, even with family members.* What I loved about her piece was her advice to teachers: *Others will encourage you to move on, to let it go, to not let this event define you. Resist this distracting discourse of triumph. May 18th will not be the sum of all your years as teachers, but it will not leave you unmarked. Nor should it.* I'd not come across teacher-to-teacher advice in my research, yet. I knew this was a perspective we needed in the book.

Upon reading her piece, I reached out to Megan through email asking her permission to publish. In that same email, I asked if she could connect me with more survivors from that shooting. While she couldn't directly connect me, she did recommend some newspaper articles that might point me in the right direction. Through reading these articles, I discovered Taylor Schumann, a part-time employee at the College's New River Valley Mall campus who was shot as she attempted to hide in a closet. I wanted to hear her story, and invite her to contribute.

I finally found a "Taylor Schumann" on Twitter. Hoping she was the right person, I tweeted her if we could Direct Message (DM) about a project I was working on about gun violence. A few minutes after that initial tweet, she messaged me *Hi Loren! How can I help?* Excited that it might be the Taylor Schumann, I wrote back quickly *Hi Taylor! Thank you for responding. I admit, I am not entirely sure you are the correct person, but I wanted to reach out anyway. I am working on a collection of primary sources written by survivors of school shootings. I wanted to check if you were at New River. If not, I am terribly sorry. Thank you so much for your time, and quick response!* I anxiously waited for her to write back. Five minutes later and no response. Then. The three dots: *Hi! Yes that was me! I was shot through my hand. I'd be honored to contribute and help however I can!* After a few more DMs, we coordinated a time to talk on the phone the next day.

On Tuesday morning, October 9, 2018, I called Taylor. Over the phone, her voice was cheerful and had a Virginia, Southern like drawl. I told her more about the project, including deadlines and scope of the project, and ask if it'd be something she'd like to contribute to. *Yes, absolutely!* She said. *But I'm not sure what I'd write about it. And I'm scheduled to deliver my baby boy tomorrow.* I asked her *are you nervous?* The question created a ripple effect. She told me about being shot through the hand. The surgeries and painful physical therapy she had to endure, and how still, today, she struggles with mobility in that hand. She added, *sometimes I worry it will affect the way I can care for my son. Like would I be able to hold him, hold his head up, feed him?* I sighed. *I think you should write about this,* I said. *I think you should write a letter to your son about the shooting, all of your fears about the use of your hand. This way you can give it to him when he's older.*

The next day Taylor delivered her son. A few weeks later she sent me the first draft of her letter titled "What He Doesn't Know about His Mother." She writes to him *He doesn't know it yet, but his life is already affected by gun violence. Specifically, school shootings.* That line chills me from my lower back to my neck. Her letter is evidence to the power of gun violence, its ripple effect through generations, but also shows her courage, her ability, as sociologist Brené Brown would say, to speak from the heart. I have to believe it's this type of vulnerability that help others who've endured the same horror.

Loren Kleinman, Editor
October 2018

No one was killed at New River Community College, but two women, including Taylor Schumann, age 22, were wounded.

WHAT HE DOESN'T KNOW ABOUT HIS MOTHER

By Taylor Schumann

Taylor Schumann was a 22-year-old, part-time employee at New River Community College satellite campus at the New River Valley Mall in Dublin, Virginia. After hearing commotion at the front desk, she hid in a closet. As Schumann tried to hold the closet door shut, the shooter shot her in the hand.

I laid on my hospital bed, fresh from what would be my first of four surgeries to repair the damage from the gunshot wound to my left hand. I still hadn't regained full vision from the shard of wood that had cut my eye. Through my blurry vision I looked at my fiancé, now husband.

"One day, I'll tell our kids about how brave and strong their mom is," he said.

All I could think of was *How on earth am I going to take care of a child if my hand never works again? Will I be able to pick them up? Comfort them? Nurse them? What happens if my limitations are too much, and I fail them?*

Now, five and a half years later, I'm sitting on my bed. It's 1:00 a.m. and I'm staring at our new baby. A boy. He doesn't know it yet, but his life is already affected by gun violence. Specifically, school shootings.

He doesn't know that his mom is still afraid to go to the movies. Or that she has to sit in restaurants and coffee shops facing the door so she can assess any danger that might walk through. He doesn't know she shakes when she hears a loud bang. He doesn't know that large crowds scare her because she can't see what everyone is doing. He doesn't know she wakes up from nightmares or that she sobs when the news of another shooting or another victim finds their way to her.

He doesn't know that sometimes her hand aches in pain when she tries to maneuver his small, newborn body, and that the nerve endings are still raw when he innocently scratches her bullet wounds with his brand-new fingernails. He doesn't know she's afraid of failing him in the everyday mundane activities that make up life, which started because someone brought a gun to her school.

He doesn't know that it scares her to think that these anxieties might be forced onto him, and that he may grow up in a shadow of her fear that he didn't ask for or deserve.

Maybe he'll never have to know. Maybe all he'll know of his mom is that she loved him with everything in her being. That she did everything in her power to keep him safe. That she worked hard to make sure none of this ever had to be his fate. Because as his mom, I never want to look in his eyes and tell him we didn't do anything to stop it.

A LETTER TO THE FACULTY OF SANTA FE HIGH SCHOOL

By Megan Doney

Megan Doney is an English professor who worked at the New River Valley Mall campus at the time of the shooting.

Dear Colleagues,

I am a community college professor, and I too am a witness to a shooting on my campus. Afterward, like a good academic, I scoured every database I could find for research on what happened to educators who'd lived through rampage violence. I needed to know what had happened to all the people who had been burned in this fire before me, because I didn't know whether I was normal. Were my nightmares typical? Would they stop? What should I say to my students about what had happened? Was this the price of being an educator in the twenty-first century?

I was dismayed to find out that there was hardly any information on people like us. The absence of firsthand narratives of educator witnesses to school shootings felt like an inexcusable, baffling elision given the public and psychological power shootings exert. We argue ad infinitum about guns, and mental health, and security measures, all the logistical and political flashpoints that catalyze public discussions about gun violence. But when it comes to the people who are in the classroom with their students when the shots pierce the air, educators who have to decide in an instant whether to flee or barricade, open the door or lock it, our voices are absent from academic literature and from public discourse. We are ciphers.

I address this letter to you, not to the students, because I know that while you have been preoccupied with caring for them, I want to reassure you that I, and others who have been on this journey, are caring for you. I offer you the following small sentiments of consolation and perspective.

Others will encourage you to move on, to let it go, to not let this event define you. Resist this distracting discourse of triumph. May 18th will not be the sum of all your years as teachers, but it will not leave you unmarked. Nor should it. How could you be human beings otherwise, if this event didn't rattle your bones with its senselessness? Writing for the website *Return Yoga,* Karin Burke reflects, "It isn't the passage of time that heals us, but the passing through experiences." People who encourage you to move on are talking to themselves, not to you.

This experience is lonely and isolating. It halts conversations, even with family members. Most people won't be able to say more than, "That must have been scary." That is as far as they can follow you into the experience. You'll feel like there is no one you can confide in, no one who can bear the additional burden of listening to you and helping to carry your grief. In his excellent book *The Evil Hours: A Biography of Post-traumatic Stress Disorder,* David J. Morris, writing about his experiences in Iraq, reflects, "At times, my sense of alienation was so strong I seemed almost radiant with it, as if a stranger could look at me and tell that something was wrong." You too will walk through the world feeling as though everyone can surmise what has happened to you, as though the wreckage is scattered across your faces. You'll see your classroom in a different way; you'll wonder how strong the glass is, or which direction you need to turn the lock in order to secure the door. You may look at your students' faces and wonder which of them has the potential to do this. You may unconsciously look for the exit signs in every classroom, restaurant, and theater. You will learn to live in this new world where safety is an illusion.

If you're like me, you became educators because you recognized something sacred in learning; you experienced the challenge of changing your own mind, the revelation of new knowledge, the expansive worldview that education allowed you. And now, the place where those transformations take place has been violated in the worst way. The sanctuary is in ruin. But you can rebuild it, and in this endeavor your students are your allies. When you return to your classroom, you're taking a public stand. You're choosing to live and to honor learning. You're choosing to arm yourselves with faith in your students and in each other. Instead of shutting down, embrace vulnerability, because in doing so you'll fend off cynicism, resignation, and fear. What do you have now to be afraid of?

Finally, it's possible to integrate this experience into your lives, in your own time. Morris writes, "Part of trauma's corrosive power lies in its ability to destroy narrative," and Isak Dinesen says, "All suffering is bearable if it is seen as part of a story." There's fertile ground for meaning and transformation in this experience. My mission now is writing the book I needed to read in the days and weeks after my school's shooting, so that all the educators who come after me—like you—won't do fruitless online searches and wonder why their experience isn't worthy of inquiry and respect. You may discover a calling of your own, one that you could not have imagined before. You can choose how to tell this story of what's happened to you and your campus.

Whatever you choose, however you cope, you're not alone. I see you. I honor you. I understand.

MEGAN DONEY, PROFESSOR OF ENGLISH
NEW RIVER COMMUNITY COLLEGE
CHRISTIANSBURG, VA

CHAPTER EIGHT

EPISCOPAL SCHOOL OF JACKSONVILLE

Jacksonville, Florida / March 6, 2012

ON SEPTEMBER 11, 2018, I received a direct message through my Twitter account from Zach Kindy, who was interested in learning more about the book project. He'd heard of the call from another one of our contributors, Mollie Davis, a survivor of the Great Mills High School shooting. After Amye and I began sharing more details about the book publicly, more survivors began to come forward with their stories.

Zach was a student at Episcopal School of Jacksonville when the headmaster, Dale Regan, was shot and killed by a former Spanish teacher. I admitted to Zach, I'd never heard of this shooting until he reached out to me. The Episcopal shooting was covered locally in Jacksonville, Florida, and didn't reach a national scale. Over the phone Zach talked about a popping noise he heard while in science class. *It was like bags of popcorn popping.* This was a common simile survivors often used to describe the sound of the assault rifle inside their school.

Hours later Zach learned that the noise he heard was the sound of his headmaster being shot, and then the shooter turning the gun on himself. *We never thought anything of him*, Zach said of the Spanish teacher turned shooter. *He was quiet, but we never thought he'd kill someone.* Zach paused. *This is why I don't think teachers should have guns in the classroom*, he added.

Later Zach introduced me to Dorothy Poucher, a young poet, who attended Episcopal when the shooting occurred. She writes about growing up in the aftermath of her school shooting and that *i am a kid in a dark room.* Since then, I've spoken to Dorothy about her writing goals and activism. I've also spent time talking to Zach about his transition and current illnesses.

Amye and I became close with many survivors, a natural development after you listen to some of the most intimate details of their lives. In the beginning of this project, I often worried that we wouldn't have enough stories, and we wouldn't be able to connect with survivors. I was wrong.

138

Unfortunately, there is no shortage of those affected by school shootings, either through primary or secondary experience. Now I realize we've only just begun, and there aren't enough pages to share the innumerable amount of stories about the aftermath of school shootings. My work with Zach and Dorothy confirmed that for me. I had not, until Zach reached out, even heard of the Episcopal shooting. But I hope our work together will inspire more survivors from school shootings that haven't made national headlines to speak out and share their stories.

Loren Kleinman, Editor
October 2018

The following staff were shot and killed at Episcopal School of Jacksonville:

Dale Regan, 63, headmaster

MARCH 6, 2012

By Dorothy Poucher

Dorothy Poucher attended Episcopal School of Jacksonville when the shooting occurred. She wrote this poem in 2017 about her experience growing up after the shooting and read it at the March for Our Lives event in March 2018.

> *i am a kid in a dark room*
> *i haven't got the time*
> *a girl sobs beside me,*
> *but i can't even hear her*
> *fear drowns out her cries*
>
> *i am a kid in a dark room*
> *someone else tells me whether i live or die*
> *i am owner of nothing*
> *not even my mind*
> *do they think i do not mind?*
> *i mind.*
>
> *i am a kid in a dark room*
> *i can not shut my eyes*
> *i see nothing, but i keep on staring*
> *wondering when you will come*
> *to claim my life*

i am a kid in a dark room
i hear but i cannot speak
is your heart still beating
in another dark room
across the stream

i am a kid in a dark room
my mother's hands calm my shaking
she cries herself, from fright
i look right through her
is it day or night?

i am a kid in a dark room
i sleep peacefully
my darkness rests deep in my chest
where i let it sit
where i have contained its unrest

i am a kid in a dark room
time pulls at my strings
tells me when i can cry,
when i can whine.
when can i scream?

i am a kid in a dark room
their words press on me
remind me it is not over just yet
coax from a deep sleep,
the beast

now I am a kid in the dark
and I am not alone tonight,
anger sits in a holster on his hip
and fear lays comfortably by my side

Zach Kindy was a student at Episcopal School of Jacksonville at the time of the shooting.

On March 6, 2012, I woke up as any student would: tired and reluctant to go to school. It was Tuesday morning and close to spring break. My brain checked out of all things school, and I was ready to spend my days sleeping and watching Netflix. I rolled out of bed and went through my regular morning routine: got dressed, ate breakfast, brushed my teeth, and sat on the couch scrolling through my phone, the news playing in the background.

After my mom and brother finished getting ready, we loaded up in the car with me in the front seat and my brother in the back. When I finally got to school, I walked through the halls to find my friends. I heard gossip about how Mr. Schumerth, a Spanish teacher, got fired earlier that morning. I never had him as a teacher, but often spent time in his classroom with my friends, who had him for homeroom.

The day seemed *normal* until about 1:00 p.m. in science class. All of the sudden we heard a loud noise, as if someone decided to pop kernels of popcorn in a duffel bag. The classroom phone rang. My teacher picked it up. We all wondered what the call would be about. *Was someone getting out of class early? Who had to go down to the office?* In the middle of the call, three bells rang. Our teacher told everyone to get down and be quiet as he set down the phone, shut off the lights, and closed the blinds. For hours we sat against the wall in the dark. The people that didn't leave their phones in their locker were scrolling down social media and texting to loved ones. As for the rest of us, we sat reading *TIME Magazine*, talked quietly, and tried to consider situations that would cause this. Someone said the weather, but it was clear and sunny. Another said it was a drill, and another said someone was going to shoot up or bomb the school. After two hours, we finally got an answer. A classmate held up her phone high in the air, crying hysterically.

"Mrs. Reagan has been shot," she said choking on her words.

How could we comprehend the fact the head of school was killed? The silence that already existed, got even quieter. There was a heaviness in the room.

Hours later, we were released from the classroom. We were told to quickly get any belongings we needed from our lockers and then go to the plaza. Everything seemed to move in slow motion as I went to my locker to grab my phone. After I got my phone, I called my mom and she told me that my grandparents were already on their way to pick me up and that she would see me once I got home. After I hung up and walked to the plaza, I spotted my grandparents' white truck. I said goodbye to my friends as walked toward them. I opened the back door, stepped up into the truck. Still not knowing quite what to feel, I sat in silence as my grandparents questioned if I was all right. But as we drove away from the school, it all hit me. Outside the window, my teachers and classmates were broken and in tears.

For the rest of the day at home, I sat and watched the news. I learned that Mr. Schumerth had gotten fired that morning and came back with an AK-47 in a guitar case. He shot the head of school, Dale Reagan, and himself. I was in shock. *How did my school, which I considered a safe place became a nightmare of chaos?* For the rest of the day, I watched headline after headline on the TV like "Murder-Suicide at Episcopal." Clips of the 911 call endlessly looped on news stations. Today I think that the fact our school's shooter was a teacher is an example of why teachers shouldn't carry guns.

The next day, I woke up still thinking about the shooting. Episcopal authorities had closed the school but reopened it for a few hours for a memorial service, so people could grieve together. I remember attending, seeing hundreds of river rocks decorated with pictures and words of love, hope, and strength. Every confused thought and question I had about the situation was never explained, never answered: *How could something like this happen? How could someone who seemed like such a nice person do something so horrible?*

The Monday after spring break everyone returned to school. I didn't know what to expect and found myself confused and slightly uncomfortable. The sky was cloudy, and it felt strange to be back. School was school, but its atmosphere was drastically different. There was an odd amount of silence. No one knew what to say to each other.

Several days later, school finally began to feel relatively normal, and over time our community healed, but unspoken scar remained. For me, this experience serves as a prominent reminder of how sometimes the safest of spaces can become unsafe in an instant.

CHAPTER NINE

SANDY HOOK ELEMENTARY SCHOOL

Newtown, Connecticut / December 14, 2012

ON THE MORNING of December 14, 2012, one of my twin daughters stayed home from school. Warm from fever, she drifted in and out of sleep as I cleaned around her. The house was still out of sorts from the girls' sixth birthday party only two days prior. Shortly after ten o'clock, I started receiving texts from my more news-conscious friends alerting me to a school shooting unfolding at Sandy Hook Elementary School in Newtown, Connecticut.

On the news there were dozens of children with terror on their faces, walking in connected ropes through the parking lot. The adults looked just as horrified. Mary Ann Jacobs, who was working in the library that day, captured that emotion in her story, writing, *It became evident very quickly that we were missing two entire classrooms of kids.*

As the minutes ticked by, and it became obvious that those "two *entire* classrooms of kids" were not coming out, I struggled to breathe. *Twenty* children, between the ages of six and seven were dead, children were the same age as my twin daughters. *Twenty*. I pressed my spine against the doorframe of my kitchen while I sobbed—praying it would hold my pain. I watched the unfolding coverage in drips, as my sick daughter was waking up, and I remember thinking she should not associate first grade with murder.

By the time my other daughter came home from school, we knew more. Six educators were also killed. We learned it was a lone gunman, twenty-year-old Adam Lanza, responsible for this unthinkable tragedy. Lanza killed his mother, Nancy Lanza, in their shared home, before driving to Sandy Hook Elementary School, shooting his way into the school, and devastating a community. He then took his own life. At 3:16 p.m. EST, President Obama spoke to a stunned and grieving nation. He fought to hold back tears. In that moment he wasn't only our president, he was also Sasha and Malia's dad. I called my mother from the bathroom, out of earshot from my girls, and I cried harder than I ever have in my life.

The shooting happened on a Friday. That following Monday, the usual skeleton crew of parents personally dropping their kids at school had tripled in size. Goodbye hugs lasted longer than usual, and many parents wiped away tears. But I really recognized the magnitude of what had happened when I saw the teachers. Usually cheery and bright-eyed to greet our children, those same faces were now swollen, sad, and far away. I realized in that moment what it meant to love and lose "two classrooms full of children." I barely contained myself as I ran back to my car. I shook with sobs the whole way home.

As the years ticked by, Sandy Hook never left me. I joined Moms Demand Action and Everytown in the weeks that followed and made ending gun violence a priority in my life. I moved forward, painfully aware of the twenty-six families who didn't have that option. Still, I couldn't get past this. I obsessed over the terror those children must have felt. I obsessed over the parents grieving them. I thought often about those two classrooms, and the others—those nearby and close to.

When we started collecting stories for this book, I knew I had to be the one to work with Sandy Hook. This was the natural progression of *something* for me, I just didn't know what. One of the first stories I collected was from Alissa Parker, the mother of six-year-old Emilie Parker, who was murdered that day. As she spoke about Emilie's "wise beyond her years" approach to life, I saw my girls in her story. As she described Emilie's love of art, and how she and her husband, Robbie, have pictures Emilie drew documenting family events, I looked at my refrigerator covered in portraits of stick-figured people with triangle dresses and three plump fingers. Every story became my story, every child became my child. And I didn't know how to separate that. Maybe I still don't.

Then, my worst fear was realized. Even though I grieved regularly for those who lost children, I often wondered about those who survived the terror of that day. Those kids in the classrooms where it happened, where it occurred. How could they possibly move on? How could they possibly grow up? In Susie Ehren's story, I found my answers. Susie's daughter was in Ms. Soto's classroom and witnessed not only the death of her classmates, but that of her beloved teacher as well. When we spoke, Susie and I both cried. I don't know if I was crying for her daughter, for my own, for Emilie Parker, or maybe all of the above. Her daughter is growing up now, and her life has been defined not by the tragedy of Sandy Hook, but by the love of the teachers who, despite their own trauma, worked to heal with their students.

As the Sandy Hook chapter began to take shape, light began to creep in. With each week, I was crying less and less in therapy. I met the bravest of women, Abbey Clements, Mary Ann Jacob, and Cindy Clements Carlson, all of whom were in the school, all of whom found the courage and strength to not only navigate their own aftermath, but that of their students. And with each story, the incredible strength of this community became evident and brought comfort to what had been a long-lasting wound.

The shooting at Sandy Hook will always be the turning point for a nation. But what has come to define this event isn't the action of one troubled young man, rather the inaction of a full legislature. On April 17, 2013, bipartisan legislation requiring background checks and the banning of some military-style automatic weapons failed in the senate. Several more attempts at gun control would also fail. But, where the government has let these children down, the community has stepped up. I have been blessed to have met so many wonderful advocates from Newtown, all of whom were brave and strong enough to stand up when no one else did and to say ENOUGH. They are parents, teachers, and community members who continue to fight every day to make sure this doesn't happen to you or to me. They are the bearers of light.

Amye Archer, Editor
January 2019

The following students and staff were shot and killed at Sandy Hook Elementary School:

Charlotte Bacon, 6	*James Mattioli, 6*
Daniel Barden, 7	*Grace McDonnell, 7*
Olivia Engel, 6	*Emilie Parker, 6*
Josephine Gay, 7	*Jack Pinto, 6*
Dylan Hockley, 6	*Noah Pozner, 6*
Madeleine Hsu, 6	*Caroline Previdi, 6*
Catherine Hubbard, 6	*Jessica Rekos, 6*
Chase Kowalski, 7	*Avielle Richman, 6*
Jesse Lewis, 6	*Benjamin Wheeler, 6*
Ana Márquez-Greene, 6	*Allison Wyatt, 6*

Rachel D'Avino, 29, teacher's aide

Dawn Hochsprung, 47, principal

Anne Marie Murphy, 52, teacher's aide

Lauren Rousseau, 30, teacher

Mary Sherlach, 56, school psychologist

Victoria Leigh Soto, 27, teacher

BEFORE, AFTER.

By Abbey Clements

Abbey Clements was teaching second grade at the time of the shooting. She is now a volunteer leader with Moms Demand Action for Gun Safety.

BEFORE

I'd been to a handful of marches and rallies—mostly in college—and always voted. I signed petitions and was aware of injustices with class and race in America. I knew about the school-to-prison pipeline, and that we had a problem with gun violence. I was aware of current events but didn't get actively involved. I was busy raising my children and writing lesson plans. I'd been a teacher for twenty years.

DECEMBER 14, 2012

I walked into Sandy Hook Elementary School to start my day teaching second graders. I stopped at the office and had a brief conversation with Principal Hochsprung about the importance of rapport between teachers and students. The two of us headed down the hall together—I walked into my classroom to prepare for the day, and she continued to a meeting in the conference room on the other side of the building.

There was a lot going on that time of year, being that it was almost winter break and the holidays. I'd heard that Mrs. Hochsprung was going to be popping into classrooms, so before the official start of math, I wanted to squeeze in time to make snowflakes for our PTA holiday luncheon. I got everyone quiet, and that's when we heard a loud crash I initially thought were folding chairs falling. We just had a holiday program, so that would make sense. What wouldn't make sense was what really happened: Someone who shouldn't have had access to a semiautomatic rifle killed his mother, then came to my beautiful school, in my beautiful town, and shot through the front door with several lethal weapons and hundreds of rounds of ammunition.

My classroom was on the right when he entered the school. He turned left, and murdered six of my colleagues and friends, and twenty beautiful children. Some children and educators witnessed the carnage firsthand, others ran for their lives or went into lockdown. The latter was true for myself and my students of only seven and eight years old. We stayed put, waiting to be rescued from what I thought was surely a gang. We huddled, tried to sing, I tried to read books. We listened. My students cried, were terrified, they laughed—confused, they scooched, snuggled into coats. We were so thirsty that we shared a water bottle. I didn't consciously think: We might die, don't worry about spreading germs. There was no time for thoughts like that. There were people on the roof—heavy footsteps. *They're here to help us*, I told my students, though I doubt I was convincing. The police banged on the door and yelled for us to get out. How was I to believe them? The kids told me to open the door. *You're shaking*, they said. I opened the door. We were rushed out, running. I don't remember the route we took out. I had kids in my outstretched arms. We passed state police with knees bent, guns in hand, in ready position, yelling: *Go, get out, run!* We were led out a door. It was cold. I had no coat. I watched my feet run. My chest hurt from breathing in the cold air.

There was nothing I did out of the ordinary that day. Even pulling two kids from the hallway, when I first heard the shots.

No active drill, no lockdown drill allowed us to escape. He turned left and we were on the right.

AFTER

A few months after the tragedy, I started getting involved in the gun violence prevention movement and I haven't looked back. Gun violence destroys people, families, neighborhoods, communities, schools, districts, towns, friendships, marriages, livelihoods, and so much more. And the aftermath of such tragedy is larger and darker than you might imagine. I had to do something to be part of the solution.

Now I'm a volunteer leader with Moms Demand Action for Gun Safety fighting to chip away at our deplorable statistics. Americans are afraid to go to school, the movies, the mall, concerts, work, church, parking lots. We're a traumatized nation.

But I work two full-time jobs to try to change that. I continue to teach at another school in Newtown, trying to build a generation of empathetic problem solvers. Educators teach peace and nonviolence. We teach conflict resolution by talking out problems. This is gun violence prevention, too.

What I do know after teaching for over twenty-six years is that guns don't belong slung around educators' shoulders, strapped across our thighs, or locked in desks ready to be used in a Hollywood-style "save the day" way. Guns don't belong in the places where our children play and learn. The presence of guns in schools is antithetical to the basic tenets of school. I don't want to live in a country where everyone has to be armed everywhere, all the time. This is the National Rifle Association's agenda. It's not mine.

THE ROAD BACK

By Susie Ehrens

Susie Ehrens's two children were students at Sandy Hook Elementary School at the time of the shooting. Her daughter was in Ms. Soto's classroom, where the shooting occurred.

The morning of December 14, 2012, was a bright, sunny winter morning. My third- and first-graders were on the bus to school and the baby at day care. I was due into the school for an afternoon gingerbread house decorating project in Ms. Soto's classroom with my six-year-old daughter's first grade class.

I remember getting calls first on my home phone, which I didn't answer as I was on a work call, then my work phone rang, which I still didn't answer, when finally, my cell phone rang. I could see it was my day-care provider and remember thinking the baby must be sick or need something. When I answered, I immediately knew something was wrong. Through sobs she said something like, "Susie, there was a shooting. Your daughter's at the police station."

I don't remember the ride to the police station, but somehow managed to call my husband. Panicked, I screamed at him, telling him to go to Sandy Hook Elementary School and find our son, a third grader, because there was a shooting. I told him our daughter was somehow at the police station and I would go there.

We had no idea what "there was a shooting" actually meant at that time.

As I pulled into the police station, I had to slam on the brakes to not hit the building. My entire body shook with fear as I ran, banging into the police station looking for my child.

I was directed to a small quiet room off the main entrance of the station where one of our good friends sat with five children—my daughter and four boys from her class. As I charged into the room, my little girl burst out crying and ran to me. I did what I could to soothe her, not knowing what had happened. When I asked, the children said, *he killed our teacher and our friends and we had to run. The gun was really big*, they said.

It's hard to explain the disconnect I felt in that moment, how the words felt alien in the air. *Gun, shooter, dead, teacher*, these are words that should never come from a six-year-old child's mouth. It didn't, and still doesn't make sense that there was a man with a very big gun in a first-grade classroom. And that this happened before 10 a.m. on a regular Friday.

As the day unfolded more details emerged. My husband, following my call, sped to the school, and got close enough to the school entrance to have witnessed some of the aftermath of first responders exiting. He never said it aloud, but I imagine that was traumatic to witness their reactions. We kept in touch via texting. The panic was growing as he hadn't yet seen our son exit the school. At some point he made his way to the firehouse and finally found our son, scared, but alive.

The mayhem, panic, and fear my husband described to me is unfathomable. At some point, when it likely began to sink in for him, was when the father of one of our daughter's friends asked if my husband had seen his daughter. She was one of the children, who, we would later learn, didn't make it out of the classroom.

That evening, the five of us gathered in our new home. We had lived in Newtown for many years but had just moved to a new home a month earlier to accommodate our growing family. Ironically, although each child had their own bedroom, for weeks after the shooting, maybe even months, we all slept in the master bedroom. My parents, my sister and her husband, my aunt, everyone just came to Newtown. I remember being surprised that my brother-in-law left his work early (over an hour away) to come to our house. It's not unusual that he'd be at a family event, but the fact that it was during the day, and he never left work early unless it was previously planned, was an indication of the enormity of what had happened. In the days that followed, our phones were never quiet—the house phone, our cell phones all buzzed nonstop. Calls from family, friends, even news outlets, all wanting to know if our children survived, how were they doing, and from the news outlets, would we give them an interview.

I held my tiny, six-year-old daughter on my lap while she told her version of the chaos to the investigating officer that day at the police station. She told us with as many words and details as she could, who was standing where, who was never coming out of the school, what he was wearing, what his hair and hat looked like, how big the gun was. And yet, even in that interview, just a few hours following the shooting, some of the details had already been locked away in her brain to protect to her, blocked from being able to speak the words, if she even had the words to describe what she had witnessed. Where her teacher was or what had happened to her was never spoken. It would be two years of trauma-focused, cognitive behavioral therapy sessions before she would acknowledge that she saw her beloved Ms. Soto shot and killed and where she was standing and where she fell and how my daughter wished for and dreamed about having been able to help her.

In the days and weeks that followed, my daughter was terrified to be in a room alone, scared of everything that made noise, scared to go to sleep, afraid to move to a room that was unoccupied. Pure, shocking, all-out fear. We attended six or seven funerals. We had to split up because the timing overlapped. We had to explain what a funeral was, and she insisted on coming to a select few. Her best friend's, and Miss Soto's.

I was in a fog for weeks. We knew very little about trauma and what to do or how to care for the kids and their fears. We heard from the therapists who were brought in to "keep the routine." "Keep the schedule." Under normal circumstances, children like structure and it would be more important now than ever. Time seemed to stand still. There were no words that made a difference, nothing that seemed to make anything better, nothing that stopped the fear from taking over.

At one point, a few of the mothers from our class suggested we bring the surviving children together. I don't remember who contacted whom, or how we found each other, but we did. Soon we realized so many people wanted to help our survivors. I can tell you there wasn't a parent among us who knew what to do with that sentiment. Our children were here. They lived. So many didn't. I felt an enormous amount of guilt, grief, and relief in equal measure. I remember thinking, how do you live a life big enough to fulfill the fate you were handed?

Our daughter has always been a happy child. A preemie by nine weeks who survived and thrived. She was strong. Whatever it was that kept her going in those early days after the shooting, kept us going. She was scared but wanted to go back to school. *Routine. Structure.* We sent her back several weeks later when the school reopened in an unused school building a town away. I went with her on the first day and for many days thereafter. I remember sitting in little first-grade seats watching them learn. They were filled with nervous energy. Every noise was like an alarm. They'd jump at the slightest sound and run for the door or the nearest adult seeking safety.

The year after the shooting, we needed to be sure each child was placed with the "right" second-grade teacher. I remember talking to the interim principal about teacher placement and how our little girl was sensitive and loving and needed someone that would hold her when she got scared. Abbey Clements was the exact right person for her at that time. We didn't know Mrs. Clements before sitting with her at Vicki Soto's funeral, and that may have been the beginning of their connection. That connection deepended throughout the year. On some days, the constant battling of fear and anxiety left my baby girl exhausted, and she often fell asleep in school, and often in the arms of Mrs. Clements. And when she cried and told Abbey she missed Miss Soto—Mrs. Clements simply held her and said, "I do, too."

That year, learning became secondary to keeping the childrens' trauma in check and finding a sense of order and peace. The only way to find a place for learning, was to find a way to clear their minds and find the peace. The kids may not have understood this, and truthfully, maybe the teachers didn't at that point in time, either, but together, they made it through and began to fight their way back. Mrs. Clements and her fellow teachers showed our children that they too, were afraid, but together, they could be strong and learn the new normal.

At home, we signed up for every event offered for our children's well-being. It felt like we tried every therapy: Trauma-focused CBT, play therapy, grief therapy, talk therapy, equine therapy, tapping, aromatherapy, MNR, and art and music therapy. Ultimately, music therapy would prove to be the most effective. Until quite recently, music was a biweekly therapy. While each of the other therapies had benefits, many had unintended consequences. And because our children were so young, it was usually well into the therapy before we saw the impact— negative or positive. For example, they didn't even have words to describe the immense grief and guilt, yet we thought they could sustain talk therapy. And there were many experts. *Many* experts who all told us they knew the solution. In hindsight, no one knew our children better than us. We did what we thought was right and what we hoped would cause the least amount of additional trauma. In the end, beyond family, it was the love of Mrs. Clements, a teacher, that softened my daughter's heart and opened her mind. In so many ways, Mrs. Clements brought Emma back to us. And for that, there are no words to truly describe the gratitude in my heart.

In the years since, I've become a gun violence prevention advocate, a member of Moms Demand Action, and have done what I can in the way of fighting and at least speaking out against politicians who turn a blind eye to the senseless gun violence in this country. I have rallied and Marched for Our Lives with my fourteen-year-old son in March 2018 in Washington, D.C. There is nothing more powerful, heartening, and pride-inducing than to see your fourteen-year-old son, the survivor of a mass shooting himself, hold up a sign for hours, while marching in the streets of Washington D.C. His sign read I AM A SANDY HOOK SURVIVOR on one side, and WE CAN END GUN VIOLENCE on the other. The overwhelming fear and joy and pride is indescribable. He is finding his voice, and I can only hope that voice wants to fight for commonsense gun laws in this country. I believe my son feels no one, no child, should ever feel as helpless and scared as he did that day.

Today my daughter, who witnessed the unspeakable, who lives with that memory every day of her life, and who fights the triggers and knows how to calm her body when it begins to tense up out of fear, struggles with the daily balance to be a "normal" twelve-year-old. To not be the one that's different. And on the inside, for the most part, that is all true. Except every night she goes to bed and says good night to the picture of her and her best friend from kindergarten on her nightstand. And her best friend isn't here anymore. She is painfully aware what death is and when evil visited here. But we try very hard to instill hope and joy and overcome the trauma with love and kindness.

My daughter has many years to decide what she wants to "do" with her life. But this year, she has decided she wants to be a teacher at Sandy Hook Elementary School. I can't imagine the courage it will take for her to walk in that school and teach and breathe life into children. The joy of her conquering her greatest fear is beyond my adult comprehension. Perhaps because my daughter knows firsthand what the love of a good teacher can do for a child. I don't know what path she'll ultimately decide to follow. What I do know, is that Mrs. Clements loved her, and that my daughter felt that love. That her teacher didn't always have the words to make things less scary. But that teacher showed up. Every day. And taught her children, taught my child, what it was to be brave and kind.

Looking back, we didn't know what we didn't know. Trauma is cruel and relentless and painful to everyone it touches. The cycle is not a straight line. It is messy and it hurts, and it's relentless in its grasp. And our children survived. Our children survived. I have no comprehension of the sadness of those families who lost loved ones. I am still not sure I understand the depths of my own trauma or the guilt of having not one, but both children survive. It has forever altered the trajectory of our lives on a daily basis. It changes the way you look at the world, how you interact, how you engage, and how you withdraw. The reasons may change over time, but the end result, is that trauma changes you at the very core of who you are.

It also doesn't help to run away from the trauma. Hold it when you need to and let it go when you can. It is a monumental task to remember that no one else can define who you are. I work on these things every day. I work on teaching and sharing these beliefs with my children. I fail more often than I succeed, but I choose to not let this tragedy define an entire generation of my family. We are not the same as we were before. Some days we are broken, some we are closer to being healed, and some we are somewhere in between. But I desperately try to find the good and instill a sense of goodness and kindness in my children. I want them to know that their hearts are good, and they can do so much good in the world.

Maybe that's what the senseless violence and thousands of deaths caused by guns every year are doing—building an army of kindness. There is no good reason to believe any of it is meant to be, or it happened for a reason, but these things happened to us. They happened in Newtown and far too many other places to count. So, at least in my house, I have a few soldiers that know love and kindness and compassion. Hopefully, we are close to finding the masses that will rise up and say enough.

AFTERMATH

By Cindy Clement Carlson

Cindy Clement Carlson worked in the Sandy Hook Elementary School Library Media Center from March 2011 to July 2017. She and her daughter were present at the time of the shooting.

I don't remember making any decisions. A colleague heard what we thought was odd, staticky laughing over the intercom so we called the office and a secretary, whose bravery we would only fully understand later, told us there was a shooter in the building. I had my cell phone on my desk and later found it in my pocket. Without thinking, I began to cover the doorway's windows with our emergency shades. I called 911. I helped shepherd our library students into the narrow space previously determined not visible from the hallway.

After evacuation by state troopers came the hurried walk across the school yard to the fire station. It was clear to me the shooter was a lone, violent domestic abuser looking for his wife. Or a deranged father with a grudge against the principal. Those images came automatically. Then at the station I overheard someone say, "worse than Columbine." That fragment of conversation defined the next few hours as the catastrophic waves of information—so many known victims, so many still missing—broke over us. *Worse than Columbine.*

At the fire station we all wanted gum. Our mouths were dry. The pieces someone came up with were broken in two to make them go around further. Later, we put a package of gum in our new emergency kit, remembering how we craved it. Water too. The firehouse was equipped with a kitchen and desperate to do something, anything, I passed a tray of plastic cups filled with water.

In the days ahead my body made the choices my mind could not. I couldn't eat. I remember taking a few bites of chicken and feeling as if I'd gorged myself. Then an unexpected period and a cold sore from the stress. We had fled the school without our bags or coats. The next day I called my doctor's office for a refill of the cold sore prescription left behind in the bag under my desk. The weekend answering service gave me a hard time until my voice broke explaining why I needed a refill.

Normally a two-cup-a-day coffee drinker, all I wanted was weak tea. The colleagues who talked of the wine they went home to? I was crackling with grief and horror and felt as if the stimulus of caffeine and alcohol would blow me apart me like a firecracker in a glass jar.

My sister-in-law sent us a care package including chocolate chip cookie bars. I lost them for two days. I figured I'd accidentally thrown them out. Then on the third day, I found them in the desk drawer with the rulers and scrap paper.

On the way to a funeral in Katonah, we stopped at a Starbucks in Danbury. My eyes filled with tears as I realized they'd chosen to wear our school colors, green and white, in honor of Sandy Hook Elementary School. It took me half a day to realize those were the regular uniforms.

I felt neon. As if to walk past me you'd read on my skin **WAS IN BUILDING WAS IN BUILDING WAS IN BUILDING.** I felt a bodily need to rid myself of my story, to hear it told aloud, to bear witness, but I held back. I walked through the Sandy Hook town center as so many did, visiting the homemade memorials, watching the media trucks. I saw people three or four times removed from the event being interviewed and I judged them for their quick willingness to characterize our situation. And yet even as I did, I felt others who had been injured or lost family members could judge me as involved only tangentially, to have been unaffected, to have had a happy ending. My family and my body were intact.

I made a new Gmail account and emailed myself thoughts because my mind couldn't hold them. Even now when I look through the hundreds of emails I sent myself I read some as if for the first time.

I developed a habit of counting off twenty-six people wherever I went. In church, at a store, even at the funerals. I needed to see twenty-six. The destruction and loss was unfathomable. My mind could not take it in, so my eyes needed to see it, to size it up, to make visual and tangible the horrible enormity.

I went to a yoga class at a studio in Sandy Hook and saw myself holding a pose in the mirror. I remember the startle of realizing that—yes—my body could do this too. I wasn't just a channel for sorrow and guilt, I could move in a calm and beautiful way. I remember feeling the hope that I could feel whole again.

What else did we need to feel whole? Did we need the union's grocery gift certificate? The two extra personal days? The tokens and trinkets from all over the world left nearly daily in our school mailboxes? In time, many realized it was therapy, career changes, massage, prayer, transfers within the district, EMDR therapy (Eye Movement Desensitization and Reprocessing), medication, and connecting with staff from Columbine, but in the meantime we watched Powerpoints about the importance of sleep, dabbed ourselves with essential oils when offered, shared gallows humor over well-meaning cut-and-paste school district wellness emails, and sat in school assemblies as authors and actors offered their time and talent intending to help us and our students heal.

Slowly, the mind and body came back together. Only years later would I fully come to understand how the traumatized brain and body work. Or don't work. Later, learning of research and writing by Steven Marans, Laura van Dernoot Lipsky, Bessel van der Kolk, Carolyn Lunsford Mears, and Bruce D. Perry I understood the dry mouth, the cookies in the pencil drawer, the inability to recognize a Starbucks uniform.

And so gradually the mind kicks back in and then decisions and realities came one after another. These subsequent months and years are the more difficult phase, the fraught part two. There's training for a wild animal in the school, for high wind, for an active shooter. There's no training for navigating the *aftermath* of a shooting.

So, attend every funeral for every child, but attend to your own child who was with her fourth-grade class that day. Go back to school right away, but don't go back too soon. Describe forgiveness, but don't prescribe forgiveness. Put this sticker on your car, but not that one. Support grief this way, but not that way. Greet victims' families in the grocery store, but please leave them alone. Catalog this book for the school library, but not that one. Arm teachers, but get guns out of schools. Tear down the old school, but keep a school in Sandy Hook. Slowly the mind grasps that the dead can never be brought back, yet you can't stop that mind from churning out ways you could make it better and it's all made worse by a town full of opinions.

When there was complaining at a PTA meeting about how donated goods were being distributed, one mom called out, "If you have your kids shut up!" And that's the crux of it. When to shut up and when to speak up.

As a staff and individually, we navigated the push and pull of how to honor the dead, where to spend your time, how to volunteer, when to make your donations, how to manage your emotional capacity, when to care for yourself. It was easier when the horrified mind took control of the body. It was easier not to have any decisions to make.

The *Newtown Bee*, the local newspaper, in a front-page editorial on the five-year anniversary, pointed out that "What we have learned is that not all good intentions came across as they were meant." It was an upsetting characterization of a community that has turned political points of view, hearts, schedules, and philanthropic priorities inside out to support whomever needed it in the aftermath. How difficult the aftermath and the decisions it entails hasn't been easily understood.

Nevertheless, individually and collectively survivors keep trying. We are grateful that our bodies and the bodies of our children are whole, and we strive to support those who are not. So many are willing to share their stories with those who have and will suffer as we have. I'm grateful to those who listen.

A CONVERSATION WITH ALISSA PARKER

Alissa and Robbie Parker are the parents of Emilie Parker, who was murdered in the Sandy Hook shooting on December 14, 2012. Alissa, alongside Michelle Gay, whose daughter Josephine was also killed that day, is the cofounder of Safe and Sound Schools. Alissa is also the author of *An Unseen Angel: A Mother's Story of Faith, Hope, and Healing after Sandy Hook.* The following is an excerpt of the interview between Alissa and editor Amye Archer.

ON EMILIE

From the very beginning, Emilie was a very different baby. She was very well behaved. She was easy. I thought I was just this amazing mother, but it turns out, she was just really easy and pleasant to be around. She slept through the night at six weeks. She could speak in full sentences by eighteen months. Because she was so highly verbal, and could communicate so well, she never felt misunderstood. Because of that, we could not remember a time that she had a temper tantrum at all.

We laugh about the fact that she would talk nonstop every day and all day, which was one of my favorite things about her. You always knew where you stood and what was on her mind. You knew what she was thinking. My dad once commented that, "It's like she thinks out loud." That was a really good description of her. She never missed a moment to talk to someone next to her. If we were at the grocery store, she would see someone and be like, "Hi, my name's Emilie, what's your name?"

In a lot of ways, she reminded *me* of better manners. It reminded me what it meant to think of other people and to be very selfless. I always appreciated that tenderness that she had toward other people.

Emilie loved to create art. Everywhere we went, she had art with her. Paper, pens, crayons, markers. She'd have oil pastels, which she loved to use. Any time we got in our van, she'd sit in the very back with this portable tray that had all of her art supplies, and she'd stick it on her lap, and that is what she would do for our drive. She would sit and do artwork. She could go through an entire notebook in a day, easily. Filling the whole thing up with pictures. But what I loved about it, is that it was like a journal into her life. We look back now at the pictures, and we see a picture of our family at Chuck E. Cheese, for a birthday, or whatever it was we were doing that day. In a lot of ways, that was really sweet.

To be able to see her inner thoughts, expressed through her artwork. When she passed away, inspired us to start a nonprofit organization (The Emilie Parker Art Connection) where almost 100 percent of the donations go toward funding art programs for kids, and more recently we've begun to focus on art therapy for kids, because art was her way of coping with struggles. And that was her way of communicating her emotions and so we decided to specifically focus on those therapies.

ON FAITH AND FORGIVENESS

After Emilie died, I remember going out to our car to say a prayer with my husband, and as we started the prayer the words came to my mind, that everything was going to be okay, and that Emilie was okay. It wasn't as if I immediately knew that everything was going to work out. I found that moment in the darkest time. That promise that everything was going to be okay. But at the same time, it felt almost impossible for that to actually happen.

I felt very overwhelmed and very confused by the fact that something so evil had so much power over the world, and I always had believed that things were fairly balanced, if not that the light was winning in the world. The shooting really challenged that idea and made me question the world that I lived in and how to live in such an evil place where such darkness could exist. I know this all sounds very heavy, but I mean it was a real moral dilemma for me.

ON SCHOOL SAFETY

After the shooting, I was filled with so much guilt, because I had seen the things that were wrong with Emilie's school beforehand. I had verbalized them to my husband, and we had multiple conversations about how if someone tried to get into the school, Emilie would be very vulnerable. I had mentioned that the doors didn't lock to him. The classroom doors could not be locked from the *inside.* So, if someone's inside the school, and wanted to do harm, the teachers would have to come out into the hallway, where the shooter would be, and was in our case, to lock their doors. I had mentioned how easy it would be to get into the school. I had said all of these things prior to the shooting.

I saw those things, and I did nothing. I dismissed them because I was one of those people who would go into their kid's school and think *that's never going to happen here.* I thought *I never have to worry about it. We live in a safe community. You're just being paranoid.* And I dismissed it, ignored my feelings.

After the shooting happened, I did not want to let my voice go unheard. So, a lot of the community was buzzing at that point with all these different pop-up nonprofits. We're all talking about coming together and creating change. I wanted to know if anyone was going to handle school safety. I'd seen these basic standards in schools as completely insufficient for what needed to happen, basic things. And this kept me up at night.

But when I went to the meetings, everything had to do with legislation and I thought, *There's so much we can do without lawmakers, without waiting for anyone else to tell us what to do, we could do it ourselves. We could prevent someone from coming into our school and creating this harm without anyone else giving us permission to do it. We could do it as a community.*

I came to Michelle [Gay] one day and said, "I have this idea. I would like to take our platform, whatever platform it is we have, and use it to help people learn from what happened at our school." Because we had learned so much at this point, and I wanted my hindsight to be others' foresight, so they could learn from our story. I wanted to do whatever I could to help protect kids in their schools.

For a while, a lot of people said, "Why are you even going to consider putting your child back in a public school?" And I thought really hard about that for a long time.

My answer came from my mom. When I was in elementary school, my mom was involved in PTA. She was the PTA president at one point, and I remember her coming to the school constantly, and she was busy, and she was involved. I would see how she was stressed, and ask, "Why is it you continue to do this? Why are you so involved at this school?" Her response was, "I believe in the public school system, and I believe in being part of the solution." And when this happened and I was thinking about what I was not only going to do with my life, what I was going to do with my voice, what I was going to do with my children, I remembered those words.

I can't run from this. I want to be a part of the solution.

Our goal was to change the conversation. Now, we're hearing people talking about locking the doors in a different way. We're hearing people use our language and to me, that is the most rewarding part. They don't even know necessarily that it came from Michelle and me. That people are changing their attitudes and their perceptions about school safety and taking it very serious. That is the best reward for me.

ON LEARNING TO HEAL

I guess for me, it was to have patience with myself. To forgive myself and to realize that you don't owe anyone else anything. I'm talking about family, and friends, and loved ones. Your energy should go toward you and your family and your healing and that it's okay to tell people no.

For me, I could see that people were deeply affected by what happened, and they were looking to me to make them feel better. So, I was doing that part. I was staying strong. And I realized that I didn't need to do that. That I was okay to be in a bad place for a while. I'm okay to not be able to do my dishes for a while. I'm okay to lay in bed and sleep every once in a while. A little longer. To allow myself to grieve. That to me, was a very powerful moment, where I realized, I didn't owe anyone else anything. I owed myself the time to heal, and that even though I was a different person completely, and that I was never going to be that same person, that taking that time to discover who I was going to be, was my right. And I could take as much time as I needed to find that person again.

YOUR NAME DOESN'T HURT ME

By Geneva Cunningham

Geneva Cunningham was in fourth grade at Sandy Hook Elementary School on December 14, 2012. The following is an excerpt of a speech she delivered to her school, Hopkins, on April 20, 2018. She was fifteen at the time of this speech. Inspired by the March for Our Lives movement, this was one of the first time Geneva spoke about the shooting in her elementary school.

My name is Geneva. I've been asked to speak today because I had a horrible thing happen to me. I didn't choose it, I had no control over it, and it wasn't about politics. This assembly is about remembering, about learning about the legislation, and about what we can do about gun violence, gun control, and horrible things we can't control. I don't know if this assembly is a good place for me to talk to you. There are so many things that so many people want to say about this issue. I have been coached to include as much about my experience as possible. But I don't know what about my experience is important. I have been coached to keep it short, to not go on and on. I have been coached to tell every little detail, so it burns in your minds. I don't think I'm going to satisfy either of these coaches today.

I wasn't pressured into doing this, but I felt I had to, because I was never able to be proactive about things when I was nine. I wanted change, but I didn't know what to do back then. I really didn't understand the whole context of the shooting. The school and parents tried to shield us from the truth, because it was horrifying and they didn't want us to be traumatized. Because of this, the surviving children of Sandy Hook didn't get anything proactive done. And I'm still traumatized, so who can say what the result of their efforts really was.

Now that I'm older, and I want people to hear about my experience, I chose this opportunity. When I see the Parkland kids doing their thing this year, I admire it. They're so much older than I was then. Now I'm at the age when people can share their experiences and demand a response. Now, I'm here.

I don't know exactly what to say to you. But that's not an apology.

When I think about that day, it is still a nightmare. The effects of that day, including the PTSD, have followed me my entire life. I don't even know if reading this speech in front of everyone is going to be an emotional disaster for me. It's risky. I don't want to have an emotional reaction in front of people who are questioning my experience.

And if I say the name, *Adam Lanza*, probably some of you don't know who that is. And some of you will sigh, because you know who it is because it's just a name. You don't see a face, a key to unlock all these memories I work so hard to master. And I want you to see me struggle up here, mastering them, as a way for you to appreciate not that I'm weak, but that pain is real.

I want to say something to Adam Lanza too. I want to say, "You took so much from my life, and I'm not giving you anymore. Your name doesn't hurt me." But it's not true yet. And I don't want people who weren't there to try and control my story.

Do I want to make a difference? Maybe my story can help some of you feel a little differently. Not so much feel as if you were there, but feel as if you can be in a room with people who were there and that you can let me talk about this thing that happened to me, and you won't think it's the only thing that defines my life. Maybe this is about seeing me as less of a symbol and more of a human being, so we can move forward with a little more empathy and productive legislation down the road.

When I was nine and ten, I tried to forget it all. People wanted to help me forget, because a loud noise would go off and I'd get so upset that I couldn't breathe, or even think. I also struggled to learn, make friends, or trust my own sense of reality. Now I want to remember because I am at the age of action and responsibility. But I have these lapses, where for some reason I can't remember everything like the well-edited movie people seem to require in order to understand or care about me or about the issues around that one bad day.

I have learned that people will seize on these memory lapses to justify their own questioning or doubt about that day, and about me. That used to make me furious, and I'm learning that part of my journey forward is to deal with those people. But today isn't about fighting doubters. Being uncertain is okay at school, even for me.

I've heard from the people in the room where the shots were fired, and they say the trauma is way worse than for people in the halls. I was in the halls. And there's a stigma in Newtown that I have to be fine, because I didn't lose a sibling. But my mother was teaching in a kindergarten room down the hall that day. She was almost killed.

And I've come to this new school, and everyone tells me, it's okay to feel this way. They're supportive, and they're also curious. They don't all have a good sense of boundaries.

But I feel I have to justify myself every time I have a response that other people notice, that I have to tell my life story so it's okay for me to feel upset. That's somehow part of why I am here.

WOMEN IN THE FACE OF GUN VIOLENCE
By Mary Ann Jacob

Mary Ann Jacob was working in the library at Sandy Hook Elementary School at the time of the shooting.

While the epidemic of school shootings in this country causes a ripple effect through families and communities, this particular form of gun violence affects the staff and faculty of these schools particularly hard. Often parents ourselves, we are faced with the monumental task of trying to heal and recover within our own families, while wearing a brave face and comforting our returning and often traumatized students.

I know this personally, because on December 14, 2012, a gunman shot his way into Sandy Hook Elementary School while I was working in the library. He blasted his way through the hallway killing our principal, Dawn Lafferty Hochsprung, and our school psychologist, Mary Sherlach, and injuring two other staff members. He then went into two classrooms where he killed twenty first graders and four more educators, while the rest of the staff was frantically hiding and protecting the children in their care.

From the library, I heard noise over the loudspeaker and thought it was Dance Party Friday, a tradition Dawn had started in our school to celebrate the coming of the weekend. I left my desk and walked over to the phone and called the office to let them know the intercom was on. The secretary, answered from under her desk and yelled—"There's a shooter in the building!" At that moment, I realized what I was hearing was gunfire. I yelled, "lockdown" to the librarian and ran across the hallway and did the same to the classrooms across from us, slamming their doors shut. When I ran back into the library, the librarian was calmly lining the kids up in the designated spot we had learned from our training.

We stayed there, listening while 154 gunshots ripped through our beloved school. We were scared to death but tried to remain calm for the eighteen children we were responsible for, most of them only nine years old. This same sheltering was happening across the building in twenty more classrooms, where more than eighty staff members were frantically trying to protect their students in the same way, while wondering if we would ever see our own children again. With us in the library was the child of a teacher from another classroom, and a staff member whose own child was in the gym.

After a few minutes one of our doors, which we thought was locked, opened and the barrel of a shotgun appeared, followed by the face of a Newtown Police officer. After quickly seeing we were okay, he signaled for us to stay put and left the room. That made it clear we were not safe, and we crawled on our hands and knees through the library into a storage room where there were file cabinets, computer servers, and school supplies. We shoved a filing cabinet in front of the door and waited.

At this point, the kids began to get scared. This was clearly out of the ordinary for a drill and I'm sure, despite our best efforts, they could see our fear. We handed out some paper and crayons to try and distract them. Some were asking what was going on and we answered honestly that we didn't know, but our job in that moment was to remain quiet and wait for instructions.

Meanwhile, at schools across town, other staff members and students were in lockdown, hearing bits and pieces of what was happening in our school. My two sons were in the high school just a mile away watching what was unfolding on their phones. They were frantically texting me, but my phone was on my desk going unanswered.

After about an hour, the police finally found us. We had them identify themselves and I opened the door a crack. What greeted me was a roomful of men with rifles in bulletproof vests. They instructed us to have the kids come out in pairs so an adult could escort two kids each. I remember taking a moment before I turned back around to face the students in order to compose my face, as the fear was beginning to become overwhelming. As we ran out of the building we were being covered by police in the hallways with guns, we didn't know what was happening exactly, we just felt terrified. When we emerged from the building there was bedlam. Police, parents frantically looking for their children, helicopters flying overhead and more ambulances than I had ever seen. Someone took the children from me, and I was face-to-face with the First Selectman, Pat Llodra. I asked her what was going on and she replied, "It's the worst thing this country has ever seen, worse than Columbine."

I went into the firehouse in a daze and began assisting staff organizing students by classroom so we could release them to their parents. It became evident very quickly that we were missing two *entire* classrooms of kids. We wouldn't learn until later that some had run and survived, but in the end, twenty children and six adults had been murdered.

When those of us who survived went home later that day, the first thing we had to do was be strong for our own children, several of whom also survived the shooting that day, and many of whom were school-aged children in other community schools. I can remember walking up to my front door, putting my hand on the doorknob, and thinking, "Pull yourself together, you are about to see your kids," before I turned the handle. Within hours of surviving one of the worst mass shootings this country has ever seen, we had no choice but to put aside our own grief and trauma to take care of those around us.

When the time came to return to school a few weeks later, the staff and the teachers were once again faced with the choice of whether to take care of ourselves or others. The school district floated the idea of bringing in substitute teachers if we were not up to returning, but not one staff member thought the kids should return to a school full of strangers. Without exception, the staff at Sandy Hook chose to be there to greet the surviving children as they returned to an unfamiliar school in a neighboring town. We held each other up as the days and weeks wore on so we could be there day in and day out for the students.

The staff was largely left to fend for themselves in those early months, with little or no mental health support. Some of us were able to connect with support while others were not. Some of the earliest help offered was from surviving staff members from Columbine who wanted to come and support us. The school system refused to support the visit so we met offsite on a cold weekend in January. We learned then that other mass shooting survivors would offer us the best glimpse of how to navigate the path we were on. We subsequently also met with members of the Amish community who had suffered their own tragedy about five years earlier. Those bonds remain strong today.

As time progressed and we grew stronger, many of us chose to add our voices to those calling for an end to the gun violence that was continuing to assault our schools, churches, offices, and homes. We could no longer stand by while more children died day after day. Eighteen months after the shooting at our school, I had reached my own personal tipping point. I watched on TV as the horror unfolded after the shooting in Isla Vista,

California. I was shaken to my core as I watched Richard Martinez, whose son Christopher was killed in that shooting, plead that "Not One More" person be taken by gun violence. And I knew then it was my time to stand up and speak out.

I joined Everytown for Gun Safety and learned about the many issues surrounding gun violence in our country today. I learned ninety-six Americans are killed by guns every day. I learned black men are thirteen times more likely to be shot and killed with a gun than white men. I learned that women are disproportionately affected by gun violence and that more than fifty women are shot to death by an intimate partner each month. That last fact resonated with me. Women, like the women at my school, are often forced into the dual role of survivor and savior. When these tragedies occur, who most often picks up the pieces of these families? Women.

So it's no surprise that the effort to end gun violence has galvanized women across the country into action. Since the Sandy Hook Elementary School shooting millions of people—many of whom are women—have joined Moms Demand Action for Gun Sense in America, an organization started by Shannon Watts in her kitchen following the shooting. We have almost as many members as the NRA, and they've been around for over a hundred years longer than we have.

In the years since the shooting at Sandy Hook, I have become a Fellow for Everytown for Gun Safety. As such, I use my experiences to teach others about the effect gun violence has on children and communities in an effort to drive change. I speak to civic organizations, churches, and medical students. I participate in panel discussions about the causes and potential solutions we need to consider. Being a survivor is difficult, and in our community, we have had our own challenges. How do you possibly talk about your experience when others have lost so much? How do you protect the stories of the children while speaking about your own experience? There are no easy answers. However, there is action. We can all act to make sure these tragedies end. And that's what I have chosen to do.

CHAPTER TEN

NORTHERN ILLINOIS UNIVERSITY

DeKalb, Illinois / February 14, 2008

MY DAUGHTERS WERE born a shade too yellow, prompting an extended stay in the nursery. *You can stay if you want,* the nurse told me. *You can stay the one extra night, or you can leave and just pick them up tomorrow.* I didn't have to think about it. *I will be back tomorrow morning,* I replied. Her disapproval was tangible as she brought in my release forms. That night, I slept in my own bed for thirteen hours straight. The next morning, I arrived early and eager. *Okay,* I thought, *I can be a mother now.* And, in the same breath, *I will never not be ashamed of this.*

Mary Kay Mace's daughter Ryanne was the youngest student murdered at Northern Illinois University on Valentine's Day in 2008. In her story, Mary Kay writes about the denial she first felt and how she refused to stay at the hospital and wait. "I would get up to leave, insisting I had to go find her. I was certain my daughter had run for her life . . . and that she was wandering around outside in a state of shock. I was determined to find her to keep her from freezing to death." In the end, she stayed.

When my girls were three, I had tubes put in their ears and their adenoids removed. They had been suffering from chronic earaches, and I let a doctor who didn't know them well enough make this decision. I didn't question him, I did what he said I should do. When the girls woke up in the recovery room, Samantha was fine. Penelope was having difficulty coming out of the anesthesia. I was allowed to go back into recovery to see her. I shook with fear the entire way. When I reached her, she looked lifeless. She had a white blanket draped over her body and she was perfectly still. The sight of her nearly killed me. After a few minutes of my touching her and caressing her face, she began to respond. Color returned in her cheeks, and she smiled weakly when she saw me. *I'm so sorry,* I told her, *I'm sorry I let them do this to you.*

When Ryanne Mace's name didn't appear on the list of wounded students, Mary Kay thought she would be reunited with her daughter. But there was an unidentified female. "A police officer came to take us into a private office to ask for her physical description. They had one unidentified female fatality. We described our daughter, and the officer went back and forth between us and another room, where I imagined they had a sort of a command center set up. The unidentified victim had a tattoo. I kept saying, "No, no, that's not her.""

Our home was built into the side of a mountain. As such, there were three staircases and three floors. A nightmare for a mother with two babies. Everything was gated. Everything blocked off. My girls slept in the attic, converted to a beautiful carriage-style bedroom, and my husband and I slept in the basement. The distance between us felt immeasurable. A baby monitor was our lifeline. I could never hear them cry without it. I obsessed over the battery back up, slept with the monitor on full volume, and dreamt about fires. I was terrified that if I didn't get to them, my girls would attempt to climb over the baby gate at the top of their stairs. I asked my father to call me every morning at 6 a.m. *If I don't answer*, I told him, *come and get the girls*. I didn't sleep soundly for six years. *Why didn't I just let them sleep in my room?*

Mary Kay remembered something. "I finally remembered another identifying detail: my daughter had a metal splint behind her two front incisors that had been left over from orthodontia," she writes. "After relaying that info, the next person we were taken to see was a hospital chaplain. I realized what that likely meant, and I felt like I'd been sucker punched in the stomach."

There was a time when I was told that I most likely would not be a mother. During that time, I saw a movie in which one of the characters said, "I don't think you can call yourself a woman until you're a mother." I remember feeling like every dream I ever had died in that moment. I wonder now, after meeting so many mothers whose children were taken by gun violence, if it can work in reverse. Can a mother ever again just be a woman?

Mary Kay struggles with what to call herself now. "Something struck me like a ton of bricks: the double meaning of the word *survivor*. I *survived* my daughter. It's the last thing in the world I ever thought would happen, and I couldn't be more devastated. I didn't want to be a survivor. I didn't want to *survive* my daughter."

A few days after I edited the final version of Mary Kay's story, I pulled my now preteen daughters from their electronics, and we took the dog for a walk in the woods. We stumbled across a gigantic pile of leaves, and the girls begged me to let them jump into them. I stood patiently with the dog, bathed in late September sun and the girls' giggles. *How lucky am I?* I thought, *I've made so many bad decisions, and yet, I was chosen. I was chosen to be their mother.* Mary Kay was chosen to be Ryanne's mother, and she will always be Ryanne's mother.

The day I made the decision to leave my babies in the hospital overnight without me, my father caught me standing outside the nursery watching them. Tears streamed down my cheeks. "Get used to it, honey," he said to me, "being a parent is nothing but heartbreak." It's the only time in my life I wished he wasn't right.

AMYE ARCHER, EDITOR
JANUARY 2019

The following students were shot and killed at Northern Illinois University:

Gayle Dubowski, 20

Catalina Garcia, 20

Julianna Gehant, 32

Ryanne Mace, 19

Daniel Parmenter, 20

UNIDENTIFIED

By Mary Kay Mace

Mary Kay Mace's nineteen-year-old daughter, Ryanne, was murdered in the shooting at Northern Illinois University.

On Valentine's Day, breaking news reported a shooting at our daughter's college, Northern Illinois University (NIU). My husband, Eric, and I were at our respective workplaces when we received separate calls from other people telling us about it. After a couple of hours trying in vain to reach our daughter by phone, we met at home and hopped into the car for the one-hour trip to NIU. We drove along with an impatient, nervous energy, hoping with all our might that we were overreacting, and she was safe.

When we were almost there, I told Eric to turn into the hospital we were about to pass. I'd suddenly realized that campus was probably locked down and that we wouldn't be able to get anywhere near it. There, we were able to ascertain that our daughter was not on the list of the wounded, but a police officer came to take us into a private office to ask for her physical description. They had one unidentified female fatality. We described our daughter, and the officer went back and forth between us and another room, where I imagined they had a sort of a command center set up. The unidentified victim had a tattoo. I kept saying, "No, no, that's not her," and I would get up to leave, insisting I had to go find her. I was certain my daughter had run for her life, leaving behind her cell phone and belongings, and that she was wandering around outside in a state of shock. I was determined to find her to keep her from freezing to death. But the officer kept persuading us to stay by telling us that we were in the right place to get the best information as they were able to piece it together. After hours of this, I finally remembered another identifying detail: my daughter had a metal splint behind her two front incisors that had been left over from orthodontia. After relaying that info, the next person we were taken to see was a hospital chaplain. I realized what that likely meant, and I felt like I'd been sucker punched in the stomach. That's when my head started spinning and my heart lodged in my throat. I kept saying over and over, "I don't understand. How can this be happening?"

It took another couple of hours before we were told that this unidentified victim had been brought to the hospital and was now ready to be viewed. The coroner told us what we could expect to see and that we couldn't touch her or even get too close. I listened, while steeling myself for what was about to happen. He was trying to prepare us for something no parent should ever have to do. His face, his voice, Eric's hand in mine, all of it felt unreal, like a bad dream from which I would never wake. The coroner opened the door. My gut tightened. I could see instantly that my child was no longer lost, she was gone. My heart detonated.

At nineteen, my daughter, Ryanne Elizabeth Mace, was the youngest of the five students murdered in the shooting at NIU. Ryanne was a beautiful person through and through. She was incredibly bright, insightful, funny, friendly, curious, trustworthy, and kindhearted. She was nonjudgmental and treated everyone with respect. And, apparently, she had just the tiniest streak of rebellion in her to have a tattoo she kept secret from her parents. If anything, that made me even prouder of her than I already was.

Ryanne had the gift of being able to make people feel comfortable. She actively sought out ways to connect with others and nourished that connection once she found it. Her friends all went to her for advice because they knew not only how stable and well-grounded she was, but also because she was encouraging and supportive. Ryanne was there for her friends, through good times or bad. But she wasn't that way just with her peers. She was able to foster good relationships with people of all ages and backgrounds within her sphere: children, coworkers, customers, teachers, and family members like my father. Ryanne and my father were kindred spirits. Despite their difference in years, they reveled in having deep discussions about philosophy. They sometimes conversed with one another in French. They made a point of reading the same book at the same time so they could analyze it in detail the next time they saw one another. How many young adults would take the time out of their busy lives to do that?

Eric and I were well aware of how blessed we were to have such a wonderful and loving kid. Ryanne was majoring in psychology with the goal of becoming a therapist because she was committed to helping others. In fact, her murderer was someone she would have tried to help.

It's very difficult to describe the debilitating grief that has consumed us over the past ten years. At times, I felt like it was actually possible to drown in despair. And even though I've gotten used to my new default state of constantly longing for her, there are still times when I have the wind knocked right out of me all over again, such as on the ten-year anniversary of Ryanne's death when seventeen people were killed at a high school in Parkland, Florida. I watched, heartbroken as parents in Florida waited for the calls and texts that would never come.

I struggle with what to call this new existence of mine, this new identity. Eight years into my grief journey, I went to a "Wear Orange" event on National Gun Violence Prevention Awareness

Day. One of the organizers who was familiar with my story tried to hand a button to me. It had the word "survivor" on it. At first, I reached out to take it, but then withdrew my hand.

Something struck me like a ton of bricks: the double meaning of the word *survivor*. I *survived* my daughter. It's the last thing in the world I ever thought would happen, and I couldn't be more devastated. I didn't want to be a survivor. I didn't want to *survive* my daughter. I think people prefer the word "survivor" over "victim" because it sounds more empowering. Maybe people believe it to be more accurate since some of us suffering the aftereffects of gun violence weren't actually shot, nor were we present during the incident. Rather, we're the loved ones of the actual victims whose lives were cut short. We are grievers. I spent years struggling to understand the "why" of the NIU massacre. I couldn't reconcile the fact that my Ryanne was the victim of a premeditated murder by someone who'd never even met her, much less had been wronged by her in some way. The "how" of it, I found out easily. The gunman bought his guns legally, despite a lengthy history of mental illness. That's what set me on my new path in life of advocating for commonsense gun violence prevention laws. Through my activism for change, I have found another identity, one I think Ryanne would be proud of, Gun Reform Advocate.

Red flag legislation was recently enacted in Illinois called the Firearms Restraining Order Act. I believe it may have stopped the NIU gunman from committing his horrific act. Even though Illinois is now safer, I will still spend the rest of my life doing everything I can to save other parents from having to identify their child on a cold, metal table. I will do everything I can to save other children from suffering Ryanne's fate. I know this is what she would've wanted. I know if she were here today, she would be alongside me. I can think of no more meaningful way to honor her memory.

SOMETHING HAS TO CHANGE

By Patrick Korellis

Patrick Korellis was taking a geology class in Cole Hall where the shooting occurred. Patrick was also the first injured student to graduate and became the alumni liaison to the university's advocacy and support group.

I sat in my geology class as a gunman with a long trench coat kicked the door open, pulled out a shotgun, and shot at us. I got under my desk as I heard my classmates screaming and crying. When he stopped shooting, someone in my classroom yelled, "He's reloading!" I ran toward the door. He shot again, and I felt a sharp pain in the back of my head. I touched my head. Blood ran down my neck, all over my hand. I had no idea where I was shot or if I would survive. I had to escape.

When I made it outside, a police officer found me and got me an ambulance to the hospital. Upon my arrival, the doctor rolled up my left sleeve. I had blood and a big bruise. I was shot in the arm, and I didn't know it. I watched as more stretchers arrived carrying my classmates. There were 150 people in my classroom, five were killed, and twenty-one others were injured. The gunman had a shotgun and some handguns. If he had a high-powered assault weapon, I wouldn't be here today.

Ever since Sandy Hook, I've been more vocal about the shooting, and meeting with my politicians to see if anything can be done. I've met with Senator Durbin four times, after different mass shootings, urging him to plead with congress to get something done. Nothing happened. He tried but couldn't get enough votes. I've connected with victims from Columbine, Virginia

Tech, Sandy Hook, Aurora, Orlando, Las Vegas, and more. We share a common bond, and we need each other.

Ten years later, on February 14, 2018, I was back at the NIU campus for memorial events to remember my classmates. I was in a room with the families of the victims, and other survivors, when news broke about a shooting in Parkland, Florida. Some of us were looking at our phones in disbelief. A shooting on the anniversary of another shooting.

These victims from Parkland were now a part of the same group I was, a group no one wants to be a part of. I did reach out to some of the victims, and some have joined a private Facebook group started by one of the survivors of the Columbine shooting that I'm a part of, too. We all were there to offer our support to these victims in the group. I really hoped this would be the last mass shooting in this country. I can't take it anymore, and ten years later, it has gotten harder, not easier. There needs to be a change, and I stand with the students at Marjory Stoneman Douglas High School that are speaking out, trying to make a change.

FROM OUT OF TRAGEDY—HOPE

By Joseph Dubowski

Joseph Dubowski's twenty-year-old daughter, Gayle, was murdered in the shooting at Northern Illinois University.

We think we know the way our stories are supposed to go. We write the scripts for our lives one paragraph or page at a time. We rehearse for the really big scenes, the ones we think will matter for us: How am I going to ask her out? What should I say? What will I say if she says "Yes"? What do I do if she says "No"?

We select our wardrobe for that job interview, or for that big promotion. We select a school, go to college, or to trade school. We plan our careers, our families, our vacations. And on a large scale, life is routine, follows a pattern, and we think we know what is expected of us in the seasons of our lives: get a degree, find and marry that special someone, start a career, have children, put children through school, attend their weddings. Based on these expectations, we think we know what should come next.

On February 14, 2008, at around 10:40 p.m., someone effectively held my script in front of my face and lit it with a match. They told us—Laurel (my wife), Ryan (our son), and about a dozen friends who had met us at Kishwaukee Hospital that night—that a girl matching our daughter's description had died after being airlifted to a hospital near Rockford, Illinois. Our twenty-year-old daughter, Gayle, who had been a sophomore in college, was dead from gunshot wounds she had received in the shooting that had taken place at NIU that afternoon. Suddenly, everything I thought I knew about my life felt like it went up in smoke.

And so began our journey through the valley of the shadow of death—Gayle's death—an event that would threaten to put a cloud of sorrow over what was left of our lives. I still recall some of the images from those six days that followed the shooting at NIU. Dark and terrible, sad and fierce, melancholy and painful. Flowers and candles in the snow, tearful nights, and tearful dawns, crushing loneliness and emptiness even while surrounded by tens and even hundreds of people tending to our every need and wish. Anonymity to celebrity, and back to anonymity again, all in a span of ten days. Ten days of hunger but not eating (at least nothing healthy). Ten days of sleeping but not resting. Ten days of endless motion, all the while feeling like the world had stopped. Then the world started again but left us behind.

There is a time after a major catastrophe such as 2/14 (shorthand, in the vein of 9/11), just as happens most of the time after anyone's death, when the cards stop coming, the phone calls cease, and the friends and neighbors return to work and stop dropping by as often—or stop dropping by altogether. I hear it from others who have lost a loved one, and I have experienced it myself. No one wants to stay in the valley. But few I have talked to over the past ten years know the way out. And not knowing the way out, they stay in the valley, and write the story of waiting for their loved one there.

But this is not the story of someone who stayed in the valley, nor of one who wants to forget the valley and the lessons learned therein. I have the advantage now of having passed through the valley and can look back on the past ten years with a sense of gratitude and awe, and hope. Gratitude for the lessons I learned about faith, hope, and forgiveness; awe of the resilience of people; and hope that comes from knowing one can overcome grief and find life enjoyable again.

Tragedy and trauma don't make us who we are; they just reveal the cracks. One area in which our "cracks" show can be our faith. Faith is simply belief, the deep-down understanding that drives our moment-by-moment existence, our choices about how we live. After a traumatic event we go back to examine what we believe to be true of God (or the absence of a faith in God), of the world around us (as a safe place), of the nature of the people around us (are they reliable?), and of ourselves (do I have what it takes to cope?).

This questioning of what is trustworthy is normal and healthy. The problem arises when we refuse to question, leading to fear and anger. We think that what we know is so, and so any attempt to question our faith is perceived as weakness, a threat. This was one of the first things that I noticed after identifying Gayle's body in Rockford that night. Her sudden death called for me to question what I believed about God, about people, about the world as a safe place, and the reliability of the people in my life. The very foundations on which my life had been built were shaken as by a magnitude 8.7 earthquake, the epicenter right beneath my feet. I don't think I could have stayed on my feet save for the people around me holding me up.

There is no mistake that questioning one's foundation and noticing the cracks is frightening business. Seeing Gayle's body—which just two weeks earlier I had seen and held so full of life, lying stiff before me—opened ugly cracks in my foundation. It demanded my reevaluating everything about what I believed God would and would not allow. I did not believe I had a "Get Out of Suffering Free" card in the game of life, but I did not expect to be dealt the card I held. I learned that our happiness is not assured by having rigid beliefs and expectations. Our ability to handle tragedy hinges on our willingness in time of testing to examine and refine our expectations according to what is truly important to us and what is certain to last. At the same time, unmet hopes, dreams, and expectations—if unresolved—can have a crippling effect on our capacity for happiness. I had no idea how to resolve them.

The death of Gayle ten years ago led me to the study of grief and resilience, as I returned to school to earn a master's degree in applied child and family studies, with a specialization in marriage and family therapy from NIU—crossing the same stage Gayle would have crossed had she lived. As a psychotherapist, I have learned that hope and expectancy are the factors most important in predicting outcomes in therapy—and in recovering from trauma. They're more important than anything I directly do in the therapy room.

This calls to mind a New Testament passage I shared with my wife the afternoon following the shooting. In 2 Corinthians 1:3–4 we read, "Praise be to the God and Father of our Lord Jesus Christ, the Father of compassion and the God of all comfort, who comforts us in all our troubles, so that we can comfort those in any trouble with the comfort we ourselves receive from God." In reflecting on that passage, I assumed that God could comfort us in our pain and loss and believed that he would when all was said and done. But with that comforting came an obligation, once we had been comforted, to do for others what God had done for us. Looking back, it seems that I had a hope and expectancy that someday, somehow—and I had no idea when or how—we would overcome the pain.

After losing Gayle, we heard things like "You never get over the loss of a child," and other despair-inducing, ambiguous, and unhelpful statements. Sometimes these statements came, unfortunately, from people whom we sought out for comfort and guidance in times of sadness and grief. If we'd simply heeded such information, we may have sought out other

information and emotions to match this untruth. (A more accurate statement would be "You will never forget Gayle." That
statement would've been more comforting—especially if followed by ". . . and neither will we.") Fortunately, we'd already
been introduced to information more helpful to us (in the form
of the Grief Recovery Method®) and quickly dismissed this dam-
aging comment.

Today I'm grateful for the wonderful family, friends, church,
community, and the university, all of whom supported us
through the healing and rebuilding of our lives. I'm grateful
for the *Grief Recovery Handbook*, which introduced us to the
actions we needed to take in order to move beyond grieving our
daughter so we could again enjoy fond memories of her and
begin letting go of the dreams and expectations of plans we
would never get to see her fulfill. I'm grateful for the gift of
forgiveness—choosing to forgive Gayle's murderer makes it
possible for us to live without bitterness and anger blackening
every day like never-ending starless night. I'm grateful for the
life circumstances that gave me time for healing my own broken
heart before having to do a lot of other things. And gratitude is
also key in recovery and growth in the aftermath of trauma and
tragedy.

Trauma and tragedy not only reveal the "cracks" in our worlds
and lives, but they also reveal our ability to adapt, to rebuild,
and to grow. Adapting and rebuilding do not mean that we forget what was. Some of us try, and in doing so we waste precious
energy and time thinking we will somehow avoid the pain. We
try keeping busy, embracing work, activism, charitable endeavors, and the like. Some, if not most, of these are for the greater
and long-term good. They provide an outlet for the fear and
anger that drive us, which in themselves are among the most
common responses to loss, whether it be the loss of a relative, a

friend, or the loss of safety/security. And most people do this because they know more about what they are doing in the wake of loss than they do about dealing with the pain itself. But, what if completing our grief and saying goodbye to the pain of grief and loss *were* possible? What if we *could* move beyond grief? What if our hearts were *not* "permanently broken"? What if we started after a mass shooting by healing broken hearts *first*, and then—with hearts scarred but healed—got busy with making the world a safer place?

Over the years since the February shooting in 2008 at NIU, I've learned much about grief and healing, and it is in this area that I see some of the greatest opportunity in the wake of gun violence. Teaching and helping others complete their grief brings greater connection between people, makes them better listeners, and improves the mental and physical health of those who experience that recovery from loss brings. And it may just be what prevents more shootings—for many a shooter was a fragile soul who never learned how to grieve.

CHAPTER ELEVEN

VIRGINIA POLYTECHNIC INSTITUTE AND STATE UNIVERSITY (VIRGINIA TECH)

Blacksburg, Virginia / April 16, 2007

AMYE AND I spent hundreds, if not thousands of hours listening to accounts of families torn apart by gun violence, including how parents could only recognize their children's faces by specific markings on their bodies when no one else could. The horror of these stories crept inside us, and for me, while different in subject matter, triggered memories of my rape. As I spoke with survivors about their experiences, my own story naturally intertwined.

When I interviewed Joe, I'd spoken to more than a dozen survivors about the deaths of their loved ones. Speaking to Joe was special, though. He was one of the first fathers I talked to about losing his daughter to gun violence. His daughter Reema was killed at Virginia Tech in 2007. Over the phone, Joe focused on Reema's life rather than her death. She loved dance and theater and had a passion for culture and languages like French. *How did you get into this work?* Joe asked. Now I faced my own silence.

I started having more interest in trauma after I was raped. I channeled my suffering into storytelling, which was how I rearranged the scattered pieces of my life. With this project, I yearned to help others do the same. But to do this, I would have to be honest with myself, and become just as much of a participant in this project as those I was interviewing.

"Did you tell your parents?" Joe asked.

"I only told my mother and my sister," I replied.

"Why not your father?"

A question I often asked myself, but never answered.

"I don't think he could handle it," I said.

"But we want to know what you're going through," he said. "We want to help."

After I hung up with Joe, he sent me photos of his daughter, Reema. They were a mixture of dance, prom, and family photos. All without captions. I go through them one by one. Joe looks happy next to his full family. For a moment, I think Reema is still alive.

I email him back, acknowledging receipt of the photos he's sent me.

Joe replies: *Thanks for sharing your story and hope that you continue to live in peace and are able to talk to your dad at some point.*

But as my mind affirmed the positive and important work we were doing, my body had other plans. And in July 2018, after close to a year of collection, I was diagnosed with gastroesophageal reflux disease (GERD). My doctor confirmed that while GERD is not solely caused by stress it's an exacerbator. For weeks after my diagnosis, I struggled to eat and keep food down. The days that included hours of interviewing, coaching, transcribing, phone and email communication, and site visits were the most physically painful for me. By the end of the week, my stomach was in flames.

As Amye and I took a deeper dive into survivors' lives, we took on their pain. Vicarious trauma was what our therapists diagnosed. According to the American Counseling Association, vicarious trauma "is the emotional residue of exposure that counselors have from working with people as they are hearing their trauma stories and become witnesses to the pain, fear, and terror that trauma survivors have endured." This definition resonated with us. Finally, a name for what we'd been experiencing—a name we both shared.

As we got closer to the end, my anxiety manifested in different ways. I had a dream about one of the young men, Jeremy Herbstritt, killed at Virginia Tech. I'm in his garden and it's flourishing. The smells are alive. He smiles at me, and then more dead appear, all cheering me on: dead parents, teachers, and children. All faces from photos shared with me by the families. Was this an approval? Were they telling me to keep going knowing I was doubting if I could go on? Was this *the* sign I was waiting to receive after asking every day if what I was doing was Okay? I took it.

LOREN KLEINMAN, EDITOR

JANUARY 2019

The following students and staff were shot and killed at Virginia Polytechnic Institute and State University:

Ross Alameddine, 20, student

Christopher James "Jamie" Bishop, 35, German instructor

Brian Bluhm, 25, graduate student

Ryan Clark, 22, student

Austin Cloyd, 18, student

Jocelyne Couture-Nowak, 49, professor of French

Kevin Granata, 45, professor of Engineering

Matthew Gwaltney, 24, graduate student

Caitlin Hammaren, 19, student

Jeremy Herbstritt, 27, graduate student

Rachael Hill, 18, student

Emily Hilscher, 19, student

Matthew La Porte, 20, student

Jarrett Lane, 22, student

Henry Lee, 20, student

Liviu Librescu, 76, professor of Engineering

G. V. Loganathan, 53, professor of Engineering

Partahi Lumbantoruan, 34, graduate student

Lauren McCain, 20, student

Daniel O'Neil, 22, graduate student

Juan Ortiz, 26, graduate student

Minal Panchal, 26, graduate student

Daniel Perez Cueva, 21, student

Erin Peterson, 18, student

Michael Pohle Jr., 23, student

Julia Pryde, 23, graduate student

Mary Karen Read, 19, student

Reema Samaha, 18, student

Waleed Shaalan, 32, graduate student

Leslie Sherman, 20, student

Maxine Turner, 22, student

Nicole White, 20, student

THE REMINDER
By Jody McQuade

Jody McQuade is the mother of Virginia Tech shooting survivor Sean McQuade. Sean was critically injured during the shootings at Virginia Tech.

EDITOR'S NOTE: The following information cited in Jody's essay was taken from information received from the media and police reports.

It's sad knowing that life could've been different, and even sadder still that Virginia Tech will not admit wrongdoing. Therefore no one will ever tell Sean they're sorry for changing the course of his life. To this day, he still deals with issues with his eye and lack of hearing. The surgeries have not corrected facial movements as a result of the gunshot wound to his face.

Some Virginia Tech officials locked down their offices at least twenty minutes before the shooter burst into Norris Hall and killed thirty people—and even before a campus-wide alert was issued about his first two killings in another building. Emails from the co-director of the university office responsible for its emergency planning showed the first victims' building was on lockdown and that some officials knew "there [was] an active shooter on campus"—while top officials were saying they saw no need to suspend classes or lock down the campus.

Emails were released by lawyers for the families of several victims who agreed to a settlement with the state in 2008. Among other things, the agreement called on top university officials to meet families and victims and explain their actions during the worst campus massacre in U.S. history. One email was sent a minute before a campus-wide alert urged people "to be cautious" after what it called a "shooting incident" at West Ambler Johnston Hall. The alert had also been toned down from an earlier draft that proposed disclosing one student had died and another was injured, according to a memo released by the lawyers. The shooter killed two people at the dormitory. Shortly after the alert went out, but before the shooter chained the doors at Norris Hall and started shooting, the same official forwarded the alert to colleagues at nearby public-school systems and added: "Unofficial word is that two people have died and the shooter is still at large. Tactical teams are staging in Blacksburg. My building is in lockdown. Bombs, shootings. . . . I'm moving to a smaller town."

Repeated efforts to reach Virginia Tech officials for comment were unsuccessful. Douglas Fierberg, one of the lawyers for the families, said one professor had phoned her husband shortly after he dropped her off at work that day—about an hour and fifteen minutes before the shooter started his rampage in Norris Hall—to say her building was on "quasi lockdown." He said the families were upset that some university officials knew to protect themselves while allowing students and staff to walk into danger. Shortly after the lawyers disclosed the emails, Joseph Samaha, father of eighteen-year-old Reema Samaha, who was killed in the shootings, spoke to reporters: "We are acting on behalf of the departed and the injured, to say: 'Never again.'" Samaha said the families thought the university should have given more-timely warnings of danger and more accurate descriptions of what that danger was. The families also felt the school ignored the risks posed by the shooter, by allowing him to return to the dorms after living off campus and by not taking action after he was charged with stalking female students, and professors complained about his bizarre behavior.

In a key part of the settlement, Virginia Tech officials promised to meet with families and fully explain their actions that day. Officials also promised a briefing on what they have done to improve safety, while the governor and attorney general agreed to outline what they were doing in response to the massacre. Former Virginia State Police Superintendent W. Gerald Massengill, who led the state task force that investigated the massacre, said he felt the university's top officials waited too long to warn the campus and probably should have suspended classes and secured buildings after the first shooting. He said the investigation focused on top officials and was not looking at whether other offices went on lockdown. In the 2008 settlement, the state did not admit any liability for the deaths or injuries.

While I occasionally wrestle with sleepless nights, my mind wanders back to the beginning . . . the place where our family's little world changed. I am thankful for the gracious support given to our family by the community and also not having to be the parent whose child didn't make it home that day.

The following is an edited excerpt from Jennifer Herbstritt's book *Leaving Virginia*, which chronicles her bike ride across America in honor of her older brother Jeremy, murdered at Virginia Tech.

MAY 27, 2008

Jeremy,

The scenery here reminds me of our hometown, Bellefonte, Pennsylvania. When I close my eyes, I see our century-old white farmhouse with black shutters.

When Dad and Mom purchased the farm back in May of 1988, I imagine they hoped to raise us there, and one day hand over property to one of us where we'd raise our own children, break bread together on weekends, and watch the grandchildren grow. The dreams Mom and Dad had for our futures were the foundation of what made our farm *home*.

We moved into that old house, the barely there neighborhood, in August of 1988. Remember when Mom worked the night shift at the hospital, and we got away with a lot while under Dad's care? Dad was often occupied with the animals on the farm, or with our brother Joe, or sister, Stephanie. As the older siblings, we could've gotten away with pretty much anything. We had free rein. Certainly, we missed Mom, and I always worried about her catching some disease at the hospital, but we had a ball watching football and baseball, playing catch, and being recruited to assist with projects inside the barn. You helped Dad in the barn, while I stayed in the house and watched Joe and Stephanie.

Soon, families started to move into newly built houses on the main road below our farm. A community was forming. And as a child, I loved meeting up with the other neighborhood kids at the softball fields at the end of our lane for a quick game of pickup on a hot summer day. I laugh about my girlfriends and I creating our own "Babysitters Club" at the park next door to those fields on a biweekly basis. We pushed one another in circles on the merry-go-round, played cops and robbers and tag in the dark. That park was the place we first formed friendships outside of our house and school. I wish I could return to those days. Life was painless then. Our biggest concerns so frivolous:

Would we have enough time after school to build up that jump (made out of snow piled three-feet deep and four-feet wide)? Would Mom and Dad catch us flying down over that jump in a line of six people, attached to one another by a sled's rope tied around the waist?

Would Mom let us back in the house after she discovered you and I dug up the entire front yard in an attempt to "put in a swimming pool" while she was napping?

Would I tattle for the 550th time if you called me "ASTCBdoubleT" (Adult, Sheep Talker, Cry Baby, Tattle Tale) just one more time? And if I did, would Mom actually wash your mouth out with soap?

We were normal kids then. We played games like most. That house was our home. There's something different about it now, though. Its vibe, eerie. But you loved it. You loved that rickety old barn and those noisy animals. We all did.

I learned a lot about life in that barn and just as much about death. Oftentimes, the lambs wouldn't survive through the cold winter months. It wasn't uncommon for an ewe to have difficulty giving birth and for Dad (and later in life you, me, Joe, or Stephanie) to have to play obstetrician. Sometimes, we'd tube-feed premature lambs and accidentally place the milk into the lungs rather than into the stomach.

I think my experiences on that farm prepared me for your death. As much work as it was there, I loved it. It was *home* with our heights written on those walls. I can't imagine you don't miss Bellefonte with all of your heart. I do too. But for me, the thought of home is a painful reminder.

We stopped for lunch today in a town called Chester, the home of Popeye. I wished Dad was still with us here because Popeye was Dad's childhood idol. One building, located in the center of Chester sticks out in my mind. It was covered in paintings of all the characters in the cartoon. We passed it as we biked toward a statue of Popeye in the park located on the east side of the Mississippi River.

After zipping by this statue, I waved goodbye to Chester and crossed the Mississippi on my bike. The instant we crossed the river into Missouri, I convinced myself a tornado would plow right through our paths. The sky was ominous. The storm was drawing nearer, the clouds had turned black, and the thunder intensified. My heightened anxiety made crossing the Mississippi River all the more exhilarating. Within ten more miles of biking, the dark sky passed and we made it to our destination, Farmington.

I should mention, at the start of this trip I expected the people of Missouri to be your stereotypical, friendly, midwestern folk. To my dismay, the gas station attendants, waitresses, and drivers whom we came in contact with today were the exact opposite. Log truck drivers seemed to make a game out of pushing us off the road. Women driving station wagons with babies in the back seats seemed to do the same while adding a long, obnoxious loud horn to the equation. Waitresses would sigh rudely when I couldn't make up my mind on my order, and attendants laughed at the fact we'd driven our car (albeit Joe) this far west despite the price of gas.

Please forgive me, but my anger has been building for months now. Take for instance the "cell phone company bitch," as we've come to call her. Not more than eight weeks following your murder, we received a letter addressed to you stating your cell phone service was going to be deactivated because of your death.

Your cell phone recording was all we had left of your voice, other than the message you left on Mom and Dad's machine the Friday prior to your death. We couldn't bear to close your account. And when I called to explain, the woman with whom I spoke insisted on closing your account. She told me, "You have ten days and that will be that. It's company policy." Ten days left to listen to my beloved brother's voice one last time!

Upon hearing this conversation and the emotion in my voice, my coworker, Kristi, took the phone and gave that woman a piece of her mind. The end result: I pay ten dollars extra each month to keep your account active. I'd pay anything to hear your voice.

Some people are jerks. The bastard who killed you was. He was an egotistical, self-seeking, worthless, poor excuse of human flesh. It disgusts me how every few days I hear of another person as selfish as him, willing to cowardly "sacrifice" his own life for the sole purpose of fulfilling his lifelong, pathetic dream of robbing hundreds, if not thousands, from a lifetime of happiness, joy, desires, and dreams. We coexist with evil people who could care less about us.

And don't get me started on Virginia Tech. I realize one sociopath pulled the trigger to the gun and killed you, but at least a dozen people could've prevented thirty-two deaths, including yours. I wonder how they'd feel if their loved one were murdered?

After all we've been through, I honestly thought your killer's private instructor would've personally apologized to all of us for not doing more. I would've thought the reciting of a poem entitled "We Will Prevail" could've been postponed past two days following your murder. How could anyone consider "prevailing" at such a time?

I also thought we'd be allowed to hold you tight as you lay still on that cold, metal table inside the cement walls of the morgue the minute we arrived on the premises, not seven days later. I also thought the senior university administrators acting as the Emergency Policy Group, who made the decision to delay notification of the first two students' murders to your student body for approximately two hours thereafter would've cried with us, apologized relentlessly for their inaction—done everything in their power to ease our pain.

I didn't expect your killer's medical records to mysteriously disappear from the university's counseling center. Nor would I expect to find myself frozen while in a settlement meeting with senior university officials where one policy group member wore a bulletproof vest, and another admitted she informed her own family members of the first two shootings prior to sending out official notification to the entire campus. And I never expected the majority of the policy group members to stare blankly at me, tears in my eyes, while through a cracked voice, I kindly requested an apology. Those senior officials withheld information from the student body they felt crucial enough their own families needed to know. I wanted them to say: "I'm sorry. I failed you. No, I failed your loved ones. I'm sincerely sorry."

In the weeks following your death, there was one man who stayed on the phone with me on multiple occasions totaling hours on end. He explained every single, solitary detail I needed to know about that terrible day: where were you lying and how he suspected you suffered, and if you were lying in a defensive position, your autopsy results, etc. He knew I needed this information. Otherwise, I'd haunt myself with such questions for my whole life. I needed the details.

He even returned all your belongings found on your body that day to our family. He jeopardized his job to provide us with the materials essential for our healing. He knew compassion, a genuine soul. I want my heaven to be filled with people like him, people who think first of others. I can want, can't I?

Anger consumes me. Please help me sleep.

All my love,
Jenny

REMEMBERING JEREMY

By Margaret Herbstritt

Margaret Herbstritt is the mother of Jeremy Herbstritt who was shot and killed at Virginia Tech. Margaret continues to keep Jeremy's memory alive through the annual event Herbie's Home "TOWN LOOP," a community run/walk and bike ride event through the Jeremy Herbstritt Foundation at thejeremyherbstrittfoundation.com. The Herbstritt family also offers a scholarship annually to a high school senior and supports Rachel's Challenge projects at high school and middle schools.

EDITOR'S NOTE: The Challenge was started by Beth and Darrell Scott, parents of Rachel Joy Scott, who was the first person killed in the Columbine High School shooting on April 20, 1999. The foundation focuses on making schools safer. Learn more about the Challenge at rachelschallenge.org.

My son, Jeremy, was energetic, requiring little sleep, and short naps. He was a happy child with a sense of humor and a contagious laugh. He *always* wanted to go outside to play regardless the weather. His sister Jennifer was twenty-two months younger than him, and I usually had both children together since my husband traveled frequently for work. I remember one cold and snowy winter day when I dressed both toddlers in heavy winter gear and pulled them in a sled around the neighborhood.

Wind was strong that day in town and blew snow into their faces. Jeremy would laugh and laugh and try to catch snowflakes in his mouth, and even though it was a short walk, Jennifer would cry and scream because it was "too cold."

Once we returned home Jennifer was so happy, but Jeremy was disappointed. To ease his disappointment, I allowed him to bring a huge bucket of snow inside the house, where he happily played with it on the kitchen floor.

Jeremy never slowed down. He liked to "build things" with assorted blocks, and then later with Lincoln Logs. He didn't walk. And instead went from crawling to climbing to running. He was somewhat uncoordinated, but persistent.

I encouraged time together as a family, which I myself experienced as a child. We had regular "game or puzzle" times. He especially liked the "mouse trap game," because of the action feature. He also liked to play cards (usually a matching game), and later as an adult he would participate in card games with my parents and siblings, a German game called 500.

At age five, Jeremy had surgery to fix a hernia he had since birth. While waiting, I heard an overhead page "Code Blue in OR." Being a nurse, I recognized that as "patient unresponsive, not breathing." My mother's instinct told me it was Jeremy. Before anyone came out of the OR, I ran through doors clearly marked "Authorized OR Staff Only." I pushed past several male staff and rushed to find Jeremy laying limp on a gurney. I resisted folks trying to get me to "leave sterile area." I had to stay. I entrusted my son to these folks, his life, and they didn't protect him. Staff revealed Jeremy had a reaction to the anesthesia and was in a coma. In later months, I learned the anesthesiologist made errors on three different children that day.

Near midnight, I saw no improvement in his condition, and told staff I wanted Jeremy transferred to another hospital. They argued and refused to listen. While I'm normally quiet, reserved, non-confrontational, I told the staff that this was not a discussion.

"Either you arrange transfer now, or I will call an administrator," I said to hospital management.

An ambulance transported Jeremy to Akron Children's Hospital, where he lay motionless for six days. I stayed at his bedside, while my husband returned to work. I had no cell phone and didn't sleep or eat much. I prayed, cried, talked to Jeremy, put my hand on his chest to feel his breathing. I wasn't allowed to hold him.

One day staff said there was a bed opening next door at a Mennonite-run center for parents with ill children. There was no charge, but donations were welcome. Everyday they made a huge crock of homemade soup and fresh bread to keep up his strength. I was reluctant to leave his bedside, but staff convinced me there was a phone in the center, and they'd call me with any change.

I was so exhausted one night I didn't remember falling asleep, and when I awoke it was mid-morning. I rushed to the hospital and saw the nurse beside his crib.

Jeremy said, "Hi, mom."

I cried and hugged Jeremy so hard he said, "That hurts!"

He had a long road ahead, but eventually recovered from the effects of respiratory arrest. Collectively, our family had to reteach him basics like how to walk (he was in a wheelchair), feed himself, and use the toilet. We used vocabulary words to help him name objects because Jeremy would point to something and make sounds only. I had to tell him Jennifer was his sister, and even point out his dog "Spot." At times, during recovery, he'd stare off, looking puzzled, and then get angry, make loud sounds, and throw objects.

During Jeremy's recovery, my husband's aunt, Sister Helen, set up prayer chains for us. And several times the anesthesiologist came to our house and asked to see Jeremy. I wasn't sure if he was concerned about him or getting sued since three of his patients that day ended up with complications and one died. Jeremy's recovery was difficult, and I wasn't sure he was going to get better.

Jeremy struggled with learning through elementary school, and at age sixteen, he told us he was going to drop out of school and work on a local dairy farm. He failed health class.

"I don't like that class, Mom, so I don't pay attention or study for exams," he said. He was always very honest.

But his school habits improved when he attended Penn State and connected with group friends. It was there he immersed himself in studies. Frequently during his sophomore year, he asked if he could bring friends over to study. When everyone came over, I made a Crock-Pot of food, bought Bonfatto subs, and they'd eat, study, argue, and laugh. I enjoyed their combined energies. To this day, I still have contact with several of his friends from Penn State.

If I could spend one day with Jeremy, I'd be in the vegetable garden with him, smelling plants, feeling damp soil in my hands, and the sunshine against my back. I'd welcome our talking. I'd listen to the radio, Bob Dylan, and watch his dog chasing barn cats. Later we'd share a meal together. Jeremy would barbecue burgers or chicken on the grill. Side dishes would include ice cream, followed by sitting on the porch swing enjoying sounds of birds, and sharing laughter together. Jeremy always made the most of his day. He was cheerful, energetic, positive, helpful, lived each day like his last. Sadly, on April 16, 2007, on Easter Monday in our church, was Jeremy's last day alive.

I talk to Jeremy throughout my "journey," asking for guidance and direction, especially regarding his siblings. At the end of each day, I ask myself, "did I make a difference in the life of someone today?" "Did I perform my best at work or home, without complaining about trivial stuff?"

I will always remember the sound of his size twelve sneakers, leaping down the stairs at 4:00 a.m., pounding each step and waking up the household as he was leaving to go milk dairy cows at the neighbors. He worked hard, saved most of his money toward his college education. Some mornings I'd drive him to the farm, and sometimes I'd give him my car.

Forever, when I hear footsteps, when I see a red Jeep, when I see a cardinal, I think of Jeremy.

IT'S ONLY THE BEGINNING
By Joe Samaha

A lifelong resident of Northern Virginia, Joe Samaha and his wife, Mona, had three children: Omar, Randa, and Reema, who was shot and killed in the Virginia Tech shooting. Since the Virginia Tech tragedy, Joe and Mona have established scholarships and funds, including the Angel Fund, in memory of their daughter Reema. Joe has been a tireless advocate on behalf of the Virginia Tech families and serves as the first president of the Virginia Tech Victims Family Outreach Foundation (VTV). Learn more about the Samaha's work at www.vtvfamilyfoundation.org.

1.

We understand loss, heartbreak and trauma.
We understand the need for long-term care post aftermath.
There are stark realities that must be dealt with.
We never thought this would happen to us.
We never imagined this would be the life we'd be living.
That we'd be left to navigate this new territory alone.

2.

When the police, media, and our extended family and friends go home and return to their own lives and move on to the next story, the next case, who can we turn to? Where is the help? The guidance? The support? How can we know what the future will hold?

The need for long-term care and response is equally important if not more important for families and survivors. Time is a factor and the ramifications and aftermath of the event all too often don't present or impact individuals until years later. As one mother asked during the first few months following the loss of her daughter at the Virginia Tech shootings, "Who is going to take care of my mental health needs?"

Once the immediate needs are met by organizations or funds, long-term physical and mental health care support will continue for a lifetime. PTSD affects the family members of the deceased and those individuals who have been injured for years to come. Years later, surgeries are still being performed to extract bullet fragments from survivors and repair other long-term injuries. Ten years later moms, dads, and siblings still seek therapy. Should they be denied assistance simply because they don't have the funds necessary to afford proper care?

Mass shootings like the ones at Virginia Tech, Sandy Hook, Las Vegas, Sutherland Springs, and Pulse Nightclub, and so many more, affect such a wide array of individuals, and unfortunately, the reach is only growing. No matter your race, religion, socioeconomic status, gender, or age, you can experience gun violence. With that in mind, we are speaking to mothers, fathers, brothers and sisters, friends, and coworkers who may not have been affected by gun violence, but who understand it could become a reality given the current trend of mass shootings in the U.S.

3.

I'm alive, but I'm not okay.
Just because you can't see the trauma and wounds,
    doesn't mean they're gone.
This is not the end of our journey. It's just the beginning.

A REEMA MIRACLE

By Mona Samaha

Mona Samaha is the mother of Reema Samaha, who was shot and killed at Virginia Tech.

Over the last decade, I've been learning how to heal from the pain of losing my daughter, Reema. However, I found myself struggling with PTSD more intensely in the years that followed.

At work, I struggled with memory loss, felt my heart beat faster and heavier, fearful for unexplained reasons. I blamed these feelings on work saying it's the heavy workload at the school where I teach. Even falling asleep became a struggle. My mind spun at any time of the day. Stress had (has) taken a big part of my entire being. My other children left home to start their own life, so I had less responsibilities at home, leaving room for my anxiety. My moments of silence in my backyard became torture. I felt fear instead of peace. I fell deeper into a world of senseless disorientation, losing my self confidence.

I was in misery, and no one was aware. To regain my peace, I had to constantly recollect myself and dissociate from my physical surroundings, from crying, and refer to my prayers and meditations. But such disassociation was not the solution. I needed to find balance between my internal and external worlds.

I struggled for three years, and with each year the symptoms worsened. The moment I would feel calm and happy about something positive in my life, I'd be reminded of the devastation. After Reema's death, I learned there was no separation between life and death. Death is part of living. I disconnected from the material world and felt ready to die any time. My daughter went though this, after all. I felt torn between these two worlds and little by little I faded.

I needed to rediscover the beauty of life, to remember it's a gift. I tried to do this through therapy, but meeting with my therapist who helped me tremendously at first, started to feel useless and stressful. With her I learned how to survive the grief, but I also had to learn how to enjoy life again. Any event I would normally look forward to like birthdays or family gatherings, depressed me. I doubted I could enjoy these moments with the amount of anxiety I was experiencing: a racing heart, distracted mind.

Then, in December 2017, around Christmastime, I asked Reema for help. *A Reema miracle would pull me out of this mess*, I thought. She was with me in my hardest time, why not now? A new sense of hope started to grow in me. I put my trust in Reema and surrendered myself to God's love and peace. I received the blessings through events that I call gifts from God. One of these gifts were learning to celebrate life in my gratitude journal. Through this process of looking for things to celebrate, I was able to begin a new phase in my healing.

Like a child learning to walk, I went through a multitude of falls, followed by lessons learned. I discovered I needed to rid myself of my shell, my built-in survival mechanism preventing me from going deeper into my healing. In order to do that, I needed to practice presence. One of the ways that helped me with this was through collective music therapy. The sessions taught me how music can resituate us in the present. But after the music was over, my mind often reverted back to the sad moments, to the stress. I realized I was happier when listening to my heart instead of my mind. Understanding what made me happy was a big *aha!* moment: just because my mind was taking me back to the sadness, it didn't mean I had to stay there. I had the power to make that shift, to make that change. This was not easy, but I promised myself to live a Reema miracle.

Learning how to live in the present is what's helping me overcome my anxiety. I remind myself not to listen to my mind when it wanders to the traumatic state. I tell myself *you are safe now. There is no need to be stressed.* I remind myself managing PTSD is a process, and while I learned to mentally heal from my grief, my body felt its emotional pain. This is especially true for someone like me, who lost a loved one to sudden, senseless violence.

Today, I thank God for enlightening me with more understanding of the healing process. For being with me at every step of my journey. I thank God for my loving husband who's always ready to comfort me with hugs. I thank Reema and my two surviving children—my reason *to be* these days. When I go to bed, I hold Joe's hand and my rosary with the other. I keep Reema in my heart and pray for God to heal me with love and peace.

JOURNAL: THEN AND NOW
by Chase Damiano

On April 16, 2007, from about 9:00 a.m. to 12:00 p.m, Chase Damiano's French class barricaded the doors in Holden Hall, the building connected to Norris Hall, one of the major sites of the Virginia Tech shooting. He took many pictures with his cell phone, including the one below that originally appeared on Wikipedia, and shares his story behind the posted photo.

Upon release from the classroom, Chase went back to his dorm and wrote an account of the shooting called "April 16, 2007." Now, at thirty years old, Chase talks about the legacy of the Virginia Tech shooting in the more recent account, "September 24, 2018."

Huddled in my French classroom. (Photo originally appeared on Wikipedia.)

APRIL 16, 2007

9:50 A.M.

We started hearing sirens outside of our building, Holden Hall. We took it as nothing, for we hear police sirens around campus all the time. It was just slightly strange that we heard them during the day. Soon, the thirteen of us heard an ambulance in front of our building. We took it as another bomb threat—we had been getting bomb threats in April that ended up being hoaxes.

We started getting concerned when the sirens increased in volume. The professor looked out the window with us and we saw police cars and ambulances out on the drill field. Students were walking away from our building. Police officers were assembling on the sidewalk. Large black vans appeared.

Two women barged into our classroom. "There was a shooting this morning at West Ambler-Johnston. The shooter has gone into Norris, and we are locking your door. Stay inside." They then left. Norris Hall. The hall connected to Holden Hall, where I was. The two halls are in the same building. We were in danger. Students were now running away from McBryde, a nearby building. Students evacuated Patton Hall, the building directly in front of us right on the drill field. Students fled with hands on their heads; one girl even fell and hit her head on the sidewalk. All in fear.

Our professor told us to close the windows. To stay away from the windows and the door. We shut the blinds, so we weren't distracted by the events happening outside. We played a game in French so our minds could be at ease from the situation. It didn't help. We were all wondering what was going on.

Gunshots were fired and we started to panic. We stopped playing our game and tried to figure out how to get the news on the projector. The main TV in the classroom didn't work, but the projector, we knew, had cable connected to it. After some struggle, we pulled up CNN, Fox News, and the local news in Blacksburg. They all said the same thing at this point: one student dead, another person wounded. We looked at the screen with horrified faces. We shut off the lights and moved tables and chairs away from the "safest" corner in the room.

We gathered in this corner and looked onward to the news.

The professor suggested that we construct a barricade in front of the door, because the door lock wasn't that strong—it's an old building. We moved our tables in front of the door in a line so that it touched the other wall opposite of the door. We made it so the door wasn't going anywhere, no matter what. The only fault in the system was that the door had a glass window. The glass was smoky so you couldn't see in or out—only the light that passed through.

We started calling our friends to collect some news. We had no computer in the classroom—our professor did not bring hers and the usual computer users didn't bring theirs, either. We had no access to the outside except for our cell phones. Most students at Virginia Tech are Verizon users; the lines were swamped. Only T-Mobile and Cingular users had good service, and we had multiple people with those services in the classroom. We all called our families, friends, and loved ones.

EIGHT CASUALTIES NOW.

My phone received messages, both voice mail and text messages, but I couldn't respond to them easily. I got through to my girlfriend and mother just to tell them that I was safe and that I loved them. I knew we were safe inside our classroom, but I still wanted to hear them.

This is when we received a knock at the door. I went up to the side of the door and asked who it was. He said it was the sheriff's department. We took down our barricade and opened the door. He told us to stay inside and stay away from the windows. He left and we rebuilt our barricade and returned to our corner. We started watching a French movie while everyone called people and answered calls sent to us. No one paid attention to the movie. We didn't want the movie; we wanted the news. We wanted to know what we had going on outside. We wanted to know what kind of history was in the making.

We heard word of people jumping out of Norris Hall. There were loudspeakers outside, telling us to stay inside with the door locked and not to go outside for any reason. Screw the movie; we watched the news again. We took pictures with our camera phones to remember.

Eventually, we heard activity in the corridor outside of our door. We quieted our voices and listened on. We heard shuffling of feet. Running. Loud stomps. A lot of panicked movement.

Then we heard laughter.

We opened our door and saw two women telling us to get ready to run. We packed up our things quickly and readied ourselves. Our only objective was to get out of Holden Hall as quickly as possible. We said our goodbyes to each other and ran down the stairs, turning the corners at high speeds. Jogging at a brisk pace. I ran out of the back door of the building and three police officers told me to run toward McBryde, and that I should be safe there. There were a lot of police cars, a lot of ambulances, and a lot of news crews. I was safe by the time I reached the Old Security Building, close to my dorm, so I walked back and soaked it all in. I wanted to remember everything that happened.

I got back to my dorm, and everyone was happy that I was safe. My French class usually gets out at 9:55 a.m. I did not leave the building until 12:00 p.m.—about two hours of hiding. Many people called to make sure that I was safe. The college closed for Monday, April 16, 2007. Classes are canceled on the 17th as well. Nothing good came out of this event at all. The news channels described the situation:

"THE WORST CAMPUS SHOOTING IN US HISTORY."

—CNN

"PRESIDENT BUSH TO ADDRESS THE NATION AT 4:15 PM."

—CNN

"31 REPORTED DEAD, MAKING IT THE WORST MASS SHOOTING IN US HISTORY."   —MSNBC

"GOV'T. OFFICIALS: DEATH TOLL IN VA TECH SHOOTING RISES TO 31."   —MSNBC

"32 DEAD IN VA TECH SHOOTING RAMPAGE; GUNMAN IS DEAD."   —Fox News

"NOT ONLY THE WORST CAMPUS SHOOTING, BUT THE WORST SHOOTING IN THE US."   —CNN

It is unbelievable to think that people do this to fellow students. Thank God that my friends are okay. This day, the 16th of April, I will never forget.

We will be in the history textbooks.

We will be on the news, being interviewed.

Our grandchildren will call us and talk to us about what happened for a history report.

Soak it all up. Never forget this day. The day when we made international news. The day where the nation looks toward Blacksburg. The day our college will never forget.

April 16, 2007

SEPTEMBER 24, 2018

Virginia Tech was the worst school shooting in recent U.S. history. But in 2007 it didn't feel that way while it was happening. On the day of the shooting, I wrote a detailed account of the events, because I knew the day would come to tell the story. That account was created on April 16, 2007, and I included photos I took on the day of the shooting as well as the story behind the picture found on Wikipedia.

I can't remember specifically how the picture of us huddled in our French classroom made it on to Wikipedia. The students were cold-emailed for interviews. From our view, news reporters grabbed at any student email address they could find. I made myself available for any interviewers that wanted to have a more direct student account.

To be honest, I felt guilt in interviewing with reporters. Specifically because I was not in an intruded classroom. I was not shot. I did not get injured. I did not die. I was in the building next door. I felt my personal account and my story were not as important as those more directly impacted by the shooter. I felt guilt in the interviews, discussing my account, and taking that picture. I felt it shouldn't be me sharing this information because nothing really happened to me. I felt extremely naive as a freshman.

The day started like any other day, and then suddenly sirens started to overtake the campus. Black vans appeared, which looked like a SWAT team of sorts. People barged into our classroom and said, "Hey, there was a shooting this morning across campus. The shooter has now gone into Norris Hall."

We barricaded the door. We were a room of freshmen and a young professor. We stayed inside, spent our time trying to get information. Too many students and faculty tried using the same phone networks. Folks had loved ones calling in. We, and certainly others, were trying to dial out. It was a double-edged sword. Yes, people wanted to know that their loved ones were safe, but those that needed it most weren't able to get cell service. Fortunately, we were able to rely on less popular phone networks. Our classroom had an opportunity to call friends, family, and loved ones, letting them know what was going on. We managed to get the news via a cable-connected projector. It was our most reliable way to get information during the crisis. We watched the shooting unfold live. The media reported one person died. Then, eight people had died. Then thirty-two people had died. It felt like I was both watching from afar and watching close by. We were distant, and right next door, at the same time.

I wrote love notes to those I cared about in my notebook. I didn't think the shooter would come into our room. Our shooter would have had to been quite intentional to travel between Norris Hall and Holden Hall. It isn't intuitive. It certainly was a possibility, but not a probability. It was logically comforting. But writing in my notebook was a precautionary measure. Just in case the shooter came knocking.

If the shooter wanted to enter our classroom, he would have been able to. There'd be nothing we'd been able to do. Barricading the door with desks and bookshelves felt safe to us. A couple hours went by, then we received a knock at the door: a self-proclaimed "sheriff." We didn't know who this person was, so we were taking a gamble. But we opened it anyway. Good thing he was a sheriff.

The sheriff said to pack our things and get ready to evacuate the building. I physically ran back to my dorm, fortunately, close by. I encountered my dorm mates. They were happy I was safe.

The college closed for the rest of the day, and they canceled classes for a week. On April 17, 2007, a convocation was held in our basketball stadium, Cassell Coliseum. President Bush and the First Lady attended and addressed our community. The anguish was palpable. Many in the crowd had their brothers and sisters, boyfriends and girlfriends, sons and daughters, and professors and coworkers die. It was tragic and heartbreaking.

To conclude the convocation, Nikki Giovanni, a University Distinguished Professor and poet at Virginia Tech, delivered a beautiful chant poem, "We are Virginia Tech". A video of her poem can be found searching **"WE are VIRGINIA TECH"** on YouTube.

Our response to her poem: "Let's Go Hokies." Our famous cheer at sporting events. That was the cheer we used when we were about to win a game. Our cheering captured an important sentiment. It indicated how our community was to react. That we will prevail, and we will get back on the horse. I was grateful for this moment. The fact we could rally ourselves out of a terrible massacre. It was a powerful reaction. It showed our spirit wasn't broken. Any community must decide how to cope, and what happens next. We chose positivity. Our cheering was our group therapy.

That night, we held a candlelight vigil to honor those who died. It took place on our Drill Field, a beautiful green field in the center of campus. We brought the entire Virginia Tech and Blacksburg communities together. Speeches turned into a moment of silence. A moment of silence broken by our game-winning cheers. Another sign that we'll get through this.

April 16th, for the following years, remained a day school was not in session. We conducted the vigil annually, through the day I graduated. It still takes place at present. April 16th formally became the Day of Remembrance in the Hokie community.

We acknowledge each year the thirty-two lives were taken from our community. I recall a particularly powerful Day of Remembrance a few years later. Students released a bouquet of balloons during a moment of silence. The balloons were a mix of our school colors: orange, maroon, and white. A single balloon stood out among the rest: a black balloon. A thirty-third balloon. Seung-Hui Cho's mental illness led to the death of thirty-three people, including himself. The black balloon symbolized that, while he did terrible things, he was a Hokie. He, too, was a part of our community.

HOW I FOUND MY WAY

By Lisa Hamp

During the Virginia Tech shooting, Lisa Hamp and her classmates laid on the floor pushing the desks and chairs against the door while the shooter shot at the door and tried to push it open. Fortunately, their barricade held and the shooter was unable to enter their classroom.

I grew up in middle- to upper-class suburbia outside Washington, D.C. in "northern Virginia." It is typical suburbia: chain restaurants and golf courses, hardworking parents and kids wearing Hollister. I felt safe all the time, everywhere I went. But on April 16, 2007, that sense of safety and security was stripped from me. I was a junior at Virginia Tech studying mathematics. I was sitting in computer science class at Virginia Tech when my classmates and I heard gunshots coming from across the hall. During the next eleven minutes, my classmates and I laid on the floor pushing the desks and chairs against the door while the gunman shot at our door and tried to push it open. In those horrific minutes, the gunman killed thirty-two students and professors, and wounded and traumatized many more.

When I walked out of that building that day, I didn't know what to do. I didn't know what was next. Process, healing, self-care, and mental health—I didn't know what these words *really* meant.

My recovery journey was far from perfect, but I eventually found my way through the fog. When I reflect on recovery, I realize I learned a lot about counseling, boundaries, self-confidence, and feelings. This stuff isn't taught in school. You learn it by observing those around you. Here are a few things I learned:

232

Recovery isn't linear.

Time, time, time. Everything takes time. Because time gives us space to process what has happened. I remember when I first started going to therapy, my counselor telling me that it was a process and it was going to take time. I got a bit frustrated inside. I thought to myself, I want to get better now, why can't I get better right now? She told me it is going to be two steps forward, one step back. But some days, it felt like one step forward, two steps back. The days will pass, the important part is to stick with it.

Be cautious when people tell you how you should feel.

Only you know how you feel. These feelings are coming from somewhere inside you because of something that you experienced. Many people you know may not have experienced what you did, so they are going on with life as normal. Meanwhile, your head is spinning with a zillion thoughts and you can't seem to relax. This is normal. Feel your feelings and confront them gently. I know from experience that pushing them away doesn't work.

Create boundaries, not walls.

I'm not talking about physical boundaries and walls, but I'm talking about the invisible kind. Who and what do you let in? This one was difficult for me. I was the black-or-white, all-or-nothing Type A kinda gal. I had to learn to embrace the gray. I had to figure out how to have healthy boundaries with the stranger at the grocery store who is asking me if I was there during the Virginia Tech shooting—do I tell them? do I talk about it?

You can't help others till you help yourself.

Just like on an airplane, when the flight attendant tells you that you need to put on your own safety mask before helping others with theirs, the same is true for recovering from trauma. I learned that you can't help others till you help yourself. The counseling that is available after tragedy at a school isn't just for the students. It's for everyone—the school administrators, faculty, and staff, as well. Everyone needs help at some point in time in their life. Sometimes it is just hard to admit it.

Create a self-care tool kit.

Create a tool kit to take care of yourself. Fill it with things you like. Journals, church, walks, music, candles, baths, coloring books, nail polish, Pixy Stix. These are some of the things I like, but your tool kit will look different. You need to tailor it to you, the things you enjoy and the things that help you relax.

After the Virginia Tech shooting, I couldn't make sense of my thoughts or feelings. The result was low self-confidence and self-worth. The result was me looking for something to control because I felt I lost control of my personal safety. The result was me trying to cope with my feelings and using food and exercise to do so. The result was me pretending to be resilient and successful, but inside, I was hollow. So, years later, when I was finally ready to process the trauma, what did I do? Trusted my gut. Listened to my feelings. Wrote in a journal. Talked and walked with my closest friends. Resisted the urge to compare myself to others. Listened to that tiny voice inside my head, that was guiding me through my recovery.

And I gave it time.

CHAPTER TWELVE

WEST NICKEL MINES SCHOOL

Bart Township, Pennsylvania /
October 2, 2006

ON A COLD and rainy October morning in 2018, my husband, a native Pennsylvanian familiar with Amish society, and I drove the more than three hours from Jersey City, New Jersey to Paradise, Pennsylvania, to meet with an Amish father, Aaron, whose son survived the West Nickel Mines shooting on October 2, 2006. After spending weeks trying to connect with these families, I was finally *in*. I was nervous the whole ride there, reminding myself this isn't *just* a different culture. It's an entirely different society, and one I was never exposed to except through the occasional farmer's market.

This shooting haunted me. I reviewed the events of the day on the drive there: October 2, 2006, Charles "Charlie" Roberts IV, a milk truck driver who served Amish farms in the Nickel Mines area, filled his pickup truck with building supplies and drove to the nearby West Nickel Mines one-room schoolhouse where he ordered all the boys to leave. He barricaded the doors and bound the remaining girls. Their teacher, Emma Mae Zook, managed to escape and run to a nearby farm for help. Roberts shot eight out of ten girls, ages six through thirteen, killing five, before committing suicide in the schoolhouse. The shooting is known by the Amish as *The Happening*.

When we arrived at Aaron's home, both him and his wife were warm and welcoming. They had a small pug mix named Coca-Cola, who growled and barked at us. Aaron's wife shooed the pup away. We all sat around their table, Coca-Cola placemats under our elbows. Aaron began to tell me the story of his son. How he was one of the boys inside the one-room schoolhouse. Roberts eventually killed himself as more authorities moved in on him.

Aaron continued to tell me about his son who struggled with anorexia after the shooting. He and his wife told us about their son's slow decline from more than 180 pounds to less than 100, perhaps a symptom of survivor's guilt. He said *you have to imagine being in a class of ten and now in a class of two and what that does to you.* This was insight I never thought about. I'd always been in a large class, and never considered the devastating impact of a shooting on a smaller school class.

We also spoke about the young girls injured that day. He told me about their progress, some of which now married and raising their own children. While survivors like Sarah Ann Stoltzfus still have some vision impairment, Barbie Fisher and Esther King have healed considerably. But the youngest victim, Rosanna King, who originally had not been expected to survive because of severe brain trauma, does not walk or talk. Aaron confirmed for me that she is still in a wheelchair, but has been said to smile at family and friends.

As the girls healed, the reverberation of the shooting echoed throughout the Amish community. Aaron told me of Amish tours that made their way from the Midwest to Paradise to visit the site of the shooting. *They came by the busload,* he said. *West Nickel became an attraction. All they wanted to hear about was what happened.*

Together we visited the site of the five pear trees that were planted for each of the dead girls. *You would never know that what these are for,* he added as we drove past. And when I asked him to talk more about the forgiveness toward the shooter and his family, a gesture that was hard for the English-speaking world to understand, he said to me under the dim dining room light, *I don't know if we would've felt the same way if he survived.* This statement was shocking considering the plethora of articles and books written on how the Amish forgave Roberts and his family, even setting up a fund for his widow to cover the costs of his funeral.

After my husband and I left their house, I saw Amye had messaged me about another shooting that took place the same day at a Pittsburgh synagogue, which I later learned was at the Tree of Life. Here I was talking to a family whose son survived a shooting at the same time another shooting was unfolding. And when I got inside the car, I started to cry. My husband cried. We held each other and cried. I thought how vital this project was in order to expose a nation to the pain endured by survivors of gun violence, a pain closer than we can often sense.

Loren Kleinman, Editor

December 2018

The following students were shot and killed at West Nickel Mines School:

Naomi Rose Ebersol, 7

Marian Stoltzfus Fisher, 13

Lena Zook Miller, 8

Mary Liz Miller, 7

Anna Mae Stoltzfus, 12

GSW'S AND THE MAKING OF A TRAUMA SURGEON

By A. Reema Kar, M.D.

A. Reema Kar was a medical student on the day of the shooting at the Amish schoolhouse in Nickel Mines, Pennsylvania. Her experiences that day led her to pursue a career in trauma surgery. She is currently an assistant professor of surgery at the Johns Hopkins University School of Medicine in Baltimore, Maryland.

Twelve years ago, I was a twenty-four-year-old medical student at the Penn State College of Medicine in Hershey, Pennsylvania. After completing two years of intense study in lectures and labs, I was assigned to the Pediatric ICU (PICU) during my first inpatient clinical rotation. I was quite eager to start finally taking care of patients, but I had no idea what awaited me on that particular day.

For me, and the entire team in the PICU, the morning of October 2, 2006, started like every other morning. I scrambled to get to the hospital by 6:30 a.m. to review the charts and labs on my patient and discuss the overnight events with the resident and fellow who were on call the previous night. We continued through our usual routine of ICU rounds, discussing every vital sign and lab value, poring over chest X-rays, and examining babies connected to ventilators. By around 11:30 a.m., we had nearly finished, and were ready for our ritual post-rounds coffee break. That's when all of our pagers went off at once. The green digital display read, "Multiple pediatric GSW's." "GSW," the medical slang for gunshot wound, was an abbreviation I had only seen and heard on TV . . . until then. As the PICU team stared at each other in disbelief, a subtle but urgent fear crept into our minds. Children had been shot? In this quiet, sleepy corner of Pennsylvania we liked to call "The Sweetest Place on Earth"?

What we didn't know yet was that less than fifty miles away from where we stood, a man had entered a one-room school-house in Nickel Mines, Pennsylvania, and shot ten Amish girls, fatally wounding some of them. The director of the Pediatric ICU answered the phone ringing at the nurses' station. He confirmed that an unknown number of victims from a school shooting were en route to our hospital. Immediately, the PICU team sprang to action, mobilizing every resource at their disposal to prepare for a potential mass casualty event.

Victims from the shooting were flown to several trauma centers in the surrounding counties. Three of the Amish girls were wheeled into our Emergency Department at the Milton S. Hershey Medical Center that afternoon. Emergency medicine doctors, anesthesiologists, pediatric intensivists, and trauma surgeons lined the hallway as the EMS teams rolled the stretchers into the ER. I stood aside, waiting for instructions, letting the surgeons and doctors control the chaos. In a blur of minutes that felt like hours, the various teams rushed to secure airways, stabilize vital signs, and care for bleeding gunshot wounds. As a young medical student, there was little I could actually do. I simply did not have the training to help. It felt as though the world was spinning around me, but that I had stopped, suspended in time in the midst of that unthinkable tragedy, utterly powerless to do anything.

When the patients, the three little Amish girls, were rolled up to the PICU, I waited at their bedsides as the nurses and doctors cleaned and examined bullet wounds. I stared, transfixed, at beeping ventilators and blinking monitors, afraid to look away for fear that all those noises and signs of life may stop if I did not keep watching. Neurosurgeons explained to us that transcranial gunshot wounds, bullets that travel across both sides of the brain, cause irreversible damage that is rarely survivable. I struggled to comprehend what that meant. It was absolutely unthinkable that these little girls were slowly dying in front of me.

October 2, 2006, changed my life. The images of pigtailed little girls in flowery dresses with grass-stained bare feet, lying in hospital beds and bleeding from bullet holes has never left my mind. In the days that followed, I visited the surviving patients in the PICU, and spent time with the Amish families in the ICU waiting room. I didn't speak Pennsylvania German, but I could play with the siblings of the victims while their parents visited their critically injured children. I could smile and give hugs, even though I was breaking on the inside. One of our patients died in the hospital. We later learned that her sister died at another trauma center from similar injuries. Our second patient suffered devastating head injuries, but she was stable enough to go home with her family. The PICU team did not expect her to survive. The last little girl recovered from her bodily wounds, but I often wonder how well a child can truly heal after such a tragedy.

I certainly could not forget, much less heal. For days, I could not eat or sleep. I could not focus on lectures and reading assignments for the rest of my Pediatrics clerkship. I could not stop seeing those girls in my mind. I felt numb and trapped, reliving that nightmare. I had never been so close to such violence, and I struggled to understand my purpose as a future physician in such a shocking context. I promised myself that day that I would never feel so helpless again. I vowed to enter a field of medicine in which I could do something in the face of such chaos. I promised to learn how to intervene in a crisis, to really help patients with overwhelming injuries, and hopefully, some-day, to save lives.

Years later, I was completing my residency in general surgery, preparing for a career in trauma surgery and surgical critical care. I probably never would have become a surgeon if it were not for those little Amish girls. I know that I was meant to be in that PICU in Hershey that morning, and to see and experience what others only watched on their television screens. The events of that day touched me in a way that nothing else before or since has done. Walking home that night from the PICU, I thought it would be the most horrific thing I ever witnessed. But it wasn't. After Nickel Mines, there was Virginia Tech, Fort Hood, and Aurora, Colorado.

Six years ago, on December 14, 2012, I realized it had hap-pened again. My throat tightened, my stomach turned, and goosebumps covered my skin as I watched, glued to the telev-ision news coverage with the other nurses and residents. Children had been shot. Again. At an elementary school. Again. This time, in Newtown, Connecticut. That's when I thought something would change. The world would not stand idly by as first-graders were murdered in their classrooms. Right?

But then there was Charleston, San Bernadino, Orlando, Las Vegas, and Parkland. The sheer numbers were incomprehensi-ble. One gunshot victim is a challenge. Two are taxing. Three are overwhelming. Fifty-nine? Incapacitating. Five hundred? Unfathomable. Inhuman. I remember wondering, will some-thing change now? Is this enough? When will this no longer be acceptable to modern society? How many lives must be lost to realize what one is worth?

My experiences with those Amish children set me on a very specific path. I became a trauma surgeon after seeing what gun violence can do to people and families. I became a trauma surgeon because I wanted to be able to do the most when the situation was the worst. I run toward the crisis, not away from it because I have made it my life's work to care for patients who are the victims of violent tragedies. Despite all of that, I look forward to the day that I do not have to treat multiple victims from a mass shooting. After training for nearly a decade to understand and assess what happens to the body when bullets blast through it, I hope I never have to see the level of death and devastation I saw in the PICU after the shooting at the Amish schoolhouse in Nickel Mines.

It takes seconds for a single bullet to carve a path of destruction. It can take me hours in the OR to find and fix the injuries, if I even can. There are days when everything I know how to do as a trauma surgeon is not enough to save a person's life. There are times when all the might of modern medicine is no match for simple human physiology. There are nights I spend in the hospital wondering why this cycle never ends.

Even though I go to work every day waiting for injured patients to arrive, seeing the blinking green "GSW" on my pager screen still fills me with dread because I have witnessed the horror of a mass shooting. I have left the hospital covered in a teenager's blood and a mother's tears. I have told a father that his new baby is safe and healthy in the NICU, but her mother may never wake up from the coma. I have watched families break down at the bedside in the ICU over loved ones lost forever. I know what it's like to go from one patient to the next, triaging the worst injuries to the OR first, deciding who might live and who likely won't. After every wound is stitched and every bullet hole bandaged, the trauma continues to spread like ripples in a pond. Every person on the wrong side of a bullet is someone's son or sister, father, or friend. As I know from personal experience, bullets do not need to pierce the skin to leave permanent wounds. Often, it is the invisible scar that is the deepest.

When will it be enough?

PAINTING THE AMISH

By Bruce Becker

Bruce Becker is an artist living in Pennsylvania. His book, *Kindness and Compassion*, about the aftermath of the West Nickel Mines shooting, conveys the unique closeness Bruce had with the Amish during that tragic time.

As the Nickel Mines shooting was unfolding, I was painting an Amish school bell in my studio. I purchased the bell the day before from an Amish woman and knew it would be the subject of my next painting. It was the first Amish subject I ever painted. I considered the fact I was painting the bell at the same time of the shooting a coincidence. And as a result, I felt compelled to help in some way.

While the shooting was considered a tragedy for the Amish, they forgave the shooter. No matter the circumstances, the Amish always react with kindness and compassion. And so *Kindness and Compassion* became the title of the bell painting, and with the blessing and approval of the Amish community, I gave public talks about the meaning behind the painting. I made prints of the painting that raised money and awareness for the Amish. And at the request of the Amish, I wound up writing a book about my experiences with them in the aftermath of the shooting.

My involvement with the Amish continues today, twelve years after the tragedy. My interactions with this event were one of a participant-observer. As an artist, I'm connected to the subject through observation. People who know my artwork, understand it represents and promotes beauty and positivity. The message from the Amish was very much the same. One of the fathers from the community said my work was "[shedding] a ray of light in a time of darkness." He must've been right. Because that message drew me into the lives of people worldwide. The message reverberated around the world, and I went from sitting in the kitchens of the Amish families discussing the loss of their children to coming home to find reporters on my porch waiting for me. I was living a life of dichotomy: back and forth from the Amish world to the English world. The Amish wanting me to tell their story and the English wanting to hear it, always in awe of their faith-based reaction.

Through it all, I was aware I hadn't suffered the devastating loss and horror directly myself. Yet every day I visited the community, I was physically in the places and with the people who had experienced such devastation. I was the messenger of this unique humanitarian gesture of the Amish. Many times, I made this very clear to those I spoke to. And to this day I remain friends with many of the Amish, and I'm welcome in their community.

FORGIVENESS IS A GIFT

By Marie Monville

Marie Monville is the author of *One Light Still Shines: My Life beyond the Shadow of the Amish Schoolhouse Shooting*. Monville is the widow of Charles Roberts, the gunman of the West Nickel Mines School shooting.

Growing up in conservative Lancaster County, my first thoughts on forgiveness came from both my family and culture. I had a simplistic view, which suggested that someone who'd hurt me would recognize the pain they caused and want to make amends. If I were the one who caused the pain, I'd want to do the same. We'd exchange meaningful words and that would be the end of it. But as an adult, I know this type of forgiveness rarely works that way. Sometimes the person responsible doesn't realize the pain they've caused others. Sometimes they don't care.

Forgiveness isn't simple. It's a choice. It's born of pain and loss. On the surface, it seems to cost everything, giving up our right to hang onto suffering. But I've learned it's not so much about *what I feel like I'm giving up*. Instead, it's about what I receive. Letting go of the agony and embracing the freedom of forgiveness is a gift. Let me explain.

One the afternoon of October 2, 2006, a group of Amish men walked toward my parents' home. When I saw them from the window, apprehension filled my heart and thoughts raced through my mind: *What questions might they ask? What demands might they make?* And rightly so. I had nothing of seeming value to give in light of all they faced. My father went outside to greet them. I continued to watch from the window, unable to hear their voices, but I saw it all: the way they placed their hands gently on his shoulders, the way they looked him in the eyes, and spoke without evidence of anger or hatred. I watched them hug my father and saw the tears that flowed down each face as they made their way back out the drive.

When my dad came inside, my family and I waited for him to collect himself from the emotion of the moment. He said that they came because they were concerned about my children and me. They wanted us to know they'd forgiven Charlie and extended grace and compassion over our family.

I was stunned. This was not my original thought as they walked toward my parents' home. They did not come to *get* anything from me. Instead, they delivered a gift: the forgiveness that found its way deep inside their hearts. The way it changed what they saw when they looked at my family. While everyone else was looking to me to account for Charlie's choices, the Amish came instead to give me something that freed me from the weight of shame, which threatened to crash into me like a tidal wave.

They helped me see that forgiveness is a choice we make to free ourselves from the weight of pain and its ability to destroy our lives. My choice to forgive Charlie, their choice to forgive Charlie, was not about Charlie. This choice had nothing to do with him. Their choice was about them, and my choice was about me. It was a choice to exhale pain, inhale healing. A choice to let go of my questions, my grief, my agony—the crushing weight that threatened to suffocate my soul. But it wasn't instantaneous. Forgiveness is messy, it's inconvenient, but it's worth it. In time, forgiveness went deep and changed everything about the way I saw my circumstances and myself. Forgiveness freed me to live above circumstances, instead of feeling constantly submerged by the pain of Charlie's choices. It enabled me to find the healing I desperately needed if I wanted to lead my kids (and myself) into a future of thriving, not just surviving.

Please hear me on this, extending forgiveness doesn't mean that someone is no longer responsible for his or her actions, and it does not diminish the aftermath of their choices. It just means that we refuse to allow them/their choices to have control over our lives. I wasn't going to allow Charlie's decisions to dictate my life's outcome. Forgiveness enabled me to live in opposition to it. It's given me the space to lead my life and parent my kids with love, to look for possibility in the world around us, and to walk in redemption. What initially seemed to cost me everything has instead, given me the greatest gifts.

CHAPTER THIRTEEN

NORTH VALLEY JEWISH COMMUNITY CENTER

Granada Hills, California / August 10, 1999

ONE OF THE more interesting aspects of this project has been working with multiple perspectives from the same shooting. In his piece, Josh Stepakoff, who was only six when he was shot, recounts the external pressures survivors sometimes feel. He speaks specifically about a woman telling him that he spoke for her daughter, her daughter who was dead as a result of another school shooting. For Josh, this perceived expectation influenced his career and most of his young adult life. For Josh, his young life was unknowingly shaped by the expectations and actions of others.

Mindy Finkelstein, who was also shot at the JCC, was sixteen at the time, and she too writes about a similar incident where she was told: *you speak for my daughter.* To Mindy, this was a heavy responsibility, one she never forgot, and that sentiment has guided her to nonprofit work in some way.

This idea, what should we expect from survivors and what role they play in the movement to end gun violence in schools, is one that hangs over this entire project. We see it over and over again. In this chapter, however, we clearly see how heavy this responsibility can be, and how that weight can impact those left to carry it. Is it fair to expect a six-year-old boy to be the voice for anyone? Is it fair to ask that of a sixteen-year-old? These are questions we must wrestle with as a society, and unfortunately, we don't have the luxury of getting it wrong.

AMYE ARCHER, EDITOR
DECEMBER, 2018

**No one was killed at
North Valley Jewish Community Center,
but two campers were shot and wounded:**

*Josh Stepakoff, 6
Mindy Finkelstein, 16*

THE PATH NOT CHOSEN
By Josh Stepakoff

Josh Stepakoff was six years old when he was shot inside of his day camp at the North Valley Jewish Community Center in Granada Hills, California.

I always believed I wanted to be a psychologist. In middle school, I read Oliver Sacks and watched movies about psychological phenomena. I was fascinated by the human mind. In high school, I took AP psychology classes and as an undergrad in college, I took extra psychology classes, volunteered in psychology experiments, and learned about child psychology and development. After earning my bachelor's in psychology, I went on to earn my master's in clinical psychology with an emphasis in marriage and family therapy. Everything went according to plan. Then, in December 2017, I had a conversation that would cause me to question everything.

I was having breakfast with two guys whom I had just met through a mutual friend. For some reason, the topic turned to guns. We were having an open and honest conversation about this very controversial topic when I suddenly grew very uncomfortable. I explained that as a victim of gun violence myself, I had felt a tremendous amount of pressure for the last nineteen years. I had been told for most of my life that I had something to offer other survivors of gun violence and that people could benefit from working with me. At one point, when I was sixteen, a grieving mother put her hands on my shoulders and said, "you speak for my daughter who cannot speak anymore." My breakfast companions looked at me with a sadness. They told me how unfair it was for people to expect something from me. Somehow, them saying it aloud gave me the freedom I had been searching for.

On August 10, 1999, I was six years old and had just finished a game of capture the flag at my summer camp program at the North Valley Jewish Community Center. I was walking down the hallway when I came face-to-face with someone I thought was a construction worker. A bald, middle-aged white man who I thought was holding a drill. In reality, at his hip was semiautomatic submachine gun. Before I knew what was happening, he started shooting. I didn't know what was happening, but I knew that I had to get out of there, so I ran. As I got outside, I was stopped by my counselor, who saw that I was bleeding. She signaled for help and I was scooped up and carried to a different building, where I laid for what seemed like hours. I clearly remember lying on the ground, covered in blankets to shield the other kids from seeing the blood. The only words I could say were "call 911" over and over again. I couldn't say anything else. I remember the teachers, with the look of fear clearly on their faces, assuring me "we did, we did."

After the shooting, I stayed in the hospital for a few days. I got a cast on my leg, had the bullet removed from my hip, and began my recovery. There are so many people who came together in this short period of time, people who were "just doing their jobs." These people saved my life, and I don't feel like I ever got to properly thank them. I don't know all of them and I don't know if I ever will, but what I do know is that I am forever grateful for the life that they have allowed me to live. I became fixated on these mystery workers "just doing their jobs." I wanted to be one of them. I didn't have the stomach to be a paramedic or a doctor, and I was still scared of law enforcement and the danger they faced daily, so the only thing left for me was to be a therapist.

Through the years, when I shared my story, people told me how much their friend or loved one would benefit from hearing it. How my story could help others. The weight of this felt unbearable at times. I felt like the only thing I had to offer to society was the one part of my life I had no control over. Still, those moments led me to the path of being a therapist. It made sense to me. I am calm, quiet, level-headed, and a great listener. I have the temperament to be a therapist.

So, I got my degrees and became a therapist, just as I had planned. I worked with clients who were in the midst of arguably the most tragic times in their lives, but I did not get any of the fulfillment that I had expected. I was finally doing the work I had dreamed of, beginning the career seventeen years in the making, and I was miserable. I realize now, that in some way, I was still allowing the man who shot me to dictate my life. I realized that every decision I had made up until that point, including my career path, had been a result of that one moment, that one bullet, that one shooter.

In the end, maybe those two strangers at breakfast on that December morning were right. Maybe it was unfair of people to expect me to speak for those who've suffered from gun violence. But, that doesn't mean I don't have something to say. If you learn one thing from me, learn that your life belongs to you and no one else. I spent almost two decades chasing a dream that I thought I would love, and it only took a few moments for me to see I was wrong. But that's okay! I am happier than I have ever been knowing that there are endless possibilities out there. So if you only do one thing today, make an effort try something new, if you don't like it move on, and if you love it, explore more. But, no matter what you do, do it for you.

DOING NOTHING WAS NOT AN OPTION

By Loren Lieb

Loren Lieb was forty-three years old when her six-year-old son, Josh, was shot while attending his Jewish Community Center during summer day camp. Loren's older son, Seth, then eight, was also attending day camp there. Seth was unharmed.

I left for work early that morning while everyone else was still in bed. I slipped out quietly so I wouldn't disturb them. My husband, Alan, would take the boys, Seth (eight) and Josh (six), to summer camp day camp at the local Jewish community center (JCC) on his way to work. I would pick them up in the afternoon on my way home. That's how it was supposed to go. That was our routine.

Later that morning, Alan called me at work. When I picked up the phone, he said, "I got a call from your mom. There's someone at the JCC with a gun." I couldn't process the words. They made no sense to me. Why was someone at the JCC with a gun?

A colleague drove me the forty minutes from downtown Los Angeles to the JCC in Granada Hills. We didn't have a cell phone, so we relied on the car radio for information. I tried to maintain my composure, which became nearly impossible after hearing a report that six- and eight-year-old boys had been shot—the ages of my sons. I now feared that my sons, who were asleep when I left that morning and whom I had not kissed or told that I loved them, might, in fact, be dead.

As we neared the JCC, streets were cordoned off for blocks, and we had to park a distance away. As I made my way through the crowd of frantic parents, a stranger told me one of the kids might be named Josh. I started to cry. The next person I saw was

256

my mom, who had been evacuated from the church next door where she was attending a literary group meeting. She maintained her composure, but the expression on her face told a different story. My two boys were her only grandchildren.

The next thing I heard was an announcement from a bullhorn calling for the parents of Josh Stepakoff—my six-year-old son. Ducking under the yellow caution tape, I approached a police officer. He placed his hands firmly on my shoulders, looked me straight in the eyes, and repeatedly said, "He's going to be okay." My mom and I were bustled into an ambulance to be taken to the hospital to which Josh had been airlifted. I begged them to tell me where Seth was, but they didn't know.

At the hospital, we were brought to the emergency room. Alan was already there, having been contacted by the police. Josh was on an examination table, draped in sheets, with IVs and tubes connected. There were X-rays on viewers. Josh was calm, sedated, perhaps. I was catatonic. I don't remember rushing to his side, hugging him, or kissing him. I stood back, terrified to approach. There was a flood of information. He had been shot. Vital organs spared. Leg broken. Growth plate not injured. Would not walk with a limp. Children repress what they can't process. Don't probe. Let him lead the conversation. My head was spinning, and where was Seth?

Hours later, we learned that Seth had been evacuated from the JCC with the other children. They were at a local park under police guard waiting for reunification with their families. Friends had taken Seth home with them. Did he know what happened to his brother? Did he wonder why we didn't come for him? Was he afraid? When we were finally reunited, he wanted to know the details. He wanted to drive by the JCC. He wanted to drive by the hotel where the shooter hid for a few hours. He wanted to see where the same shooter had murdered a postal worker. We didn't know how to respond. We declined his requests.

The following Monday, one week after the shooting, the boys returned to day camp at the JCC, and enrollment was higher than the week before. We wanted the kids to be with their friends. We wanted to resume our normal routines, but, of course, normal was different now.

Josh was on crutches with a full leg cast. He didn't want to be seen in public because well-intentioned strangers would ask him how he broke his leg. Without emotion, he would simply reply, "I got shot." Putting the pieces together, the questioner's face would fall. The JCC shooting, just a few months after Columbine, had received intensive media coverage. Everyone knew about it. We stopped going out.

Loud noises, sirens, and helicopters were triggers for Josh. We chose television shows carefully. The house and windows had to be securely locked. His bedroom light on all night. We never talked about "the thing that happened." It was the elephant in the room. It was probably hard for Seth, too, but I don't know for certain because we never talked about it. All we knew was that his eight-year-old self was envious of gifts Josh received from well-wishers around the world, and that he wanted to ride in a helicopter.

Many years later, I realized that I knew very little about how the shooting had impacted Seth. I felt guilty for not talking with him about it. He had concerns about personal safety and for a time expressed interest in becoming a police officer. On a few occasions, he accompanied Josh to therapy appointments, but I never asked him about *his* feelings. When I finally did, he agreed to talk, but never made the time or he didn't have much to say. I don't know if it was because his feelings had faded with time, or because he needed time to think about it, or he didn't want to think about it.

Although I had relatives in law enforcement and another who was a competitive shooter, guns were not part of my world. My sister and I grew up in a comfortable suburb of Los Angeles. Our parents were city dwellers from New York. After their deaths, I found records of their early donations to Handgun Control, Inc. Growing up, after our house was robbed a second time, my parents responded by getting a large dog, not a gun.

In the weeks after the shooting at the JCC, I learned a protest was being planned in Washington, D.C., to demand changes to our nation's gun laws. I immediately got involved. It was cathartic for me to feel like I was drawing attention to a problem I hadn't even known existed until my child was shot. But once I knew, doing nothing was not an option. I made phone calls, attended meetings, raised money, talked to hundreds of people, gave media interviews, and helped to form the San Fernando Valley Chapter of the Brady Campaign to Prevent Gun Violence. The culmination of the efforts was the Million Mom March, which occurred just nine months after the shooting and was the brainchild of New Jersey mom Donna Dees Thomases. My family attended the March in D.C., and we have continued to participate in protests, marches, and vigils.

Being a gun violence prevention activist has become a way of life, even though it was difficult to be a working mom with two children spending much of my free time working on gun violence prevention. After the shooting, Alan and I were keenly aware that we could no longer assure our children that we would keep them safe. It was a painful acknowledgment. Surely, parents across the country continued to make this solemn promise to their frightened children, but for us, the promise now would be hollow. I hoped that seeing me work so hard to for gun violence prevention would help my kids, and show them that it's important to fight for what you believe in.

Over the years, friends reached out when there was a mass shooting—wondering if I was okay, fearing that the news would "bring me back" to the JCC shooting. What they didn't realize was that, as a gun violence prevention activist, gun violence was always on my mind. What changed, however, was my reaction. Intense grief and disbelief are now accompanied by overwhelming anger with the gun lobby, do-nothing politicians, and Americans who wring their hands, offer a prayer, and do nothing more. Since Josh was shot, almost 2.5 million Americans have been injured or killed by guns. The ripples and collateral damage reach many, many millions more. Can any one of us truly say that we haven't been impacted by gun violence? I don't think so.

THE CONUNDRUM OF SURVIVORSHIP

By Seth Stepakoff

Seth Stepakoff was eight years old when his younger brother, Josh, was shot and injured at their local JCC day camp. Seth was not injured in the shooting.

As we move through our lives, series of events, and interactions shape who we become. Most people can look to singular events throughout their life that had a significant impact. For me, it was the day my brother was shot by a cowardly Neo-Nazi. A man with such disdain for human life, that which differs from his own, thought best to attack a group of children.

My brother was only six when he was shot, and I was eight. We were at our summer day camp at the local Jewish Community Center. I did not see nor hear it happen, as I was in another portion of the facility. But I remember the day as vividly as yesterday. Immediately after the incident, those who were not injured were taken to the city house above the Northridge Park by the police station. There were lots of detectives walking around with guns and legal pads asking what we saw or heard. My friends' mother picked me up from camp and I remember my brother not being with us. I remember getting the call from my parents. They called from the hospital. My mom first, barely able to speak, told me that Josh fell and hurt his knee. I knew something wasn't right. Dad was next, I don't remember how he said it, but in no uncertain terms, he told me my brother had been shot.

In the days that followed, I spent time with Josh in the hospital and made great friends with the staff. We had a whole other room just for the gifts my brother received. Josh had a full leg cast from his foot to his pelvis. In the back where the exit wound occurred, there was a little door in the cast—a cutout used to access the layers of bandage underneath. Every day, if not multiple times per day, that bandage had to be changed. As the wound healed it, healed around pieces of bandage which meant that every time was an excruciating experience requiring the help of the whole family. Mom and Dad changed the bandage while I kept Josh busy, usually with a walkie-talkie.

While I remember the little things, what has stuck with me through the years is the shocking disregard for human life. In a world of freedom from oppression, there are those that are oppressed by their own ideologies and dogmas. Dogmas that drive them to kill for pleasure. Of all things that I carry with me to this day this undoubtedly shapes me the most. This idea that anyone at any time can suffer at the hands of another person because of hatred. I'm tremendously proud of my brother for his resilience, fortitude, and continuous drive. Yet, I've had to watch him and the rest of my family live with the aftereffects of the shooting for two decades. Living with PTSD is an unfortunate state, a complete hijacking of the brain. It's hard to process the idea that people aren't just out to kill—they're out to kill *you.*

As the sibling of someone who was shot, you're left with the conundrum of survivorship. There's one part of me that's tremendously grateful that I won the location lottery. That I was in the right place at the right time. I will never have to experience the physical pain, and more so the enduring psychological pain. The other part of me wishes It would have been me. Then, quite honestly, I wish it were no one. I wouldn't wish this experience on anyone. But the truth is, it can happen to any one of us at any time. We were the perfect family until someone with a gun changed everything.

A CONVERSATION WITH DONNA FINKLESTEIN

Mindy Finkelstein was a sixteen-year-old camp counselor at the Jewish Community Center (JCC) in Granada Hills, California, on August 10, 1999. Her mother, Donna, was forty-seven years old at the time. The following is a conversation between Mindy, Donna, and Amye Archer, editor.

AMYE: *Let's start after the shooting. After Mindy was treated for her injuries and released, what were those first few days and weeks like?*

DONNA: In the beginning, it was all about getting well and dealing with the wounds as a mother. Even though Mindy was hospitalized, she was sent home and I was supposed to clean her bullet wounds. That was another part of this. It was beyond awful. I was very busy taking care of the medical aspect of it.

MINDY: It was hectic, and it was much more about the physical recovery versus dealing with what happened on an emotional level. Also, this is nineteen years ago, so Columbine had happened, but it wasn't as prevalent an issue as it is today. I think parents now dealing with kids have a very different conversation with their teenagers about shootings than we had at the time.

AMYE: *What role has PTSD played in the aftermath of your shooting and in your recovery?*

MINDY: One of the biggest issues I face is since I was shot when I was sixteen, my brain and my subconscious kind of set in at that specific time in my life where my safety net was my parents

263

and my safety net was my house. So, when I'm taken away from that or I feel like I'm being taken away from that, my brain reacts very similarly to when I got shot.

I've had two big breakdowns from PTSD in my life. One was when I went away to college or tried to go away to college, and I ended up having a breakdown and was hospitalized and then had to take a year off school. Then most recently, almost three years ago, I was getting married and the summer before my wedding had a massive breakdown. My now-husband and I were considering postponing our wedding or not getting married because I was so sick. I was having really severe panic attacks and was in therapy and on medication.

DONNA: I went up there [where Mindy was living] for a week and I was going to hospitalize her.

MINDY: I got through that time. We got married and we're happy and we have a baby now. But I'm in treatment and I do see a therapist and I'm on medication. I'm very self-aware. My husband is now, too, and my parents are, about when situations arise that could potentially set off my PTSD. In fact, having a baby was, everybody was a little concerned that perhaps I would have something similar because it's a big life change. That usually is what does it for me. But I got through pregnancy and having a baby with no issues, so it was great.

AMYE: *How do you feel about the new generation of school shooting survivors, namely the Parkland community, speaking out about this issue?*

MINDY: I worry. I was the same age as them when I was shot, and I was thrust into this survivor role and victim role at the time. I was not prepared for it at all. We didn't have much experience with school shootings.

They've grown up with school shootings, so they were fully aware of how they felt about what was taking place. I think the Parkland kids have this maturity level to them that I did not have at that age. And not to say I wasn't mature, but they have a very different perspective on what took place at their school. So that's part of it.

I do think they are so well-spoken that they are a media's dream. You have these kids that were trained in debate class, who were trained by their teachers in the most incredible way, and it's doing a really incredible service to those of us who have been in the fight for so long.

However, what they don't realize and something I didn't realize is once the media goes away and once people stop talking to you about it, you crash. So, I'm nervous for them because they haven't had time to grieve. They haven't had time to be outside of the limelight.

DONNA: A school shooting has to cause trauma, because it's not a natural experience. Being in a shooting is not a natural experience. So even for me personally, whenever there's a loud noise or a boom or something or wherever I go, I'm frightened. It's always on my mind and it will be for them, too. But I think it's inevitable they'll suffer from PTSD, but what I think and what I see is empowerment and it gives some meaning and purpose.

AMYE: *What would you say to, unfortunately, the growing population of shooting survivors like yourself? What do you think is one or two of the most important things they can do to make sure that they're taking care of themselves after these kind of events?*

DONNA: How I took care of myself was by becoming an activist and knowing that the work specific to what I do in all of these years may have prevented other potential loss of life due to gun violence. I have some issues from all of this. I didn't go into therapy. But I feel that by talking about it and getting the word out about voting and doing all the things that we can to prevent future gun violence is taking care of myself. Does that make sense?

MINDY: I think for parents of survivors it makes really a lot of sense to be as involved as possible. I think for people that were wounded, I think that it's really an incredible opportunity to be able to speak for those who can't speak for themselves. I always tell the story of how the father of Mary Reed who was killed at Virginia Tech told me I represent his daughter because she can't speak for herself. I always remember that and feel that every time I speak and do some form of activism for gun violence prevention.

However, I really want to stress that I think it's one of the best things that you can do is to acknowledge what happened to you and not put it behind you as though it didn't really happen, and reach out and talk to other survivors because one of the things that I find the most helpful and feel the most relief is actually being in a room with other survivors of mass shootings because we've gone through such a bizarre but similar experience. It's one of the few times that I feel a sense of relief from it is being open and honest in those conversations versus just talking to others.

AMYE: *Mindy, since you just had a baby girl, I have to ask. Do you feel hopeful?*

MINDY: I think I have to. If I didn't feel hopeful, why would I have a kid?

DONNA: Hopeful that we're going to end gun violence?

AMYE: *Hopeful that my . . . I want to change the culture of this country so that my kids, not only will survive high school, but won't have to parent in fear for their own children. So, I guess my question is will it be better for them?*

DONNA: I just continue to do the work I do. What I do is I talk to parents and students about safe gun storage in the home. That's my focus and that's where I feel I can make change. There will be more school shootings. There will be. I don't feel hopeful that that's going to change.

I'm hopeful that this generation, the Parkland kids, gets more young people out to vote and more engaged and informed about voting and what all of this means going on around them. Whether it's going to curtail gun violence? No, I don't think so. And the other issue we're focusing on now is teen suicides. What's changing is it's getting people to recognize the importance of a gun in the home and being a responsible gun owner because that's the big push now.

MINDY: I think it depends on what you're hopeful for. I hope that my daughter will go to a school that doesn't experience gun violence. I hope that she doesn't have to go through the same thing I did and that laws will be changed in order to make them less often than they are. But, like my mom said, I don't think they're going away. I think I'm realistic to know that they're here and they're here to stay. But I am hopeful that people don't have to go through what we went through, and I'm very hopeful that my family doesn't have to go through it again.

CHAPTER FOURTEEN

COLUMBINE HIGH SCHOOL

Littleton, Colorado / April 20, 1999

COLUMBINE. **I WAS** twenty-one years old and in my last semester of college at Penn State University when I first heard that word. I lived off campus, so the bus ride in every day was around fifteen to twenty minutes depending on traffic. The news broke right as our ride started. Another student's cell phone rang, and he announced it to the group of us. A school shooting. A hostage situation. A world away in Colorado. *A school shooting?* I had never heard of such a thing. When I got to campus, there were whispers, but not one of my professors turned on the classroom television. I remember running straight home and watching in horror as newscasters interviewed anyone they could find, and a helicopter showed terrified students running from the school.

Because Columbine was the first school shooting that I remembered living through, it became a touchstone in my life, as it was for many of my generation. I often thought about those teenagers, especially since I was so close to them in age. As I graduated, found work, got married, and moved forward with my life, I was acutely aware that our lives were progressing at the same rate. *Or were they?* I wondered how they recovered and how they grew. How could they possibly move on from Columbine? That question began this entire project. *What happened to those kids who survived Columbine?*

I would find many answers. First, they were followed by the shooting. To be from Columbine meant something after 1999, a theme that shows up over and over again in this chapter. Coni Sanders, whose father, Dave Sanders, was the only teacher murdered at Columbine, writes, "Even now, when someone finds out about Dad, they stop and tell me where *they* were that day and what *their* experience was. They have no idea how hard that is." Still, it's hard not to personalize Columbine, since in many ways it feels like we experienced it collectively, as a country. In fact, didn't I start this chapter in that exact way?

They were also followed by the trauma. Ted Zocco-Hochhalter writes about his daughter Anne Marie's paralysis from one of the shooter's bullets and how the trajectory of that bullet forever changed his family. "Six months after our daughter was shot at Columbine, Carla [Anne Marie's mother and Ted's wife] committed suicide with a gun. The tragic irony in that act haunts me to this day," he writes.

Finally, what happened to those kids at Columbine was that they turned into amazing advocates, many working behind the scenes to help curb gun violence. Student Jami Amo, now a parent, has turned her attention to Moms Demand Action. "I realized that someday I need to be able to look my children in the eyes and say that I did everything I could to change this," she writes. Another student, Heather Martin, is the cofounder of The Rebels Project, one of the largest networks of support in the country for survivors of mass shootings. Many of our contributors from other communities told me how this group helped them find normalcy and a sense of belonging after their own mass shooting.

Coni Sanders earned a master's in psychology and works with offenders of violent crime, mostly men, to help better understand the root of violence. "In losing my dad, I found myself and my purpose in this harsh world. Holding the hands of felons, helping them find their own *why*," she writes.

Even the teachers who lived through the shooting found a way to give back. Paula Reed, a teacher who saw several of her students murdered or wounded, was one of the teachers and community members who visited the teachers at Sandy Hook shortly after their shooting. "The teachers I met have mettle," she writes, "they are hurt, and sad, and angry, and confused, and all the things the teachers at Columbine were, but I hope we looked like we had half as much grit back when we were six weeks out."

When I finished compiling the stories in this chapter, I felt a light surrounding Columbine that I hadn't felt in twenty years. They call themselves the Columbine Rebels for a reason. Each person in this chapter has blazed their own trail in some way. I am in awe of what they've accomplished.

Amye Archer, Editor

January 2019

The following students and staff were shot and killed at Columbine High School:

Cassie Bernall, 17, student

Steven Curnow, 14, student

Corey DePooter, 17, student

Kelly Fleming, 16, student

Matthew Kechter, 16, student

Daniel Mauser, 15, student

Daniel Rohrbough, 15, student

William David "Dave" Sanders, 47, teacher and coach

Rachel Scott, 17, student

Isaiah Shoels, 18, student

John Tomlin, 16, student

Lauren Townsend, 18, student

Kyle Velasquez, 16, student

RIGHT PLACE AT THE RIGHT TIME
By Coni Sanders

Coni Sanders's father, Dave Sanders, was the only teacher killed at Columbine. He was shot several times as he ran toward the gunfire in an effort to save as many students as possible.

I don't want to be a hero any more than Dad did, but last week a man who'd spent twenty-four years in prison called *me* just that. I suddenly felt life had come full circle since the day Dad was murdered and hailed a hero for saving hundreds of kids at Columbine High School.

Dave Sanders, my dad, was many things to many people. But to those who knew him best, he was just a normal guy. He loved coming home after school and watching TV with his dog, a mini poodle, while drinking a rum and Coke. He wore polyester pants, butterfly-collared shirts, and goofy owl glasses. He was everything to my mother. I don't think he ever said no to her. If she wanted something, he would make sure she had it. As for us kids, if we needed guidance, he made sure we got it. To his students, he was more than Mr. Sanders, he was someone who tried to help them find their path in the world and who enjoyed reaching the "tough kids" by encouraging them to play sports and do well in school.

To his grandkids, Dad was the great entertainer. Every weekend, they would come over and he would have treats under their pillows such as puppets for the puppet theater he and Mom had made from wood. And he loved making their favorite bedtime snack, worms and dirt (Oreos, ice cream, and gummy worms).

He was also the only teacher killed at Columbine High School on April 20, 1999. The world's first glimpse of Dad was the One Bleeding to Death, as described in a sign made by students trying desperately to resuscitate him and keep him alive inside a second-floor science classroom. More importantly, and maybe most importantly, my father, Dave Sanders, was a hero. He ran toward the school that day while students ran away, fleeing for their lives. My father ran toward the screams, toward the shooters, toward the guns. And in doing so, he saved hundreds of students, while losing his own life. A colleague told us that his last words were "tell my girls I love them."

In the days and weeks after Columbine, my family was swirled into a media nightmare. Our lives were no longer normal, no longer private. We'd spend years not saying where we were from or using our last name because people would want to talk about the worst day of our lives. Even now, when someone finds out about Dad, they stop and tell me where *they* were that day and what *their* experience was. They have no idea how hard that is.

Many reacted to the shooting by blaming the parents of the murderers, guns, violent videogames, prescription medication, music, and a myriad of other desperate grasps to help us understand why this happened. I felt differently. I kept wondering what was happening in the boys' heads? What made them wake up on a Tuesday and try to blow up their school? How does that thought process turn to action and *why*? The boys who murdered Dad were on *Diversion* (a program for first-time offenders of crime), after they broke into a van. They received therapy and interventions, yet they still murdered people. Who could've helped them? I believed the key to *why* lay within.

I struggled to make sense of my own life after losing Dad. He'd always wanted me to go back to college, so I decided to honor him. I was in my third year of my bachelor's program, working toward my business degree when I took abnormal psychology. It was an eye-opener and I felt compelled to learn more. It was exhilarating thinking I might finally find the answer to the *why* I'd been searching for. What I found was—the *why* isn't simple. I decided that if I couldn't determine *why* Columbine happened, I'd at least try to prevent such atrocities.

The college I attended had a "Psychology of Violence" program. I took every class I could on the criminal mind. I didn't tell anyone at the college about my Columbine connection. I feared that they'd change the curriculum to be sensitive or worse, give me a sympathy grade. Plus, everyone might want to share their "Columbine experience."

Then, one day, I was outed. We hosted a guest speaker in my homicide class, and it happened to be the lead investigator for the Columbine massacre. She walked into the classroom and hugged me and asked how my mom was. I wanted to crawl under the table. My professors were angry at me for not sharing. I spent the rest of my time in school hearing everyone's story about where they were when Columbine happened.

One day, the dean contacted me and said that I'd "accidentally" minored in psychology and asked if I wanted to change my degree program. I did. I graduated with honors and received an Educational Perseverance award, which revealed my Columbine connection in front of everyone at graduation.

I immediately enrolled in a Master of Psychology program. I wanted to have every tool I could to reduce violence in our society. When I finished, I had to find an internship site. I initially thought I'd go into grief counseling, but most grief counselors are volunteers. With $130,000 in student loan debt, a volunteer job wouldn't work. After sending my information to every site in town, I was desperate. So, when a little private practice that worked with offenders of violent crime, mainly domestic in nature, asked me to interview, I went. I didn't know it at the time, but the universe was putting me exactly where I could do the most good.

The night before my first day, I tried to calm my husband's fears about the fact that I'd be sitting in a room with men convicted of violent crimes committed mostly against women. There really wasn't anything good to say about it, but he reluctantly agreed that I should go.

The next day, I expected to walk into a room of men in wifebeater tanks, dirty jeans, and face tattoos. I never expected what I found. A room of men from different backgrounds, some wearing business attire, some in jeans, none in wifebeater shirts and, in that group, no face tattoos. I was confused. These men were supposed to be scary and horrible and deserve punishment. Some talked about remorse for their actions, others about a desperate love for their children, and many wanted to learn more about how to be better men. They talked about what they thought before they did something terrible. One said, "It wasn't like I just woke up one day and decided to do this." Unlike the boys that murdered Dad, I learned most crimes aren't planned out.

Shortly after starting this new work, it hit me. I'm the teacher like Dad, and these men are students who need me. I finally found where I belonged, in a room full of convicted felons, offering the same things Dad did to those "tough kids" he so often sought out: kindness and encouragement without judgment and an opportunity to work hard to improve their lives.

Last week, a man who spent twenty-four years in prison and calls me "White Bread" and swears I have more street cred than his homies, called me his hero. He said he was in the right place at the right time when he walked into my office. I cried. He had no idea why. At that moment, it occurred to me that Dad was in the right place at the right time to save hundreds of his students, the way I've been in the right place at the right time to save my clients. In losing my dad, I found myself and my purpose in this harsh world. Holding the hands of felons, helping them find their own *why.*

Today, more than a decade after walking into that room for the first time, I've had thousands of clients go through my program. I meet each one of them as a person, not a felon, a batterer, or a gang member, but as a human being in need to compassion and guidance. My dad, Dave Sanders, the hero, the teacher, the loving husband, father, and grandfather, taught me this.

ESCAPING COLUMBINE
By Jami Amo

Jami Amo was a fifteen-year-old freshman at the time of the shooting.

It's been nineteen years since the shooting at Columbine High School, yet the memories of April 20, 1999, have been woven among the fibers of my being. The cracking voice of the boy who came into the cafeteria shouting that someone had a gun, the unsettling thud of nearly four hundred people dropping to the floor simultaneously, how after being directed to run, those of us who had piled into the elevator had to close the doors in the faces of classmates desperate to flee. I can still smell the smoky hallway outside the library, thick with the stench of explosives, punctuated by gunfire. I still feel the distortion of time as we waited for the doors to close again. I remember the vibrations felt in between the rows of cushioned theater seats as a bomb went off in the cafeteria. And then after about an hour, the escape route, through a hallway to an exit.

I lived directly across the street from the high school, but the police had set up a perimeter to protect the crime scene, preventing me from crossing the street to my apartment building. Unable to go home, I spent the remainder of the day, and a portion of the night, wandering the neighborhood. I went to a neighbor's house, turned on the news, and watched as my school filled the frame. Helicopters circled above. A sign plastered in a science room window, read One Bleeding to Death. A classmate jumped from a second-story window of the library, desperate for his own medical attention. The SWAT team postured outside the building for what seemed like forever. The images were surreal. I couldn't watch anymore.

I ran to the nearby elementary school to scan the crowd for familiar faces and the list of known survivors for names I recognized. Classmates were telling stories from the terror inside, after they were evacuated from my school, which had now become the focus of the nation. I heard hushed whispers and cries about whom they'd seen shot, who was already dead. A friend waited for her brother's name to appear on the list of survivors. Evening came, the waiting crowd dwindled, the last students were evacuated from the building, and the injured were identified. As darkness spread across the sky, only a small group of people remained, including my friend and her parents. Those twelve families were facing darkness indeed, as they would never again meet their child's gaze, never again share an embrace, never again exchange *I love you.*

Our community was left to reconcile the horrific events of the massacre and bury our dead amid a throng of reporters and their cameras. Of course, we were shocked. People around the world echoed what we felt: this was an unconscionable tragedy, something must've gone terribly wrong for this to take place in an American school, and we must do something to prevent another. If it could happen at Columbine, it could happen anywhere.

However, there was no sweeping legislation, and shootings kept happening. I turned to drugs and alcohol to cope with the overwhelming devastation I felt. I struggled to make sense of it. After all, I had escaped the building unscathed and hadn't had any relatives or closest friends die. Why hadn't I gotten over it as it seemed so many of my classmates had?

Ten months after the shooting, in the hours after midnight on Valentine's Day, two of my tenth-grade classmates, a pair of sweethearts, were gunned down in a sandwich shop. The case remains unsolved. It was another shock to the community, and by the time a prominent student athlete committed suicide a few months later, I actually believed we'd been doomed, each of us, marked by fate.

The trauma from the shooting and the ensuing events weighed heavily on me. I felt guilt for surviving. I even felt guilt for feeling traumatized. I was haunted by the memory of Steve Curnow in the cafeteria at the beginning of the lunch period. Plagued with regret for things I didn't know I should've done. I should've noticed the duffel bags in the cafeteria, I should've said something to Steve when he got up to leave for the library. I carried an endless stream of "should've's" along with so many "what ifs" and "if onlys."

Throughout high school, I refused to address my growing depression. I dulled myself with drugs and alcohol. Being under the influence allowed me to pretend my situation was under control, that I was okay. I barely held part-time jobs. I thought being away from the building would help me move on, so I skipped classes. I didn't seek therapy. I thought I could do it myself. I was convinced there wasn't any help to be had, because there wasn't a therapist around who could tell me something I didn't know about my own feelings. I was sure that I could self-medicate until I got over it.

Eventually, I learned to move past controlled substances and into healing. I allowed myself to feel the pain I had stifled for so many years, and I admitted that I still struggled with the aftermath of the shooting. I was living with post-traumatic stress disorder, and I was finally able to acknowledge it. My heart still pounds every time I use an elevator, I startle at every loud noise, and the state of heightened vigilance my body lives under leaves me on edge and exhausted, yet unable to rest. Over the years there've been hundreds of shootings in schools across the country. I brace myself for the onslaught of flashbacks and vivid nightmares in the weeks and months following each one.

In 2010, I became a parent for the first time, and found myself having new feelings about the shootings, more complicated feelings. I wasn't only the teenage victim anymore, I had also become the frantic parent, wondering how my children would cope if they were among those who survived. After the tragedy at Sandy Hook, I was struck like never before with a deep sorrow. I was dismayed the deaths of those young children didn't inspire a resounding call for change from legislators. I became more than cynical, I felt hopeless, and pondered my own children's fate.

I watched one afternoon as my son's kindergarten class was herded into the closet with their teacher for a lockdown drill. To follow protocol, I, as a classroom visitor, had to crouch under a shelf near the back of the room. I knew it was a drill, but I panicked. I did my best to push my feelings aside because there was another parent volunteer there, too, who had no idea I was at Columbine. That day, a wound opened inside of me, inflicted by the realization that we adapted our lives to allow for shootings in our schools, the people in charge didn't care, and this cycle wouldn't end. I wondered how long it would be until a shooting happens where I live, and which of my kids would be there.

I'm not sure why it took me so long, but in recent years I started to truly feel the weight of the damage done at Columbine. Here I am, alive, married, with my three beautiful, healthy children. The children of Dave Sanders have had to miss their father for nineteen years. There are no children for Lauren Townsend, Daniel Mauser, and Kelly Fleming. There was no graduation for Steve Curnow, Cassie Bernall, or Daniel Rohrbough. There was no marriage for Isaiah Shoels, Rachel

Scott, or Corey DePooter. Since the shooting, I've had nineteen years of holidays with my family while the families of Matt Kechter, John Tomlin, and Kyle Velasquez had only those sixteen years' worth of memories with their sons. There are those who still carry physical reminders of their wounds. Some of them never walked again. Layer after layer of damage done to the students, the staff, the families. And every town that has experienced a shooting is fraught with the same pains, rippling throughout for years to come. Hundreds of thousands of people have felt the same sorrow, borne from shock and terror, and growing sharper, perhaps concentrated, in some way, with time.

Almost twenty years after the shooting at Columbine, there was a mass shooting inside Marjory Stoneman Douglas High School. It was obvious immediately that something in the response among survivors was different. I began to question if my lack of action was, in fact, part of the problem. My silence wasn't helping to prevent gun violence and it wasn't changing the minds of legislators or voters. I realized that someday I need to be able to look my children in the eyes and say that I did everything I could to change this. I decided it was time to speak out about my experience and the trauma of gun violence, and to join the advocacy groups I'd silently supported for so long, Everytown for Gun Safety and Moms Demand Action.

It is difficult to put into words what I feel when there's another school shooting, ushering some other community into our survivors collective. I feel angry, initially, and beyond heartsick for the loss of such precious, young life. I feel uneasy when I think about the painful experiences that will befall so many of the survivors of school shootings, the triggers that will send them into a panic at inopportune times for years to come. I question if they're better prepared, having been trained to expect an active shooter in drills since grade school. I wonder if they resent us for having been unable to prevent it from happening. I fear the pattern of the news cycle that will leave their stories untold, and I dread the day when mental health support services will leave them behind too soon. I hope they will not stumble into the same darkness I did. I wonder how long the nightmares will plague them, and I think about how they will manage to send their own children to school one day.

ONCE A REBEL, ALWAYS A REBEL

By Heather Martin

Heather Martin was a senior at Columbine High School at the time of the shooting. She is the cofounder of The Rebels Project, a nonprofit organization connecting and supporting mass trauma survivors from across the country.

EDITOR'S NOTE: For more information on The Rebels Project, visit the website therebelsproject.org.

Two days after the mass shooting inside Columbine High School, I turned eighteen. Because we were seniors, April 20, 1999, became the last day of school at Columbine for the class of '99. That meant I didn't have a built-in, easily accessible support system as I started my life as an adult. Of course, those who went back to the school where the shooting occurred had a whole set of different struggles, neither one more difficult than the other, but going into the world surrounded by people who had no idea what I'd experienced felt isolating. And while I had some very supportive friends, it just wasn't the same.

Like other survivors, I tried to get back to normal as quickly as possible. This need for normalcy is our way of trying to find solid ground after our worlds have crumbled beneath and around us. Only three months after graduation, I moved out and attended community college hoping to start fresh. Because the college was local, I was often blindsided by people bringing up the shooting during casual conversations, class discussions; it was even mentioned in my college textbooks. The word "Columbine" became a trigger for me, and any mention of the event caused me to shut down and shut off.

In one class, the assignment was to write an argument paper on gun violence and gun laws. Somehow, I worked up the courage to tell the professor that I couldn't write about the topic. I even told her I was a Columbine graduate. Her response—write the essay or fail the class. I failed the class.

On another day, the fire alarm went off and I froze at my desk with tears streaming down my face. Eventually, I made it outside, where I found a friend who offered to tell my professor why I wouldn't be coming back to class after the drill. The professor shrugged and said she would mark me absent. After having been met with such disregard for my feelings and my experience, one that I was just barely beginning to process, I shut down even more and stopped talking about it. This led to intense feelings of isolation and embarrassment. In the months and years following the shooting, after all the "what-if" scenarios had played out in my mind and dreams, I kept asking myself why I wasn't over it, why was I still scared of loud noises and libraries?

I worked to stay busy. I worked three jobs in addition to being a full-time student. Looking back, I think these jobs helped me to avoid school, academics, and thinking about the shooting. To help me feel in control of my life, I developed an eating disorder. At one point, I didn't eat for two weeks and ended up in the hospital. However, I refused to quit any of the jobs I was working.

Eventually, I dropped out of college, even after attending formal therapy. I spent years struggling, feeling more and more lost as each new shooting happened. One huge step toward my recovery was being invited back into the school for the tenth anniversary, where I was able to connect with classmates I hadn't seen in years. With my newfound informal survivor support system, I was able to reenroll in college, where I majored in English and obtained my teaching license. Then, in my final year of college, there was a shooting at a theater in Aurora. Two days later, I received a text from a friend, a fellow 1999 graduate from Columbine High School, asking: "how do you feel about starting a support group for survivors?"

Two minutes later, I replied: "I'm in."

Thus began another huge step in my journey to healing.

I was just beginning my first year of teaching when Jennifer Hammer and I started The Rebels Project, named for the Columbine High School Mascot—the Rebels. Both of us had barricaded ourselves with fifty-eight other students in a small office adjacent to the choir room for just over three hours on April 20, 1999. We knew panic, we knew fear. And we knew that we and many of our classmates were still struggling, even thirteen years later, from the trauma we experienced on that day. The shooting in Aurora opened up the floodgates for us, and we were ready to help in a way that only other survivors could understand.

Desperate to provide a resource that we hadn't had, The Rebels Project began holding monthly support meetings where survivors could talk to other survivors and relate to each other on a level deeper than when outsiders asked "Oh, you were there? Was it scary? What did you see?" Because of the success of the monthly support meetings, we began fund-raising to bring survivors from around the country together for a weekend gathering. From there, we started traveling to impacted communities to offer our support.

One of the unique qualities about our nonprofit is that our leadership team is made up of all survivors, from Columbine: Amy Over, Zachary Cartaya, and Missy Mendo, from the Washington Navy Yard shooting: Sherrie Lawson, and from the Aurora theater shooting: Chelsea Sobolik. Together, with the help of survivors from around the world, we work to provide systems of support for survivors in need. While I wish I could say that these are easy to provide given that we have all experienced a mass shooting, that is not always true, though it does help us immeasurably because in essence, it's the helplessness survivors feel that drives this work.

We counteract that helplessness in the best way we know how—by reflecting on what we experienced, on what worked and didn't work for us, and on how best to fill the gaps that each of us has experienced throughout our recovery journey. As a survivor network, The Rebels Project helps fill those gaps for others, so the journey is less lonely and less isolating. The Rebels Project offers survivors a way to support others and help alleviate the helpless feeling we experience after every subsequent shooting.

In April 2017, we had a little over four hundred members in our private online support group. Now, we have over nine hundred from approximately fifty different survivor communities. We always say that we are so happy that new members are finding us, but so terribly sad that there is a need.

Since starting The Rebels Project, I've learned so much about my own recovery journey. I've also learned how much connecting with others can help heal. The importance of connecting with others is invaluable. Today, we travel the country meeting with survivors and speaking at various conferences so others can help fill some of the gaps we experienced along the way. The best part is that each member contributes and can offer their unique insight, which in turn supports other members, so we always have someone to reach out to when we need it, in many ways transforming us from victims into survivors. Of course, we wish we weren't needed. But the truth is: we are. Now more than ever before.

ARRIVALS AND DEPARTURES
By Ted Zocco-Hochhalter

Ted Zocco-Hochhalter's daughter, Anne Marie, was critically injured in the Columbine High School shooting. Carla, Ted's wife and Anne Marie's mother, took her own life six months after the shooting.

As the years come and go the school massacre known as Columbine continues to affect people in different ways based on each individual's personal experiences of that day and the healing process they've gone through since April 20, 1999. Count me among that group of people. The massacre ended that day, but even after the last shots were fired and the last explosives detonated, the events of April 20 continued and multiplied for everyone affected including me.

I was in Seattle on business when Columbine began. I really disliked the travel my job demanded. My kids were growing up and my first wife, Carla, was suffering from a deep and pervasive mental illness first diagnosed in 1996. I felt guilty being away so much.

The meeting I anticipated would take at least eight hours, only took four. Meaning I might be able to make an afternoon flight home. I called United to see if that might be possible. It was. My reservation would get me to Denver about 5:30 p.m. instead of flying out the next day.

All that remained was calling Carla and asking her to pick me up in Littleton. I borrowed my colleague's cell phone and dialed. A couple of rings and she picked up. Carla asked me if I'd been watching the news. I responded that I hadn't. She began telling me about Columbine.

"There's been a shooting," she said in a panicked voice. "Anne Marie has been hurt, and I don't know where Nathan is." My initial reaction was disbelief. My hands began to shake, and my stomach churned with nausea—the bile rising in my throat. My daughter was shot at school? Who did it? Where was Nathan? None of it made any sense.

Carla tried to get to the school but had been turned away at a checkpoint by someone she didn't know. This person told her they thought Anne Marie's injury was to her ankle and advised Carla to go home and wait. She went home believing Anne Marie would be okay. I explained to her my meeting ended earlier than expected and that I'd be home later that afternoon. Her relief was palpable.

I felt helpless. I was two hours away by air; I had at least a three hour wait until my plane took off. My anxiety meter was close to being pegged. Frantically, my colleagues and I tuned into different stations on the car radio in an effort to get whatever sketchy information we could. The stations were saying shooters were inside the school and there were injuries and maybe fatalities.

That's when it started sinking in that it was something that would change our family and our lives forever. I knew that once I got to the airport, I could call my family back from a pay phone. I had to trust they were handling everything until I got there. The rest was out of my control.

My colleagues didn't know what to say as they dropped me off at departures. They wished me well, and I thanked them. When I reached my gate the scenes on TV were playing out. Media helicopters hovering over the school were filming images of kids running across the lawn and down the sidewalks with hands clasped over their heads. I searched furiously for any sign of Nathan. I tried to imagine what Nathan wore that morning, the colors of his clothing, book bags, anything. His height should make him distinguishable, his gait unmistakable. Any sign that he was alive and okay.

Police were everywhere and herded terrified kids to a nearby fenced area out of harm's way. Squad cars lined up in a row outside the cafeteria with police pointing weapons at the school. Ambulances were there, too. I looked around at others in the boarding area. No one spoke. Their eyes were glued to the screen. They wore horror on their faces.

The media was saying all kinds of things. No one seemed to know who or how many people were shooting. I had trouble breathing. The fear, concern, and helplessness exacerbated my need to get home. I couldn't control the panic the anxiousness and waiting were causing. It's as if there was a timer, an hourglass in my brain and it was quickly draining of sand. I *had* to get home.

There was a pay phone in the waiting area. My hands shook as I pressed the numbers. I asked Carla if she had any new information. She told me Anne Marie had been shot in the chest, not her ankle, and she was on the way to the hospital. She still didn't know where Nathan was. I didn't know if Carla could handle anything more serious.

I hung up and called my sister, Belva, who told me Carla was being taken to the hospital by some neighbors to be with Anne Marie. I asked her about Nathan. She didn't know where Nathan was or whether he was all right. Her husband, Marc, was at Leawood Elementary School, a nearby reunification point, looking for him. She told me Marc would pick me up at the airport when I arrived in Denver to take me to the hospital.

Belva also told me Anne Marie was shot while eating lunch outside the cafeteria with her friends, Jayson and Kim. When they realized shots had been fired, Jayson and Kim ran toward the cafeteria for shelter believing Anne Marie was with them.

When they realized she wasn't, Jayson ran back for her. He had to abandon those plans when he came under attack himself. Later I would learn one of the shooters had looked straight at Kim before turning and shooting at Anne Marie, whose back was to them. We hung up, and I went to sit down again.

A man sat beside me and began talking about how horrible this was. I don't know why, but I blurted out that my kids were in that school. To my surprise he gave me a hug, whispered in my ear that he wished me well, and moved off somewhere out of sight. He never told me his name and I never saw him again. His act of kindness helped me feel a bit better and reduced my anxiety somewhat.

Eventually, it came time to board. My pulse was racing.

I found my seat. A woman sat down in the seat next to me. I didn't converse with her. Her husband and little boy sat in the row in front of us. She was preoccupied with taking care of her son and didn't try to start a conversation with me, either. I was grateful for that. The plane backed away from the gate and, as we began to taxi toward the runway for takeoff, I suddenly felt faint, and began to tremble again.

It wasn't until we were in the air that I finally asked a flight attendant for information from Denver if she could get it. She asked me why I needed information. That's when I broke down and began to cry. I can't remember exactly what I told her, but I know it tumbled out of my mouth as if someone else was saying it. I'm surprised she even understood me.

The woman beside me overheard. She told the flight attendant she was a doctor. I tried to explain to her what was going on at Columbine and that I needed info because my kids were in that school. She demanded I be taken into first class so I could get off the plane first. The flight attendant agreed.

A horrific headache set in.

After I sat down in the first row next to the exit door, the captain of the aircraft came out and sat next to me. I remember him telling me he had a daughter about Anne Marie's age and that he couldn't imagine the emotions I must be feeling. I saw tears well up in his eyes. I couldn't bring myself to say anything. In a very calm voice, he said that the flight would be changing, that we were going to go "as fast as this bucket of bolts will go," about two thirds the speed of sound.

He'd declared an onboard emergency. That meant we were going in with absolutely no delays. Someone in Denver wanted us to taxi into a holding area because we were arriving way ahead of schedule. The captain told them to either find an empty gate or he would find one himself and dock there. The last thing he told me before going back into the cockpit was that our descent into Denver would be fast and very steep. I didn't believe him, but I should have. He wished both me and my family well and went back into the cockpit.

At least I didn't feel so alone anymore.

The aircraft began accelerating. The flight attendants hovered, not knowing what to do. No announcement was made regarding an onboard emergency. Some passengers were visibly antsy. Even the flight attendants looked a little nervous.

My headache intensified.

We touched down hard in Denver and careened off the runway into the taxi lane. I was scared. The plane arrived at the gate. I could feel the jet walk bump against the aircraft.

As we prepared to deplane, I stood there nervously waiting for the door to open. When it finally did, I ran toward the Concourse up the Jetway.

Four Denver police officers were waiting for me. My sister, Belva, had called ahead to let them know I was on this flight and that they were to detain me until her husband, Marc, got there.

When I saw them I thought the worst had happened. The four of them surrounded me protectively trying to reassure me no news was good news, and that Marc was on his way. All we could do was wait. Finally, I saw Marc. He told me Nathan was okay. I almost collapsed with relief.

Soon we were in Marc's truck and on our way to the hospital. He told me Anne Marie was in emergency surgery and that her condition wasn't good. I went numb. Good news, though, was that Nathan was safe after Marc found him at the reunification point. He told me it was a chaotic scene. Nathan had been on the very last bus coming from Columbine, and the police refused to release him or any of the kids. It wasn't until Marc told them about Anne Marie that they let them leave. Now, Nathan was safe and waiting for us at the hospital. It's hard to put into words my gratitude to Marc and Belva for what they did. They helped reunite my family under the worst of circumstances, while still worrying about and tending to their own children.

In Marc's truck, we listened to the radio. Media reports were still sketchy. When we arrived at Swedish Medical Center, we had to sneak in. Media vans were everywhere.

Carla and Nathan were there. Trying to get to them was emotionally like slogging through knee-deep mud—my legs were shaky, unsteady. I hugged Nathan tighter than I ever had. He seemed to be holding himself together pretty well given what he'd been through. Carla seemed eerily calm, almost too calm. But given her earlier near panic on the phone with me, I was glad to see her this way. She relayed what little she knew. Anne Marie's wounds were much worse than we first believed. I *had* to see Anne Marie. She'd already been moved to the Critical Care Unit. That's where we headed. Marc then left to be with his own family.

The door to Anne Marie's room was closed. Access to the room was restricted even for us. Chances for infection were just too great. Straining to get a closer look through the window, I could barely make out Anne Marie's face. She was almost unrecognizable; ashen. Her face was all I could see. Everything else was under blankets. The room was dark, the only ambient light coming from the nurse's station outside and from the monitors on each side of her bed. Her eyes were closed. A tube trailed out of her mouth down the side of the bed to the unit keeping her breathing. One of her lungs had collapsed. Tubes inserted into her lung through the side of her chest stuck out from under the blankets; each of them containing pinkish fluid from her lung dripping slowly into a plastic bag. There was no movement from her, not even a twitch. If I hadn't been reassured by hospital staff, I would have thought she was dead.

I couldn't breathe. My knees began to buckle. I had to lean against the wall to steady myself. Nathan, Carla, and I silently embraced, each of us with our own thoughts and emotions. A while later Nathan left to be with his friends, perhaps to commiserate on the events of the day.

Much later that night, three paramedics who rescued so many injured kids earlier that day asked through the hospital public affairs officer if we might let them see Anne Marie. They wanted to pay respects and to make sure she was still alive. They needed reassurance and to see for themselves that their actions were not in vain. There was no hesitation in granting their request.

John, the paramedic who rescued Anne Marie, shared some harrowing details of her rescue. He had thought she was dead and almost passed on trying to rescue her. Then, he saw a slight movement of her hand, and she mouthed the words "help me." He picked her up and got her out under police cover who opened fire on the library above as he got her into the ambulance.

The emergency room doctor told us when she arrived, Anne Marie was bleeding out internally. He also told us they thought she was already gone, so they opened her chest more to try and determine a cause of death than anything. They detected a faint heartbeat and immediately moved her to the operating room. That she survived the radical procedure was astonishing.

The trauma surgeon who performed her lifesaving surgery in the OR had combat experience. That factored into Anne Marie making it through what can only be described as something she should not have. Even then, he told us Anne Marie might not make it. I got the distinct feeling he was preparing us for the worst. He told us she may have brain damage because during surgery her aorta had to be clamped off at intervals in order to make repairs to vital organs and to her vena cava vein. That procedure also cut off oxygen to her brain. There was no way to tell until she regained consciousness. He also cautioned she might suffer respiratory failure, which would be fatal. She suffered multiple injuries to vital organs including possible spinal damage.

Every doctor tried to prepare us for the worst. They told us her odds of making it through the night were less than 25 percent. They expected her to die. The hopelessness we felt was like falling into a very deep abyss. The doctors told us we should start thinking about whether or not to donate organs if Anne Marie didn't make it. Carla refused to talk about it. I let it be. It could be dealt with later—if it came to that.

The visiting area was swamped with people throughout the night. It got so overcrowded the Critical Care nurses called security to maintain order. Reporters were swarming outside the hospital trying to get a scoop. There were no opportunities to escape, to even take a breath. Carla and I began wandering the halls late into the night. The back halls were almost deserted at that hour and provided a brief respite. We didn't speak. We just walked. Our thoughts were our own, and that's the way it stayed throughout that excruciatingly long night.

When April 21, 1999, dawned, it was cold and rainy. A pall hung over the families whose lives were irrevocably altered by Columbine, including ours.

Anne Marie made it through the first night. There would be more nights to come where we wouldn't be sure she'd survive. We were told she would not be out of the woods for at least the first two weeks minimum. That she eventually did get out of those woods is a miracle.

Anne Marie's injuries caused other life-threatening issues. The pericardial sac around her heart filled with fluid that had to be surgically removed. Her lung collapsed again. She couldn't speak because of the intubator. She was fed via a tube through her nose into her stomach. For the first two weeks, she was heavily drugged and almost comatose. She couldn't move on her own.

Anne Marie's pain was palpable. We could only imagine how she was dealing with any of this emotionally or psychologically. Nathan's pain was emotional and psychological. All he wanted to do was to be with his friends who'd gone through what he had. We seldom saw him for those reasons. We didn't leave the hospital. There was a pervasive fear Anne Marie could die at any time. We would never be able to forgive ourselves if that happened and we weren't there. Carla's illness rendered her virtually incapable of participating in making any decisions at all. The responsibility, for the most part, fell on me. There's no shame in that. Nor is there any blame. It just was.

The tragedy at Columbine changed us as a family. For Carla, the physical and emotional toll of the tragedy must have been too much. Six months after our daughter was shot at Columbine,

Carla committed suicide with a gun. The tragic irony in that act haunts me to this day.

It's been said when events shake us to our core, we either rise to the challenges they present or not. I'd like to believe I rose to the challenges thrown at me by Columbine. There are latent emotional and psychological scars, to be sure. With every new mass shooting, those emotional and psychological scars get ripped open every single time. It's like I'm reliving the events of Columbine on an endless loop.

I did not believe I would ever experience true love and happiness ever again. Then Katherine came into my life, and we were married three years after Columbine. Three new children entered my life, as well: Shawn, Jessi, and Robert (Bobby to his family). Bobby did me the honor of allowing me to adopt him on Valentine's Day 2005.

Nathan is doing well. It wasn't always that way. He struggled with his experiences that day for a very long time. He didn't say much about his own experiences then. He doesn't say much now. That's his coping mechanism, and I honor that.

Anne Marie chose a separate path. Tragedy tends to do that to families—sometimes it binds you, sometimes it breaks you apart. I can only hope she's doing well.

There are no fairy-tale endings to events like Columbine. There can be progress. There can be healing. There can be recovery. There can be happiness and newfound love. Those are the things I try to focus on now. I've faltered along the way. I've stumbled more than a few times. I've even fallen down on a few occasions. Getting back up was sometimes slow and painful, but I did it every time with the love and support of family and friends.

ROADS NOT TAKEN

By Paula Reed

Paula Reed was an English teacher at Columbine High School for thirty years. Two of her students were among those killed in the shooting. This piece was written after Paula met with the teachers from Sandy Hook six weeks after they suffered their own mass shooting.

As an American literature teacher, it's pretty much de rigueur that I love Robert Frost's poem "The Road Not Taken." I've always tended to view the paths as friendly, dappled in shade, but mostly sunny. As described, one is more worn than the other. I've thought about it differently this past weekend.

I found myself saying several times to various people that they are entering a dark forest, and they must keep in mind that, no matter how dark it gets, every step in is a step out, because the only way out is through. I went to assure them that sunlight lay at the far edge of the forest. I kept my focus there on the way to Sandy Hook.

Of course, many of their questions were less about what lay ahead than what path to take now. I could tell them the paths I'd taken, but there were other ones I'd passed up, and you know, "way leading unto way" and all that, I could tell them I wish I'd taken some, but I can't really know whether those would have gotten me through the wilderness any faster, any easier, with any fewer contusions on my soul.

I wish I'd said yes to meds sooner. I wish I'd found a better fit in a therapist, rather than giving up and going it alone. In part because I didn't go it alone. I wonder how much more arduous my choices made my husband's journey.

I wonder who I would have been when I reached the other side if I'd taken those other routes. Would I have become an author? Would I have left Columbine in 2002 never to return? Would I have left at all, even those two years?

I mean, who would I be now, and would I like her as well? All modesty aside, I very much like who I am now. Would it really have been better to medicate earlier and take a therapist along with me? It's so hard to know what to tell people.

I do know that I would spare them the pain of the journey through these woods, but I can't, and it wouldn't be my place anyway. They'll find their own ways. They'll call to one another in the darkness, as we did. And I will keep cheering them on, shouting "Keep coming! Keep coming!"

And they'll make it. The teachers I met have mettle. They are hurt, and sad, and angry, and confused, and all the things the teachers at Columbine were, but I hope we looked like we had half as much grit back when we were six weeks out.

The paths before them are dark and scary, and none are all that well traveled (thank God). The folks at Sandy Hook, too, will choose. They will be glad they made some choices and wish they'd made some different ones. I hope we all stay in touch throughout the journey. I so want to greet them as they come to the far edge.

CHAPTER FIFTEEN

THURSTON HIGH SCHOOL

Springfield, Oregon / May 21, 1998

I DRIVE MY twin daughters to school every morning. The bus stops at the end of our road, but as they've gotten older, making that 7:41 a.m. pickup has gotten more and more difficult. The extra twenty minutes is appreciated by all. We live in the country, farther from the city than I would like, which means there are at least two or three long, winding roads leading to the school parking lot. Having grown up in a city, albeit a small one, a school having its own large, roomy parking lot is an unfamiliar concept in itself. But this parking lot, the one it takes me a whole thirty-seven seconds to navigate, has becoming the staging area where my twelve-year-old twin daughters still love me and bathe me with goodbye kisses before reaching the front of the school where their friends can see everything. I slow the car to the curb, wish them a good day as their chestnut ponytails bounce away from me. I watch until they are swallowed by the double glass doors.

This simple act—the dropping off—has become increasingly difficult as the number of school shootings increase each year. They were six when Sandy Hook happened, and taking them to school on Monday was an act of bravery. It was probably the hardest thing I had to do. But then, it grew easier. With each year, each kiss goodbye, the intensity of Sandy Hook seemed to fade a bit. Then, this book.

I spent two weeks in August editing Jolene Leu's story, in which she described dropping her daughter off for her first day of high school at the same school, Thurston High, in which she herself had survived a shooting almost twenty years earlier. In 1998, fifteen-year-old student Kip Kinkel, killed his parents and then went to Thurston, walked into the cafeteria, and shot and killed two students and wounded almost two dozen more. Jolene witnessed it all.

In our initial phone call, Jolene and I talked extensively about the cafeteria. This was *the* room, *the* place, her anxiety, her trauma. When her daughter attended orientation, a week or so before classes started, the sign-ups were held in the cafeteria. Jolene told me how much she struggled just to walk into that space again, all these years later. Then, only days later, she watched as her daughter walked through the doors and into the school.

Now, every time I drop my girls off, I imagine what it must be like not just for Jolene, but for so many of our contributors who, at some point, had to either return to school themselves, or in an unimaginable act of bravery, drop their own kids off at a school. Do they watch those chestnut ponytails bob away from them and wonder if they will ever come back? Do they assess the doors? Pull over in the parking lot and make sure there are no alarms? How do you survive something like a shooting inside what should be the safest place in America, and then willingly bring your children there?

AMYE ARCHER, EDITOR
DECEMBER 2018

The following students were shot and killed at Thurston High School:

Mikael Nickolauson, 17
Ben Walker, 16

IF I DIE BEFORE I WAKE

By Jennifer Alldredge Ryker

Jennifer Alldredge Ryker was a junior at the time of the shooting.

ONE

I am seventeen, a junior, and habitually late for school. I usually slide into my seat at least twenty minutes late with a latte from the student-run café or from the machine in the teachers' lounge I discovered last year. I don't get raised eyebrows anymore about being late, I accept my fate as they add up into detentions and I use that time to do my homework anyway.

My grades are decent enough to be on the honor roll. I love to argue and debate. I have a lot of attitude, but I'm also a pretty good kid, honestly. I'm usually either teacher's pet or sent outside the classroom for speaking out. I take Shakespeare and sci-fi classes for fun, I'm a choir geek, vice president of the poetry club, and a mat girl for the wrestling team.

I'm also part of an awesome freaks and geeks group of friends. We are more like outcasts banded together for protection and yet we end up being a band of proud misfits having a blast and dealing with teen angst simultaneously. Some of the guys are Boy Scouts. The girls are in choir and band. At one side of the table are the Magic and role-playing kids. The other side are athletes, usually wrestling and track and bowling. The table behind us are our goths and skater kids.

Today, I actually show up early to school and sit in the cafeteria with them. It's my boyfriend's seventeenth birthday, so the girls

304

and I are planning on how to crash his party. I stand behind him, with my arms wrapped around him, and visit. Student elections are happening, lots of the popular, rich kids walking around campaigning. We roll our eyes and keep talking.

I hear gossip from someone that a kid was expelled from school yesterday because he brought a stolen gun to school and kept it in his locker. That sounds pretty stupid, we all agree. We have so many kids that live on farms and out in the country, many just leave their rifles in their trucks in the parking lot.

The side door of the cafeteria that leads to the choir and band rooms opens but it does so often no one thinks anything of it. *Pop. Pop. Pop.* It sounds like fireworks echo through the room. We turn to face the sound, it's a kid with a rifle shooting, spraying from one side of the cafeteria to the other and back. I assume it must be a prank. This is really weird and not funny at all.

Suddenly, a hot, searing pain shoots through my hand and something hits my boyfriend's chest. I stare at my hand black and red blood pouring out and I'm being pushed down by my boyfriend as he gets up. I realize I've been shot. As I fall, I'm shot again, this time through my back. I try to scream, but no sound comes out, instead blood does. I learn later, several people have nightmares about me with blood coming out of my mouth.

I fall to the ground. I stare at my hand thinking, I should put that between my legs and apply pressure but then I can't figure out how to move. I look at my friend and say, *I've been shot,* and he says *yeah, me too.* Months later, he says we never had that conversation.

And then it's quiet. I think the screaming and the shooting has stopped. I fall asleep.

I wake up and my head is in my friend's lap. She rocks me back and forth crying and telling me to wake up and not die. I think she's being melodramatic, and I try to tell her I just need to sleep. I'm tired. I'll be fine.

I wake up again to the sound of people running. I open my eyes and it looks like firefighters and EMTs. I realize I still have a butterscotch Life Saver in my mouth, and I shouldn't be falling asleep with something in my mouth or I might choke. I spit out the Life Saver. An EMT notices and realizes I'm still alive. I find out later that the rules of triage mean he should be passing me over for someone else who is considered less of a lost cause. He takes a chance on me. I wake up again and I'm being lifted up while being on a stretcher into an ambulance. I'm worried they're going to drop me. They ask me my name and where I've been shot and even though I can think the answers, I can't get the words out.

I wake up in the ICU. My contacts have been taken out, and I can't see. I have tubes coming out of me everywhere. One tube is lodged down my throat, so I can't speak. A respirator is breathing for me. My right arm is in a cast. Tubes for IV, wires, I am connected to machines everywhere, heart monitors. *What. Is. Happening? Where am I? Why am I here?*

What is going on? My mom rushes toward me. She tells me everything is going to be okay. She says the hospital is taking really good care of me and not to worry. I try to talk, and she rubs my forehead and tells me to calm down. She says there is a tube down my throat so that's why I can't talk. "Don't panic," she says, "It's there to help."

I wake up again and apparently don't remember the last time or several times that this conversation had taken place and we do it all over again and again. Sometimes it's my mom and dad, sometimes just one or the other. The TV is always on. The news is always playing. At one point I keep seeing pictures of my boyfriend and my school and my friends and my own picture. My mom hands me my glasses and although my writing hand is in a cast, I'm handed a paper and a pen from my mom so I can at least communicate.

I write with my left hand, *Am I going to die?* My mom says, "Oh honey, no. You're going to be okay."

She tells me there was a shooting at my school. She tells me I've been shot. She lets me know that both of my lungs collapsed, so once I'm strong enough, they'll take me off the respirator and try to get me out of the ICU. I was brought back after flatlining several times. I needed lots of blood. The doctors saved my fingers, but they gave my dad a choice of what position they should be fused in—straight or slightly cupped. My dad chose cupped so they wouldn't catch on things and I could still hold things. I was going to need more surgeries and they didn't know if I would be able to regain any more function.

My mom lets me know some of my friends are in this hospital and have been coming by to check on me. My boyfriend has been sent to the other hospital in town and has faxed over a note. My dad reads little bits at a time and gets choked up. I cry, he cries, my mom cries.

It turns out my boyfriend and his brother and several of our friends had tackled the gunman and taken the gun from him. He had another gun on him and shot my boyfriend with the handgun too. They beat him up and subdued him until the police could arrest him. They were calling the guys heroes.

Two kids died. One of them was engaged to my friend and going into the army in a few weeks. The gun had been put to his head and the trigger pulled. The other kid had been shot in the walkway to the cafeteria. The shooter had killed his parents the night before. He shot his mom multiple times in the garage while she was carrying in groceries. He told her he loved her. He shot his dad earlier when he found out his dad was going to put him into military school. His parents were teachers at the other high school. He told his friend not to go to school the next day, he had been planning this for a long time. He stored guns in his room his parents never even knew about. He had been obsessed with shooting the school and violence. It was rumored he had been diagnosed with schizophrenia. I hear his parents didn't know what to do with his violence obsession and anger. I would spend years hating them for not helping their son and not addressing his issues.

Reporters swarm the hospitals. Some pose as doctors and pretend to be family or friends to get inside. My parents shield me from the chaos as best they can.

The days pass. I get off the respirator and the feeding tube comes out. I'm still on machines to drain the liquid from my lungs with chest tubes and an IV. I'm moved out of the ICU, and respiratory therapists come into my hospital room routinely to work on my lungs with these huge buffer wheels against my back. I have a cup with a ball in it that moves when I suck into the straw to measure my lung power. It wears me out fast but the room chants, "Suck, Suck, Suck!" to encourage me.

Friends, ex-boyfriends, family, teachers, coaches, and childhood doctors come to visit. The amount of love and care is so amazing. Letters, flowers, stuffed animals, and phone calls pour in. The best phone call is when my boyfriend calls from the other hospital. An hour or so later, he walks through my hospital door. It's an unforgettable moment. We hug after being apart for seven days. We both cry. I think the whole room cries with us.

After ten days I get to go home. It isn't the intended restful time to heal. Instead, it's angst of not being with my friends and boyfriend. It's painful. I'm still working up to lung strength to be able to take big breaths again, my hand throbs constantly. I take a half of a Vicodin and I fall asleep face-first at a restaurant into my strawberry waffle breakfast. The phone rings nonstop with reporters.

I go back to school right away, but it isn't at all what I expect. I don't know why I'm surprised. I was an outcast before. Now, it's even worse. People don't want to make eye contact with me. The popular kids are still worried about their elections and their friend—the shooter. They care more about their friend and grieve harder for his family than they do for any of us, the twenty-five of us who were shot. Reporters stand outside, camped in vans. They stick microphones in our faces. The chain-link fence is covered in notes, flowers, ribbons. I feel lost. I shadow my boyfriend in his classes. I'm glued to him. He's my superhero. No one understands our bond but us. We are unbreakable.

TWO

Returning to "normal" wasn't easy on many levels. In the weeks and months that followed, it seemed as if some wanted to extort us—the injured. We felt so much anger and frustration. Other students seemed almost excited for the attention. The Portland Trail Blazers and President Clinton visited. We, the injured, were cast aside and used as props when needed. Or maybe, we slunk back as best as we could because it was all too much.

That summer, the other injured kids, minus one who was still in the hospital after being shot in the head, went to a Young Life camp together. It was probably the last time we all really got together as a large group for fun. We did obstacle courses, zip lines, and sang songs. We were kids. Treated like kids and got to act like kids. It was fun, a warm environment, but we had aged. We may have been just teenagers, but because of what we went through and how close we came to dying, we were somehow different. We were fragile and invincible all at the same time. We had flashbacks and anger and tears together.

We went home. Back to the media. Back to the chaos. Back to senior year. We had almost died at the school. Some did die. Our childlike innocence was gone. Everything was annoying, buzzing chaos in a larger picture that no one understood. Everything seemed trivial and surface level. It was hard to not be confused and angry at everything and everyone.

We graduated high school and a month later, my boyfriend left for his three-and-a-half-month Marine Corps boot camp. We wrote letters back and forth in achingly slow snail mail. A friend drove me eighteen straight hours to see him graduate from boot camp in San Diego.

I turned down an internship for *Good Morning America* so I could stay with my boyfriend, and he stayed in the marine reserves rather than active duty to do the same. I went to community college and worked at a jewelry store. I joined Gun Control Incorporated and traveled as a spokesman. I argued on the steps of the Capitol for background safety and safety locks. I traveled for Ribbon of Promise and spoke on behalf of ending youth violence. I got to meet families of other school shootings. I went onto talk shows. I spoke at summits.

My boyfriend became a spokesman for the NRA. In the same time span I had met Jim and Sarah Brady, responsible for the Brady Bill, I also sat down to dinner with Charlton Heston. I learned there were extremists on both sides, but the ultimate goal of gun safety and common sense was severely important to both of those organizations.

In November 1999, I testified against our shooter. I shook the entire time, but I stood in front of him and read my statement. The body has a memory. Of the trauma. Of the physical pain. When I was done, the judge had tears in his eyes and asked for a break. It was a very emotional time. Many of us spoke. Many parents spoke. Most of us cried. There were hugs and hand holding, people with folded arms. One parent appeared to have a heart attack and needed paramedics in the courtroom. One of the shooting victims went into labor and never got to give her statement.

Part of the plea bargain was that we downgrade some of the charges from aggravated attempted murder to a lesser charge and in exchange, he couldn't plead insanity or appeal. He was sentenced to 111 years without parole. Relief. Complete ecstatic joy and relief came with that sentence. The appeals did come, he switched lawyers, and so far, they've all been denied.

My boyfriend and I got engaged during that same time frame, but now with the sentencing over, we could finally announce it. We married one month after the attack on the Twin Towers— October 2001. My husband went on multiple deployments, often gone for a year at a time. We had two kids, Miranda and Logan. They're both blond haired, blue eyed and charming with their dimpled, devilish grins.

I've told my kids about the shooting at my high school. It became a reality they might have to deal with. It was becoming too common. I told them how their daddy tackled the gunman and that's why I always called him Superman. I let them know that's why my hand is shaped the way it is and why I can't show them how to hold the pencil. They learned about gun safety at home and went target practicing. They also do active shooter drills at school. Their dad was actually the inspiration for the active shooter response program known as A.L.I.C.E. (Alert, Lockdown, Inform, Counter, Evacuate). They learn about our shooting and hear about their parents in school, which is really odd and slightly a sense of pride.

My husband and I clung to one another through the hardest times in our lives. We survived the shooting, deployments, and deaths in our families. Our daughter had a spinal injury while he was away during a deployment. There were multiple hospital trips and after surgery, she wore a spinal halo vest for several months. She was finally declared stable right before he came back home. We took vacations as a family, and we tried as best we could with what we knew to stay strong. We didn't address or heal many of our personal and marital issues, which made things toxic. This eventually led to our divorce.

I wasn't showing my kids how to handle issues or be healthy. I needed to learn coping skills. With the help of an amazing therapist, I started to acknowledge and deal with things that I had stuffed away since the shooting and beyond. We discussed EMDR therapy and spent months analyzing focus memories. I practice mindfulness. I practice grounding. I breathe. I take walks. I listen to music. I write and draw in a journal. When I get upset, I write it down and then rip it up and throw it away. Perhaps the most helpful and motivating of all has been connecting with other survivors.

Today, I work a desk job. I share joint custody of my kids and have a healthy routine. I share a house with my boyfriend, with our two cats, and our dog. I've lost some family and friends along the way but gained a sense of confidence and new friends and family. I don't have my life mapped out anymore. There are unknowns. I went skydiving. I go hiking. I went camping at the Painted Hills for the solar eclipse. I've stepped out of my fear and when I find myself cocooning back into my safety net, I look up activities and I get back outside again. I take the kids on adventures to the coast, camping. I'm living.

DIARY OF A WITNESS IN TWO PARTS
By Jenny Gregory

Jenny Gregory was a freshman at the time of the shooting. She witnessed the shooting through a classroom window.

1.

In my last year of nursing school, I read about PTSD (post-traumatic stress disorder). I came across a medical term called "survivor's guilt." I was amazed there was a term for how I felt all these years after the shooting at my high school. Since that day, I replay over and over again how I could've helped my class-mates. How I didn't. I've avoided talking about the shooting because I think, deep down, I want to forget it. I want to forget my shortcomings. But I always return. Somehow try to put the pieces together, and answer my own question:

Why didn't I do more?

When I arrive at school, everyone is chatting, laughing, and dragging their feet to get to class. I glance at the clock and notice it's time to head to class or be marked tardy, but nobody is moving. Maybe it's okay to be late. I look into the cafeteria and search for my latest crush, but my elongated gaze is interrupted by a loud noise.

BANG, BANG, BANG!

"Fireworks! Oh, someone is going to get into trouble!" I say to a friend. I see a boy sprinting out of the cafeteria, holding his arm.

I point, "I bet it was him."

I keep hearing loud cracks, and peer closer into the cafeteria through the window. Something doesn't look right. Why is everyone ducking? A girl runs out with a handful of other students. She's crying. "Someone has a gun. Someone is in there shooting at people," she yells.

I turn back toward the cafeteria when another loud *bang* rings out. *Was that a bomb that just went off?* I run as fast as my legs carry me, far from the threat. But then I stop. I'm confused, and not sure what to do next. I look down the corridor and see the health occupations classroom.

Why didn't I run down and grab Mr. Duffy? I knew he used to be a nurse, and that the classroom was stocked with some emergency supplies. I sensed people were hurt back in the cafeteria and would need these. Instead, I turned away. I spent years questioning this decision.

I ran in the opposite direction until I saw a familiar face. A friend who'd been dropped off late. They didn't know what was happening.

I started laughing while telling her what I witnessed. I don't know why I laughed. I didn't think this was funny, but I couldn't stop.

2.

We walk to homeroom, a short distance from where we stood. My homeroom teacher shuts and locks the door behind us. She scurries us and about five other students to a spot behind her desk.

We watch the SWAT team run by. She turns on her radio. There are voices already talking about the incident. I'm wondering how they know so much, and we know so little. My thoughts are interrupted by a radio announcement. "We have the name of the shooter at Thurston High School. His name is Kip Kinkel." I freeze. *Kip?*

I wasn't surprised. He was friendly, quiet. He was also just expelled for having a gun at school, but it never entered my mind he'd hurt people. I will be forever bothered by this initial reaction and curious if there was anything I could've done to help prevent this.

I look out the classroom window and see two girls walking slowly down the breezeway. I recognize the girl limping and cringing. I've known her since grade school. We make eye contact. Her eyes beg for me to be her second crutch.

I don't go. I debated whether I should help her. On one hand, she clearly needed help. It was the right thing to do. On the other hand, I was afraid of getting shot. Afraid of what I'd see by the cafeteria, which was where she was headed. I was afraid of leaving the safety of my teacher's desk. In the end, I chose the path of the coward. Out of all my missed opportunities to be helpful, I feel the most shame about this.

Survivor's guilt is not spoken about often when describing victims in the aftermath of shootings. But it's a common affliction. I'm proof and feel guilty labeling myself a "victim." I'm not entitled to PTSD. I don't have any rights to it. I witnessed this event through a window. The real victims died, were wounded— were actually in the room.

While my story pales in comparison to theirs, I still suffer (and choose to silently). I think I'll always carry this guilt with me. But, today, I use my guilt as a reminder. To be better. To choose better. To choose differently if there is ever a next time, next time.

A LITTLE MORE HEALED

By Jolene Leu

Jolene Leu was a junior at the time of the shooting.

On a warm, sunny September morning, I dropped my daughter off for her first day of freshman year, at the same high school I attended twenty years earlier, where I spent four years, and made lifelong friends. The same high school where in 1998, during my junior year, a student walked into the cafeteria and shot and killed two students and wounded twenty-five others.

At seventeen years old, I'd sit in the cafeteria every morning with my friends while we waited for classes to start. It was there, in that cafeteria that the shooting occurred. I remember the yelling, the smell of smoke. I froze, while everyone around me jumped into action. I stood, watching. Stuck in place for what felt like forever. Then, after the smoke cleared, I finally made the decision to run. I got out of there with blood on my clothes, but the blood wasn't mine. I left my friends and my then-boyfriend in that cafeteria and never went back.

When it was over, nine of my close friends were wounded including my boyfriend, three severely. My boyfriend had a gnarly scar from exploratory surgery in which they made sure the bullet passed through him properly. Shortly after he was released from the hospital, we went to see a movie and he sat there as long as he could. Uncomfortable and still in pain, we ended up leaving the movie early. I felt horrible for him and my other friends who were suffering the physical effects of that day. I sometimes felt an enormous amount of guilt that I escaped without physical injury. *I shouldn't have run. I should have gone back in.* I realize now that I was suffering from survivor's guilt, and that it put a great distance between me and the friends I loved.

I moved on as best I could, burying the events of that day deep inside myself. I graduated, met my husband, and started my own life. But the trauma was still there, bubbling up when I least expected it. In October of 2002, my husband and I found out we were expecting. The predicted due date sent shivers down my spine: May 21st. The same date as the shooting. I was determined I wouldn't have my first child born on that day. I could've chosen to look at it as something positive, but I refused. My daughter was born two days later, on May 23rd.

Later, when the time came to send my daughter off to kindergarten, I was an overly paranoid parent. It didn't help that her first day of kindergarten, the school went under lockdown because of an incident in the neighborhood. By age eight, I had given her a cell phone to take to school. We made it through middle school with minimal lockdown drills. Still, I panicked with each false alarm.

Then, within days of my daughter starting at Thurston, the high school went under lockdown. The threat wasn't on campus, just in a surrounding neighborhood, but I freaked out. This was different, this was the same building. *Was it happening again?* I immediately texted her to see if she was okay. While I waited for what felt like an eternity for her to text back, I thought about the cafeteria, the kids who didn't escape, who couldn't run. *Would she be one of them? Would she know to run?* I started to panic. Then, she responded that she was okay and that everything was fine. It took me an hour to stop shaking.

My kids know about my experience in the shooting at Thurston High School. They know I never liked violence or crowds and that I would get *exceedingly* upset with each new mass shooting. But I tried not to let it completely control me. I wanted their school experience to be their own. I supported my daughter going to Thurston because of all the great memories I had there before the shooting, but it wasn't until she started attending that I realized just how deep I had buried that day.

2018 was the twentieth anniversary of the shooting. I left the house early, as usual, to drive my daughter to school. As we passed Thurston, blue ribbons hung on the chain-link fences outside of the school and across the street at the park. It wasn't until I saw the banner that read THURSTON STRONG that it all hit me. As I watched my own daughter walk past the ribbons and into the school that held so much of my past, I began to cry both tears of sadness and joy. I realized that despite our tragedy, my community and my classmates persevered. And that in some way, Thurston High School will always be a part of me. And I'm okay with that. In fact, I might even be a little bit proud.

RUNNING

By Aubrey Bulkeley

Aubrey Bulkeley was a fourteen-year-old freshman at the time of the shooting.

I stood in front of my closet staring at my least favorite clothing. I told myself, "Aubrey, just pick something. It's not like there's going to be any cameras." So, I donned a pair of washed-out jeans, tank top, and plaid button-up shirt. Like most days, I left my house before my family and walked through my uniform, suburban neighborhood to catch the school bus.

At school, I wandered the breezeways rehearsing lines for theater class. Once my friends arrived, we stood in our usual spot in front of the counseling offices, across the courtyard from the cafeteria.

Before the first bell, I heard what sounded like firecrackers coming from the cafeteria. As the commotion continued, I watched people rush out of the cafeteria, scattering in every direction. There was so much yelling. None of it made sense.

Several of my friends wanted to see what was happening, but I knew heading toward the cafeteria was a bad idea. Despite my unease, I remained in my familiar corner of the courtyard, attempting to comprehend the disjointed details.

Through the cafeteria windows, I saw a puppet-like figure holding a rifle. The *pop, pop, popping* sound paused. Then a reverberating boom. A scream erupted from within me as I ran in the opposite direction of the courtyard, stampeding down the hallway alongside my classmates trying to escape an unknown threat.

My best friend was running in front of me. Suddenly she stopped, attempting to go back. I shoved her down the hallway shouting, **"KEEP RUNNING."** The throng dispersed the farther I ran. Once I reached the south parking lot, I gathered behind the last row of cars with a few friends. We debated what to do next. No one, not even teachers knew what was going on. The high school spread the distance of a football field, and we had no active shooter procedures. A teacher came out of his classroom from the last wing of the building. Waving wildly, he yelled, "Get back inside." This was the first time I had seen an adult since I heard the popping noises.

Instead of going in the closest classroom, I made my way to Spanish class. I was supposed to have a test. Once there, an authoritative announcement came through the intercom: Close the curtains. Turn off the lights. Hide. My classmates and I piled behind a half wall. We were in lockdown long enough that administrators checked on us four times—taking head counts and compiling witness lists.

Still in lockdown, but free to move about the room, a student told me I should call my parents. My mother answered with a panicked, yet expectant "Hello?" In a detached tone I told her I was all right, and she should go to the church across the street from the school.

After the call, another student in the room turned on KDUK, the local radio station. The host said on air, "This is not a joke. There has been a shooting at Thurston High School." These words confirmed the sights, sounds, and feelings I experienced.

Being locked in a dark classroom became tedious. I gazed out the back window to pass the time. My parents managed to get on campus and were right outside. I immediately told my teacher and, because of the lack of procedures, rushed out to meet them. While we embraced, a classmate came out and told me I had to give my statement in the library before I left. My parents and I walked through the empty breezeways. Police tape hung between the poles cordoning off sections of the school.

In contrast to the empty breezeways, the library was jammed with people. A classmate sat at a table with a police officer, giving him his bloody shoes. I waited while my parents talked with people trying to get more information. I observed everything and absorbed nothing.

After we left the library, I walked flanked by my parents. As we got to the end of the breezeway, I spotted the camera. At that moment the photographer snapped my picture. My thoughts from earlier in the day had been realized in a sick twist of irony.

Sometime that evening, a detective came to my house to take my statement. Sitting at the circular dining room table, he had me draw a picture of what I saw through the cafeteria window. My mother gasped at the image. Then the adults spoke over me: How shocking it was kids our age witnessed such a thing. Yet, living through it, I had become an adult even though I wasn't mature enough to be. I didn't tell my parents anything more of what happened that day. That picture was their only window.

CHAPTER SIXTEEN

HEATH HIGH SCHOOL

West Paducah, Kentucky / December 1, 1997

THE LAST TIME I felt like I belonged anywhere was on the morning of December 1st, 1997. Before the shooting. I'm on the phone with Kelly Carneal Firesheets, the sister of Michael Carneal, the fifteen-year-old boy who shot and killed three students at Heath High School on that same morning. Michael is still alive and is in prison. Kelly tells me how teachers, parents, and counselors, never really knew how to classify her. *The grown-ups whispered in the hallway, "What the hell do we do with Kelly?"*

Kelly's is a story of not belonging, but that's not just her story. It seems like that idea, the not belonging, is Heath's story. I was a junior in 1997, and I don't remember hearing about the shooting at Heath High School. I confess that I, like many adults my age, always remembered Columbine as *the first.* I had no idea that while I was living out my teenage years in my corner of Pennsylvania, there was a growing trend of school shootings sweeping across the country. And I'm not the only one. In their extensive and well-respected database of research on school shootings, the *Washington Post* estimates that 220,000 students have experienced gun violence[1] at school since Columbine. *Since Columbine.*

There are hundreds of students, maybe thousands, not counted in those numbers, including those killed, those wounded, and those who live with the emotional scars of the shooting at Heath and the many shootings that came before. *We're not included in that number by the way. We're culturally irrelevant in post-Columbine America*, Kelly writes.

This idea is repeated in story after story in this chapter. Christina Hadley Ellegood, whose fourteen-year-old sister, Nicole, was murdered that day, remembers, *Every time I went to a counselor, I was told they had no idea how to help me. There was no one else like me in America. I was the only person to survive a school shooting and lose a sibling in the same event.* Contributors told me unbelievable stories of the students returning to school only twenty-four hours after the shooting. *They called on the community to help clean the school, to scrub away the shooting.*

Before Columbine, there was Heath. A tight-knit community who had to heal and survive a mass shooting with little or no assistance from the rest of the country. They found a way forward, together. Still, when I think of the systems and supports we have in place now: the readiness response, the protocols, the extensively trained first responders, the checklists of alarming behavior, the drills, the training, I can't help but feel sad in some way. Is this the world my girls will grow up in? A world in which the best I can hope for is that they'll be well taken care of after a mass shooting?

Amye Archer
December 2018

The following students were shot and killed at Heath High School:

Nicole Hadley, 14

Jessica James, 17

Kayce Steger, 15

TERROR SPRINGS ETERNAL

By Hollan Holm

Hollan Holm was a fourteen-year-old freshman at the time of the shooting.

Our prayer group met that morning in the lobby of Heath High School before class started. We prayed and were headed back to class when I heard a series of pops, like a firecracker or a small balloon. I heard two—maybe three—pops and everything went black. I woke up lying facedown on the tile floor of the lobby.

I saw drops of a red liquid hitting the white tile in front of me and wondered if someone was pouring something on my head. When I touched the side of my head I pulled my hand away and saw blood—my blood—and hair in my hand. I had the awful realization that I had been shot in the head. My gut churned, and I thought I was going to die.

My mind flashed back to news coverage of the 1991 Luby's Cafeteria shooting in Texas that I remember watching on television. I was in third grade when that happened, but the stories about how those survivors played dead to avoid being killed came back to me in that lobby six years later. Afraid the shooter at Heath would shoot me again, I played dead, too. I said what I thought would be my final prayer: begging for forgiveness for whatever sins a fourteen-year-old can have and praying for blessings for my family.

Then I closed my eyes, slowed my breath, lay still, and waited to die.

I spent almost twenty years after I graduated from high school trying to put the aftermath behind me. Trying to run from it.

What we didn't know over twenty years ago was that we couldn't run away from it, couldn't forget it. You can never put it behind you. No matter how much you want to. Because three months after Heath, there was Westside Middle School in Arkansas, and we saw the same kinds of images on the news that had been broadcast about our school. And then, five months after Heath, there was Thurston in Springfield, Oregon.

And the next year, despite how hopeful I was that we would get through just *one* school year without another shooting, with only a couple of months left in the school year there was Columbine. When we were out on our own as young adults there would be Virginia Tech. And by the time we were parents with young children, we would watch the coverage of the horror at Sandy Hook, learning a new way to be afraid and sickened.

Whenever there's another shooting, I'm back there over twenty years ago, in the lobby of Heath High School. I'm fourteen years old again, and I've been shot. Terror springs eternal.

In December of 2017, I watched the coverage of the twenty-year anniversary memorial of the Heath shooting from a laptop in my kitchen and was overwhelmed at how little has changed in twenty years. My daughter had come home from school that fall, early on in her kindergarten year, and told me about a new safety drill she learned at school. One in which she and her classmates had to be quiet and hide in their classroom with the lights out from "the bad people." An active shooter drill was now as commonplace as the tornado drills or a fire drills we had to practice in elementary school. Now two generations were living with gun violence in schools.

In January of 2018, there was the shooting at Marshall County High School. Not forty miles from Heath. The shock of it happening again, so close, and so similar to our trauma twenty years earlier wrecked me. I saw that same trauma echo across the faces and voices of my parents, friends, classmates, pastors, teachers, and first responders, and you realize how far the impact of one event ripples out. I heard stories of the impact of gun violence on my friends that I had never heard before. My gut churned again.

Like so many others from Heath and McCracken County we had lived these stories, felt this pain, and experienced these fears before, and we relive it every time there's another shooting. And in the midst of all this, I got angry.

Angry that the only solution the party in control of our state and national governments offer to the problem of gun violence is thoughts and prayers—and more guns. Angry that the party in control of the levers of government at the federal level and in my state will not act on commonsense gun solutions to stop this horror show which now repeats day after day in grisly syndication.

I'm also outraged at the utter indecency of National Rifle Association (NRA) president Oliver North speaking at a fundraiser on August 3, 2018, not twenty miles from Benton, Kentucky, home of Marshall County High School. This was just six months after the shooting at Marshall, while the horror and the trauma were still fresh and raw for that community.

This was nothing short of a show of force, and it came as no surprise from an organization that once held its annual convention in Denver the day after Columbine families buried their children. At best, the decision to fund-raise off the NRA president's words was tone-deaf in the extreme, at *worst,* it was a calculated attempt—an attempt to demonstrate to victims and their families who calls the shots in government in Kentucky.

The NRA is not interested in ending gun violence. The NRA uses fear of gun violence to help its most prominent donors, the gun manufacturers, sell more guns. The NRA then uses fear of gun safety reforms to help those manufacturers sell more guns and help firearms sales spike after major shootings. The only school safety reforms NRA-funded politicians will propose, like arming teachers in the classroom, are those that—you guessed it—*sell more guns.*

When the NRA's only tool is fear, every problem starts to look like a target. The NRA wants to make a conversation about gun violence prevention a conversation about taking away guns. Gun violence prevention advocates don't want to take away guns. We just don't want your guns to take our lives or the lives of our children.

Gun violence prevention advocates have plenty of common ground with the NRA's members. And together we can start by passing real, commonsense gun safety solutions.

We can start by strengthening and enforcing laws that keep guns out of the hands of domestic abusers, because 54 percent of mass shooters are linked to domestic or family violence.[2] Sixty-eight percent of NRA members believe people who've been arrested for domestic violence should NOT be granted concealed carry permits.[3]

We can start by requiring background checks for all gun sales because 34 percent of mass shooters were prohibited from owning or possessing a gun at the time of their shootings.[4] Seventy-four percent of NRA members have supported background checks for all gun sales.[5]

We can start by requiring safe gun storage so our children can't hurt themselves or others. Sixty-six percent of gun owners believe it's essential to keep all their guns in a locked place when there are children in their home.[6]

Universal checks for gun buyers, bans on sales to known or suspected terrorists, and a bar on gun sales to violent criminals, are all gun safety laws that experts rate as some of the most effective changes we can make to prevent mass shootings.[7] All are supported by greater than eight in ten Americans.

Twenty years of gun violence in schools is twenty years too many. Mass shooter drills have now become as commonplace as tornado and fire drills. I will not accept this as the future for my children or any child.

We don't have to accept this as the new normal. It's not normal. It's not okay. We need to remind our elected officials who they work for. It's not the NRA. It's not the gun lobby. It's us: the voters. Their constituents.

Our legislators and politicians need to remember who we are: we are the students, teachers, and parents of this nation. We need to put them on notice that their thoughts and their prayers are not enough to stop the violence. We need action. And if they continue to ignore our voices, then it's time for them to retire, or be retired by us at the ballot box.

THE NEW NORMAL

By Christina Hadley Ellegood

Christina Hadley Ellegood was a sophomore at the time of the shooting. Christina's fourteen-year-old sister, Nicole Hadley, was killed that day.

I survived the school shooting at Heath High School, but lost my younger sister, Nicole. We were only nineteen months apart, fourteen and fifteen at the time of the shooting. It never occurred to me that morning would be the last time I'd see my sister alive.

My memory is foggy, but I do remember a panicked girl running up the stairs. She said someone had a gun. She pointed outside our window. I thought she meant someone brought a paintball gun and shot at a school bus. I don't remember hearing screams or seeing people running from the school, but I was told later this happened. As I was looking out the window, the bell rang initiating the start of class. I said goodbye to my friends, still not concerned, and headed to class. I walked down the stairs where a large group of students had gathered. A friend of Nicole's looked at me and said she thought Nicole was shot. I was confused. I calmly walked to my class, put my backpack down, and then walked to the lobby to see what was going on.

I saw a body in the lobby and knew that person must be dead because of how they were laying. Then, two more people. I couldn't see their faces, but knew they were seriously hurt. Then, I saw Nicole. She was lying on her back and not moving. She'd been shot in the head. I'm told there was a lot of blood around her, but I don't remember. I do remember what the bullet hole looked like.

I also remember steeling myself for sobs and hysteria, but they never came. Instead, time stopped. I know I was the one who called my mom to tell her that her daughter, my sister, Nicole was shot, but I don't remember how or when.

A friend took my mom, my brother, and myself as well as two friends to the hospital. My dad was in Nebraska on business. My mom called him before she left home to let him know that there was a shooting at the school, and that Nicole was injured. Even though I saw Nicole lying there, and I must've known she was gone, I was telling people I didn't know if she would be okay. It was like if I didn't say it, it wasn't true.

At the hospital, we called my dad to tell him that Nicole was brain dead and would never recover from her injuries. I remember everyone being very calm. No one was crying, instead everyone sat stunned. My parents quickly decided they wanted to donate Nicole's organs. Being an organ donor was very important to my sister. It was something we had discussed as a family. I then asked if I could be the person to tell our friends, all of whom had been waiting in the emergency room reception for hours. I met them and said Nicole was brain dead and that my parents were going to donate her organs. They screamed and cried.

My sister was put on life support so the doctors could perform tests and line up the people who would receive her organs. Nicole was on life support until my dad arrived at the hospital. Throughout the day, the nurses and doctors went above and beyond to help all the kids and parents that were in and out of Nicole's room. I went into Nicole's room a couple of times. She looked very peaceful, like she was sleeping. There was quiet. And then, she was gone.

At fifteen years old, I had no idea how much my life had changed. I had no idea that in the upcoming weeks, months, and even years, I'd have to learn to deal with the media, to share my grief with the world over losing my sister.

In the immediate aftermath, life was chaotic. There were reporters camped outside of our front door for weeks. Our phone rang nonstop from early in the morning to late at night. There were people coming in and out of our house all day. I returned to school a week after the shooting. I had my mind set that I was not going to let the shooting make me a different person. I felt the shooter took something away from me that couldn't be replaced, so I wasn't going to let him take away another second. I also felt I had to be there to support everyone. I was a happy person before that awful day. I was determined to stay that way.

The school shooting at Heath was the first to be broadcast around the world. It would be another year before the Columbine tragedy played out on live television. Our small community had no recovery plan, no easy path forward. There were no experts in the field of school shootings, no trauma response units or busloads of mental health experts coming to save us. We relied on one another, and we did what we thought was best. That's why the school administration thought it would be best to have us return to school the very next day. Maybe they thought moving forward or getting back into a routine would help. It didn't.

Shortly after Nicole's death, my parents sent me to counseling. Every time I went to a counselor, I was told they had no idea how to help me. There was no one else like me in America. I was the only person to survive a school shooting and lose a sibling in the same event. I was living with the trauma of surviving a mass shooting and mourning my sister. I was told I would go through the stages of grief. I was reluctant. I didn't want to accept I would have to change my life or change who I was.

Looking back, I do believe I went through those stages, but not how I thought I would.

When I was first told about the healing process and the stages of grief, I thought I'd quickly go through each stage, never having to deal with sadness and loss again. I was very wrong. I didn't start to deal with the emotional impact of that morning until twelve years later. I finally realized I was not going to be a truly happy person until I dealt with the anger and sadness that built up inside. It took me several years to really start to get to a place where I felt like I had dealt with my feelings. There were times when I thought I'd moved on from one issue and it would come back. I dealt with many layers of emotions and feelings before I could heal.

Meanwhile, at school we didn't talk about the shooting or what we were going through. Every day, we walked silently past reporters lining the school grounds. I completed my sophomore year at Heath and then the decision was made to have my brother and I attend a private school. There, I never talked about what happened at Heath. I made up my mind that I didn't want people treating me differently because I lost my sister at Heath.

Another way in which Heath was different is that our shooter survived. Many school shooters and mass shooters end their lives by suicide. Our shooter didn't. He was sentenced to prison with a chance of parole after twenty-five years. Knowing he could be released is scary.

The hardest part has been learning to forgive the shooter, because I didn't feel like he was sorry for what he did. I'm still not convinced he feels remorse. For many years I told people I'd forgiven him, but I lied. I couldn't. When I was finally able to forgive him, many, many years later, I felt at peace.

It's now been twenty years since Nicole was killed. I'm very happy and live a blessed life. I'm married with two step-daughters. There are still times when my sister is greatly missed like at my wedding and my brother's wedding. She missed being an aunt to my stepdaughters and my niece, who is named after Nicole. I know someday my brother and I will have to explain where her name came from and why it's special. I look forward to that day.

In 2016, on the nineteenth anniversary of the shooting, Heath was back in the news regarding a memorial that was built for Nicole and the other victims. When the memorial was originally built, no one would've imagined that school shootings would plague our country. But they did. A few years after the memorial was built a fence was put up around the school for security. This made it very difficult for anyone to visit the memorial. Shortly after the anniversary, I was able to get the Board of Education to agree to build a new memorial, a project which I oversaw. The community came together with donations and support we were able to build a new memorial across the street from the school. The new memorial was dedicated on the twentieth anniversary of the shooting. I also organized the first memorial service of the shooting. There was a service followed by the dedication of the new memorial.

During the process of building the new memorial, people who survived the shooting at Heath finally started to talk about the shooting, and for a lot of people it was the first time they dealt with their trauma. Perhaps, the new space gave us permission to process what happened. Now, when people go to the memorial, they talk about how peaceful they feel. And it makes me happy that I had some small part in that.

A LETTER TO THE HEATH HIGH SCHOOL CLASS OF 1998

By Kelly Carneal Firesheets

Kelly Carneal Firesheets was senior at Heath High School when her brother, Michael Carneal, opened fire on a group of students praying in the lobby of the school, killing three of Kelly's friends and injuring several others.

Let's put it out there. Senior year was a mess.

Most people get nervous about their high school reunion. I had permission to be extra ambivalent about it. The truth is, I felt weird about going back and seeing you. I remember you all so well. We were a few days away from finals, holiday break, and the second semester of our senior year. This was supposed to be the best times of our teenage lives. There would be prom, and graduation, and senior pranks. But then, my little brother brought a gun into our school and sent the entire world to hell in a handbasket. Our class was hit so hard. Jessica died. Shelley was gravely injured. I don't know how many of you were there, but pretty much everyone was affected. And then there was me. I became known as "The Girl Whose Brother Shot People."

The grown-ups whispered in the hallway, "What the hell do we do with Kelly?" But if you, my friends, my peers, didn't know how to deal with me, you never let it show. You scraped me off the ground and dragged me to safety. You came to my house and sent me cards and flowers. You hugged me and you cried with me. You held my hand when I went back to school. But most importantly, you treated me like a normal person. You danced with me at prom, helped me learn lines for the senior play, and rehearse my graduation speech. You fought with me, laughed with me, and gossiped with me about who was kissing who. You loved me so well, and your love made me brave. It seemed normal then, didn't it? The things we did seemed normal because they were the things we had to do. But we were just kids, and what we did was nothing short of heroic. We live in a flashy world, but your small and simple acts of love were the most heroic things.

The rest of the world hasn't always been so kind to "The Girl Whose Brother Shot People," and I don't think I've really felt loved, or understood, or like I belonged anywhere in the twenty years since. The night before our twentieth reunion, I went to the school, sat on the sidewalk, and cried an ugly, heavy cry. I've never found a way to communicate the pain inside of me. That was the best I could do. My heart is still broken, and I needed to go home and grieve the fantasy that one day I will "be okay." This will never be okay.

But twenty-four hours later, I stood in the middle of our high school reunion and cried happy tears. You're so beautiful! You've turned out so well! And what a special gift to have so many of the most important people in my life in the same place at the same time. I looked at your faces and was overwhelmed with how you greeted me with warmth and kindness (then and now). For a moment, I belonged. I know I'm a painful reminder of what happened, but somehow you still want me around.

Twenty years later, my heart is still broken. I'm afraid it always will be. But my life has been full of good stories, too, and a lot of that is because of you.

This would make a nice and tidy ending to my love letter, but I need to say some hard things to you. What my brother did twenty years ago was unimaginable. The world was shocked. No one knew what to do, what to think, or how to help us. But now I'm afraid it's becoming normal. *The Washington Post* estimates that since 1999, more than 200,000 people have survived a school shooting.[8] We're not included in that number, by the way. We're culturally irrelevant in post-Columbine America. But Heath High School became an archetype. Our story reads like the blueprint for so many other school shootings.

You know all those nameless students who run from their schools with their hands on their heads, traumatized, with tear-streaked faces? The world occasionally wonders what happens to them. We don't wonder. Those students will grow up to become us. Many of them will face profound challenges. Some of them will have pain they can never quite articulate. But at the same time, most will turn out to be very normal, functional, and likeable adults. They'll get married, have kids, get jobs, and pay taxes. Those 200,000 survivors are not doomed. But they have a long journey ahead of them, and no one knows that trail better than us. Because we blazed it. We're the grown-ups now. We're the seniors. The leaders. Everything we did was uncharted territory, but those 200,000 people walking behind will walk with a guide.

After our reunion, I had the privilege of meeting with five students from Marshall County High School. They're smart and brave. They're hurt and afraid, but they have a gritty determination that makes you want to stand up and cheer. Their stories and experiences are incredibly different from mine. But we are all survivors. They want someone to tell them it's okay to feel and to hurt so much. They also need someone to tell them that life will move forward, that they have a future. They need to know their lives aren't ruined, that this trauma may sometimes define them, but it will not own them. I used to pray that someone would come along and give me hope for the future. When I talked to those survivors, I realized I've become the answer to that very prayer. I'm the hope. I'm the future. But only if I show up.

The showing up is the hard thing, isn't it? Most of us haven't shared our stories, and I understand why. I've spent the past twenty years trying to be anything but—*everything* but—"The Girl Whose Brother Shot People." I'd prefer to be invisible. I've hidden my story because I'm ashamed. I don't want to be defined by the worst moment of my life. It's something I couldn't control. I know some of you feel that way. But I also know some of you don't think you have a story to share. You've confessed to me you don't think about the shooting anymore. To you, it was an upsetting thing that happened, but it doesn't affect your life today. Let me give you permission to say that out loud. In fact, that may be the most important story of all. I will admit I feel a tinge of envy, but knowing you are okay gives me so much relief and happiness. Imagine what a gift that story would've been to your younger self, to know you're not irreparably damaged, and that you'll be okay, normal, even. Your stories are important, they are the road map for the 200,000 people desperately in need of a future and some hope.

I'm not here to tell you what to say. Only to ask you to use your voice. I know it's awkward. This is hard, but trust me when I say that it is the good kind of hard, and it makes a difference. You matter so much. Your voice matters so much. And your love is a powerful, healing force. You're the answer to so many prayers, especially mine. Thank you for being my friends, my heroes, and my home.

Much Love,
Kelly Carneal Firesheets

I'M DONE PICKING SIDES

By Sarah Stewart Holland

Sarah Stewart Holland was sixteen years old at the time of the shooting.

I was a sixteen-year-old junior when three of my fellow class-mates were shot and killed in the hallway of my high school. Twenty years later, on January 23, 2018, I was a thirty-six-year-old mother of three watching the community I love go through the trauma of gun violence *again* after two students were killed in the hallway of Marshall County High School, located only thirty miles away from my alma mater.

Now, twenty years out, I have chosen to deal with this in what many might see as contradictory.

First, in the heavy days after the shooting at Marshall County, I helped start a local chapter of Moms Demand Action for Gun Sense in America, a nonpartisan grassroots movement of American mothers demanding new and stronger solutions to lax gun laws and loopholes that jeopardize the safety of our children and families.

But I didn't want to stop there. I didn't want to pick a side. I wanted to understand both sides better, so I also decided to learn more about those who value gun rights, and I didn't think I could do that by continuing to avoid guns. So, in the weeks after the shooting, I fired a gun for the first time in my life.

Unlike many people in this area, I didn't grow up around guns. There were no guns in my home. No one in my family hunted. My entire childhood experience with guns was con-tained in the images I saw in television and movies, as well as the one time my cousin showed me the gun of a family member which I refused to touch.

All of that changed on December 1, 1997. Suddenly, a gun and the young boy who wielded it changed my life and the lives of everyone I knew. Guns were no longer neutral items that played little to no role in my day-to-day life. They were scary and powerful and the symbol of a controversial political debate I became well-versed in at a young age.

The tragic events at Columbine—a year after our own shooting at Heath—re-traumatized us and galvanized the nation. Suddenly, the debate surrounding access to guns and gun violence in schools was happening all over the country. I watched Michael Moore's documentary *Bowling for Columbine*. I traveled to Washington, D.C., with my mother, classmate, and her mother for the Million Mom March. I argued and debated the Second Amendment with my college classmates, law school classmates, and coworkers for most of my young adulthood.

At the time, as a young survivor of a school shooting, I believed that you had to pick a side. You were either with the NRA or against them. You were either for gun control or against it. You were either a gun nut or a someone who cared about kids.

So, I picked a side. I spouted the talking points and I watched nothing change except the increasing frequency and intensity of mass shootings.

However, some things did change. I changed.

I moved back to my hometown of Paducah, Kentucky, after almost a decade spent attending college and law school and working on Capitol Hill. I became a mother. I ran for office and won (and then lost). And I started a podcast, *Pantsuit Politics*, with a dear friend from the opposite side of the political spectrum. All those experiences taught me that no side holds a monopoly on good ideas, kindness, or patriotism.

So, when the events of January 23rd shook me to my core, I was ready to look at the issue with a very different perspective than I did twenty years ago.

I'm done picking sides. I don't want to "win" an argument. I want to work for change. Moms Demand Action has given me a sense of hope that I haven't felt in a very, very long time. Modeled on Mothers Against Drunk Driving the premise is very simple: it's a marathon not a sprint. Our work is to raise awareness and effect legislative change supported by data. We support the Second Amendment and have no interest in shaming those who feel differently than we do about universal background checks and commonsense gun laws.

I'm also done being afraid of guns and living in ignorance about how they work. My work in this community and on my podcast has taught me that there are so rarely only two sides to a story and that no matter how right I think I am my perspective is limited. I have also learned that curiosity is rarely a bad thing. I decided I had been judgmental about those who owned guns but I had not been curious. Through the generosity and training of fellow gun owners, I am trying to transform my previous fear of guns into a healthy respect.

The worst part of January 23 was the feeling that nothing changed. Hopelessness in the face of trauma is the worst kind of pain. But I realize now that things have changed, and while I can't control the future and I certainly can't control other people, I can control myself.

I felt powerless after the events of December 1, 1997.

I don't feel powerless anymore. There is no power in picking a side. There is tremendous power in learning everything you can about a situation you care about, embracing all perspectives, and doing your best to move forward.

CHAPTER SEVENTEEN

BETHEL REGIONAL HIGH SCHOOL

Bethel, Alaska / February 19, 1997

WHEN I FIRST reached out to those who survived the shooting at Bethel Regional High School, I struggled to get a response. A small community in Bethel, Alaska, the students, staff, and teachers who were there the day Evan Ramsey brought a shotgun to school and killed a classmate and his principal, seemed to be unreachable. I researched the story, sent emails, still nothing. For weeks. Then, a response. Two responses. Three responses. Yet in their response, there was a hesitancy. *How did you get my name? How did you find us? What will this be for?*

One of the most interesting responses included a caveat. *I'll participate if you can assure me that this book will not be used to demonize the killer.* That struck me as odd. The idea that the shooter, who shot and murdered two people, should be protected. Then, I started reading about Evan Ramsey, and it suddenly made sense.

Just like guilt, there is also plenty of blame to go around in each of these shootings. Each community has their own theory, and within that community, every person has another. The parents should have seen something, the friends should have taken him more seriously, the bullies should have been caught, the teachers more attentive, the police more diligent, the guidance counselor better trained. But with Bethel, it seemed pretty consistent among those I spoke with that Evan Ramsey was a product of his own life's worst circumstances.

Ramsey's early years read like a blueprint for a bad outcome. His father was called the "Rambo of Alaska," after he went on an armed rampage and was imprisoned when Evan was only five. Evan and his brothers were taken from his alcoholic mother, and placed in foster care. The brothers were split up, and Evan reportedly lived in eleven foster homes, and had been sexually and physically abused in more than one.[1]

I wept while reading about Evan. There were signs from the very beginning. Fannie Black writes in her story that in third grade, "he threw a temper tantrum and broke one of the windows in the classroom because he wanted to stay in the reader's nest and not go back to his desk." My heart broke for the unloved boy who brought a gun to school. I thought about the unloved boys in my daughter's school, the one whose parents refused to buy him new shoes, even after we offered to donate a pair, the boy whose homework is never done, the boy who couldn't read in third grade.

I remembered the unloved boys I went to school with. The one who sat in the very back of the class with unwashed clothes and hair, the one who skipped class and hung out in the back alley smoking cigarettes even in elementary school. The one who dropped out at sixteen to work full time and support himself. As a teenage girl, I spent much of my life trying to love those boys. Now, as a mother, I want to care for them. Clean their clothes, teach them to read, and do their homework with them every night. I want to care for Evan Ramsey. But then there are those he killed, the families he destroyed. I want to care for them, too. Sometimes, it feels like I am drowning in sorrow.

AMYE ARCHER, EDITOR
JANUARY 2019

The following student and staff were shot and killed at Bethel Regional High School:

Ron Edwards, 50, principal
Josh Palacios, 15, student

IN THE PATH OF GUN VIOLENCE
By Fannie Black

Fannie Black was a junior at the time of the shooting.

I never thought Evan Ramsey would shoot me, still when I saw him holding a rifle pointed at the ceiling, walking toward me in my high school hallway, I was immediately afraid. I was scared I might get injured either in the crossfire or crushed by the mob of fleeing students. I ran for the nearest exit, but it was blocked by students. So, I snuck into the nearest classroom, the art room, with two other students, one of whom was in the same grade as Evan and me. We stood around the teacher's desk staring at each other in shock. Then, more gunshots. We had no idea what to do.

We stayed there, trapped, terrified, unable to make sense of what was happening for about thirty minutes, before we decided to creep out. Police officers in the hallway directed us to the cafeteria in the District Office. When I got to the cafeteria, I searched for my friends. There were still other students trapped in the building. There was just a lot of confusion.

After Evan Ramsey was apprehended, we were sent home. One of our classmates, Josh Palacios, and Mr. Edwards, our principal, didn't make it. I didn't cry when I heard of their passing, because it was just so unbelievable. I don't think we came back to school the *next* day, but I know it wasn't long. We had an assembly to honor Josh and Mr. Edwards, and counseling was offered to those who felt they needed it, but I didn't take it. Little did I know at seventeen, how much I needed the counseling I'm now getting in my thirties.

In the days and weeks that followed, I wondered why I was so certain Evan would not harm me despite my being in his direct path. I reflected on our shared history, searching for answers. When Evan was brought into my third-grade classroom for the first time, I felt connected to him. It was as if I could sense that he had a rough going in his short life, something that I could definitely identify with. That same year, he threw a temper tantrum and broke one of the windows in the classroom because he wanted to stay in the reader's nest and not go back to his desk. I remembered wanting to tell the teacher to just let him have his peace.

I often saw him being bullied on his way home from school. He just wanted to go home, and a group of upperclassmen followed him, taunting him, trying to get him to fight. Evan wouldn't fight. My response was the same as almost anyone else's, to just stand there and watch silently. I remembered all the times that no one stood up for Evan, all the times that other students poked and prodded until he blew up, all those times I chose to watch and do nothing.

I wondered, if I had stepped in, even just one of those times, would things have turned out differently? I was angry, angry at Evan, angry at teachers, angry at myself, and angry at a system that seemed to have no support whatsoever for a child who experienced things no child should.

After the shooting, information on Evan's history emerged: his traumatic childhood, the abuses he suffered, and his experiences in the foster care system. This child was angry, as anyone in his shoes would be. He was already being pushed down, and it seemed like the world around him wanted to push him down even further. Maybe this was the reason for my response in the shooting, my inexplicable calm in the path of gunfire. Maybe

Evan sensed somehow that I recognized the hurt boy he was inside, and that I would never hurt him.

I've spent twenty years watching the world prepare the next generation of students for school shootings. I am glad they're holding drills and training for students now, because we were so unprepared twenty years ago. Still, it makes me sad to think we still need those kinds of drills today, and that this issue has become more widespread. Schools are better prepared to handle this, but they really shouldn't need to be since schools are supposed to be one of the safest places for parents to send their children.

I am not anti-guns, but anti–gun violence. I am part of a subsistence living family where hunting rifles are considered a commodity, yet I don't believe access to firearms should be a right. I believe owning a gun should be a privilege. More guns is not the solution. And arming teachers is absolutely not the answer.

I believe more mental health support could have prevented our shooting. But that care must be provided not just for students like Evan, for teachers as well, and not just in response to a tragedy but well before a tragedy even happens.

The fact that preventing mass school shootings has become a political issue just leaves me shaking my head in bewilderment. People's lives are forever impacted by events like these, and it has been morphed into a political argument about gun laws.

Seeing young people getting involved and fighting for changes is one positive aspect of this issue, along with all the anti-bullying movements happening across this country. But there is more that needs to be done at the district level regarding gun violence in schools. I personally have not done anything yet, since this was a part of my past I kept buried for as long as I could. And there are hundreds, if not thousands more like me across the country—survivors just beginning to heal, decades later. If we had the support we needed right away, and if we accepted the limited support offered to us, would we be able to speak now? When our voices are most needed? Through therapy, and by slowly opening up to my family and friends about my trauma, I'm finally finding my path to healing, but it is a tough, long path that I would not wish on anyone.

CHAPTER EIGHTEEN
BARD COLLEGE AT SIMON'S ROCK

Great Barrington, Massachusetts /
December 14, 1992

GALEN GIBSON WAS eighteen years old when he was shot and killed at Simon's Rock. He was poet with a glowing smile. I learned about Galen after reading his father, Gregory Gibson's book *Gone Boy*, which told the story of his family's healing journey after Galen's death. The book also explored a new take on gun violence, one that he's been often criticized for, such as his communication and PSA with the shooter, Wayne Lo.

I first reached out to Gibson in April 2018 with a request to learn more about his personal experience with gun violence and his advocacy work. But before that, I was curious to know more about his relationship with his son's murderer. Through email Gibson informed me that *at the end of April I will be working with the man (in prison for two consecutive life terms) who killed my son to make a video PSA in which he says, more or less, "When I was so crazy, I thought God was commanding me to kill people, it was still a simple matter to get a gun."* It was an intriguing response to advocacy work: the shooter noting the ease to which he purchased guns and how such *ease* contributed to the shooting.

With the inception of such movements like #NoNotoriety, which calls for media to not mention the names of those that have committed mass shootings, Gibson's interview with Lo challenges this. Their conversation becomes less about Lo achieving infamy and more about what the public can learn from a school shooter in terms of gun sense, remorse, and healing. For Lo, he didn't realize what he'd done until he'd read Gibson's book. For Lo, *Gone Boy* was transformative and proved to Lo the devastation of his actions. And since Lo's incarceration he's turned to art as a way to give back, donating all the proceeds from the sale of his work at the Hyena Gallery to Gibson's the Galen Gibson Fund.

I think of the he relationship between Gibson and Lo as restorative justice. This process allows both the victim and the perpetrator to begin a process of rehabilitation together, thereby allowing the perpetrator to make amends and take accountability for their actions. Gibson has been able to help more people affected by gun violence by continuing his restorative justice work in prisons. Needless to say, I'm inspired by Gibson's great heart and his drive to change the way we think about healing, justice, and advocacy. I don't know what could be more healing than knowing the source of all this pain, and then using that knowledge to help those still suffering in silence.

Loren Kleinman
November 2018

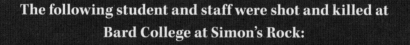

The following student and staff were shot and killed at Bard College at Simon's Rock:

Galen Gibson, 18, student
Ñacuñán Sáez, 37, Spanish professor

SICK OF IT ALL

By Gregory Gibson

Gregory Gibson is the father of Galen Gibson. Galen was an eighteen-year-old poetry student murdered at Simon's Rock in the doorway of his college library. Gibson is the author of *Gone Boy*, an exploration of gun violence in America, and the story of a family moving beyond grief. "Sick of It All" is the first chapter of *Gone Boy*.

I always had a knack for making plans. Not long-term plans, but an endless supply of existential ones, in an ongoing calculus of strategy. Whenever the situation changed there'd be a new plan. Sometimes there were several in an hour.

So, it was not surprising that, when the dean of my son's college called, late on a Monday night in mid-December of 1992, and told me there'd been a terrible accident at the college, and that my son had been shot and killed, I soon had a plan.

At first, I could not speak. I handed the telephone to Annie, my wife, and as I stood there, gasping for breath, the idea came to me. I was going to drive out to the college and bring Galen back. I was going to spread out his old sleeping bag in the back of the van and lay his body on it. I was going to get the body and bring it home so we could clean it up and bury it, so we could wash those bullet holes with our tears. Three hours out and three hours back. I'd be home by dawn. That was the level at which I was capable of planning.

Annie put the telephone down and walked to one end of the hall, then back, a wild, distracted look about her. This was not one of those revelatory moments in which husbands and wives learned deep truths about one another. Shock had driven us down inside ourselves. The truth was more physical, literal. Annie was standing beside me, as she had been for eighteen years.

She picked the phone up again and called her mother, who gently pointed out to me that my proper place during this time of crisis was at home with my family, not at the other end of the state trying to haul the corpse out of a murder investigation. So, I stayed home that night, with Annie, and our son Brooks, and our daughter Celia.

Initially, the news of Galen's death was so enormous that we could not assimilate it in any meaningful way. We stumbled woodenly about the house, trying to make the necessary phone calls to relatives and friends. Brooks, a sophomore in high school, went out for a long drive with another boy. We let Celia, our baby, have one last night of untroubled sleep. She was nine years old, the special pet of eighteen-year-old Galen.

We could not cry. We kept telling ourselves that it was a mistake, that it had happened to someone else. We kept thinking, throughout that long and terrible night, that in the morning we'd wake, and it all would have been a dream. But when the morning came, it brought a deluge of news reports. Our waking nightmare became common knowledge, an absurd violation, and an inescapable fact. Galen was dead. The radio said so.

Somehow, on the small, sleepy campus of Simon's Rock College, a student had gone crazy. Somehow, he'd ordered bullets through the mail. Then he'd gone to a local gun shop and bought a military-style semiautomatic rifle. Somehow, he got the gun back onto school grounds undetected. At about 10:15 on the evening of Monday, December 14, 1992, he began walking through the campus, shooting people. First, he shot and seriously wounded the guard at the front gate. Then he murdered a professor driving past. Then he walked to the library where he murdered Galen and wounded another student. Then he wounded two more students. Then, somehow, he surrendered and was arrested, unharmed. His name was Wayne Lo. He'd emigrated from Taiwan, China six years before.

Beyond establishing the place and time of our son's death, these few stark facts were of little use to Annie and me. We desperately needed an exact account of how this terrible thing had come to pass, but we got no word from anyone on the scene. Our imagining of the event took the form of a grotesque cartoon, drawn from the terse hyperbole of news reports.

Thus, Galen had died in a "campus shooting spree" at his "exclusive Berkshires school." The killer was a "troubled, angry youth . . . an outcast." He "proceeded across the snowy paths . . . panic in his wake" and "sent a blast into Gibson's chest." Galen "staggered to the front desk . . . blood soaking through his shirt, and cried 'I've been shot.'"

The report ended with "steel gray hearses" removing the bodies at dawn, and with Wayne Lo being taken into police custody. His head was shaved, and he was wearing a sweatshirt on which was printed the motto, "Sick of It All."

This version of what had happened raised more questions than it answered, but we were too stunned to ask them.

WHAT YOU DON'T GET ABOUT LOVE, LIFE AND DEATH, AND SURVIVAL

Anne Thalheimer was eighteen years old at the time of the shooting. While she was working on a paper in her dorm room, she got a call from the resident director that said, "Turn out the lights, lock your doors, and get down on the floor. Someone is shooting on campus." Anne wrote an autobiographical comic called *What You Don't Get*, about love, life and death, and survival. This is a short chapter from her comic book.

MAY 2008

GREGORY GIBSON

THERE ARE DAYS WHEN MY WORLD
FEELS REALLY WEIRDLY SMALL.

may 2009.
YEAH. OKAY. IT'S TRUE. I HAVEN'T BEEN MUCH FUN TO BE AROUND LATELY.
I HAVEN'T BEEN AROUND MUCH LATELY.
I'VE BEEN A LITTLE LOST.
TWEEET!!
RED THREE CUTTING MAJOR!
I KIND OF GOT LOST IN THE DERBY STUFF A LITTLE.
MAYBE THAT'S OKAY.
IT'S BEEN A WHILE SINCE I HAD A WORLD-ENDER DAY.
I CAN FUNCTION.
MOSTLY.
I HAVEN'T HAD AN UNEXPECTED TRIGGERY MOMENT SINCE FEBRUARY.
AND THAT, REALLY, THAT WAS MY OWN FAULT.
REALLY.
I WAS READING ABOUT SOPHIE LANCASTER ONLINE
=click=
... TO GOTH CULTURE
=click=
... TO SCHOOL SHOOTINGS
... and i fucking should have stopped clicking there

but i didn't 'cause it's me and I'm stupid
and it's like a scab that i can't stop picking.

and i knew what I would find,
and i fuckin' clicked the link anyway.

THERE'S MY FAULTY PROGRAMMING.

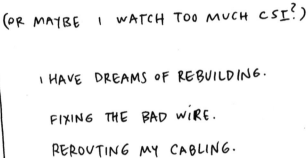

(OR MAYBE I WATCH TOO MUCH CSI?)

I HAVE DREAMS OF REBUILDING.

FIXING THE BAD WIRE.

REROUTING MY CABLING.

OVERRIDING MY DEFAULT.

IF I COULD JUST REPROGRAM
THIS WEIRD LITTLE MACHINE...

(it's funny. every time i draw myself at autopsy
peeking inside myself, i never have a heart.)

I WANT TO BE THE KIND OF PERSON WHO IS CAPABLE OF FORGIVENESS.

I'M NOT THERE YET.

I DON'T KNOW IF I'M GONNA GET THERE.

AND THIS FREAKING BOOK IS BRINGING ME

RIGHT.

BACK.

THERE.

BACK TO MY RAGE.

MY FURY.

MY HATRED.

BACK TO WISHING FOR WHAT I CAN'T HAVE.

(FEELING INHUMAN)

BACK TO ALL MY WHAT-IFS.

EVERYTHING I TRIED TO OUTRUN.

I WISH I COULD GO BACK TO TALK TO MYSELF CIRCA LATE DECEMBER 1992.

LOOK. YOU'RE NEVER GONNA GET OVER THIS. YOU'RE NEVER GONNA BE THE SAME PERSON AGAIN. THIS IS GONNA FUCK YOU UP FOREVER. IT IS. THAT'S OK.

'CAUSE BEING FUCKED UP BEATS BEING DEAD.

IT'S TRUE. I FEEL KIND OF SELF-INDULGENT. I MEAN, GOD.

IT'S BEEN HOW LONG?

i was eighteen when it happened. and I'm gonna turn thirty-five in october.

(I'M GETTING OLD.)

IT BAFFLES ME THAT SOMETHING FROM SO LONG AGO IS STILL SOMETHING SO PRESENT IN WHO I THINK I AM.

AND YET SO DORMANT.

(SIDE NOTE: DON'T EVER ASK ME IF I'M OVER IT YET.)

I'M PRETTY HIGH-FUNCTIONING.

UNTIL YOU START TALKING ABOUT GUNS.

and then all bets are off.

USUALLY, ANYWAY. I WAS AT A PARTY THIS YEAR WHERE SOMEONE'S HALLOWEEN COSTUME WAS "SCHOOL SHOOTING VICTIM."

HUH.

INSTEAD OF HAVING A MELTDOWN I KIND OF DIDN'T FEEL ANYTHING.

IS THAT BAD?

(DOES THAT MEAN I'M GETTING BETTER?)

↑ i went as Pippi Longstocking.

cats

IT'S GOTTEN SO TANGLED UP IN EVERYTHING ELSE. ALL THE WEIRD SOFT PARTS OF MY HEART.

growing up poor

derby
finishing grad school

parents divorcing

not being afraid of dying

cancer

lover leaving you

shooting murder

AS IF ALL I HAVE IS DAMAGE? I KNOW THAT'S NOT TRUE.

AFTERWARDS NOBODY COULD FIGURE OUT WHAT TO SAY, EVERYTHING SOUNDED HOLLOW. NOTHING FIT.

AND SO THERE WAS A LOT OF HUGGING HAPPENING INSTEAD.

AND I THINK AT SOME POINT I HAD JUST HAD ENOUGH.

BUT I COULDN'T FIGURE OUT HOW TO SAY IT.

AND ENDED UP STAMPING DOWN MY URGE TO JUST VIOLENTLY SHOVE EVERYONE AWAY FROM ME.

AND GOT HUGGED TOO MUCH. AND STARTED FLINCHING WHEN IT HAPPENED.

I DON'T HUG.

THIS FLINCHING PERSISTED FOR YEARS.

I TRIED DODGING WHEN PEOPLE CAME AT ME.

AND LET THEM DRAW THEIR OWN CONCLUSIONS.

LATER, AS AN ADULT, THE PROFESSOR WHO'D TAUGHT THE CLASS I WAS IN WITH ▓▓▓▓▓▓, HAD A HOST OF QUESTIONS.

DO YOU THINK THAT?

I DON'T REMEMBER ANYTHING.

IT WASN'T A DODGE. I REALLY DON'T REMEMBER.

IN TRUTH, THE WHOLE CONVERSATION MADE ME WILDLY UNCOMFORTABLE.

UM.

UH. YEAH. I GOTTA GO.

I DON'T KNOW WHAT SHE WAS LOOKING FOR— ABSOLUTION? PEACE?

HUH.

BUT I'M PRETTY SURE SHE DIDN'T GET IT FROM ME.

FOR A LONG TIME I WAS REALLY INVESTED IN FIGURING
OUT HOW MUCH THE ~~SHOOTING~~ — IF YOU'LL FORGIVE
              MURDERS
THE COLLOQUIAL— FUCKED ME UP, AND HOW MUCH
              I CAME TO IT PRE-FUCKED.

BOOK, BLAH BLAH, DEAD PEOPLE,
BLAH BLAH BLAH. . .

WHAT I FEEL LIKE I'VE
BEEN FOR THE LAST YEAR

I TALKED A LITTLE ABOUT
IT WITH A FRIEND WHO
MADE IT OUT OF ONE OF
THE TOWERS ON 9/11.

AND IT'S TRUE — EVERY EXPERIENCE SHAPES
THE PERSON YOU BECOME, EVERY PIECE.

AND YET...

DOES IT REALLY
MATTER WHERE
THIS QUIRK
CAME FROM?

IT USED TO.

BUT PARSING IT DOWN GOT A LOT LESS
INTERESTING AFTER MY DAD DIED.

UHH...

IT STOPPED
MATTERING
SOMEHOW.

NO. I GUESS NOT.

I DON'T KNOW WHAT MY LIFE WOULD HAVE BEEN LIKE
IF IT HAD NEVER HAPPENED.

I CAN IMAGINE GALEN, HAPPY,
          WITH A HOUSE FULL OF KIDS,
                    JOYOUS.

ÑACUÑÁN, IN HIS OFFICE,
        STILL TEACHING, PLANNING
           A TRIP TO PARIS, MAYBE.

BUT ME?
I HAVE NO IDEA.
I NEVER DARED IMAGINE.

WHAT WOULD I
HAVE BECOME?

WHO WOULD I
HAVE BEEN?

A LETTER TO GALEN GIBSON

Mark Fredrick was a close friend of Galen Gibson from the Unitarian Universalist (UU) Church youth group in eastern Massachusetts. Mark wrote this letter to Galen in 2018.

Dear Galen,

It's been twenty-five years since we, your family, friends, Unitarian youth group members, and classmates, last saw you. Been that long since your last Moxie, the old-school soda; since you read a book, anything.

You're probably wondering what happened.

Your last memories might be it was a Monday night, you were studying in the library, heard a commotion and tried to exit the building to find out what was going on. Then you were shot and killed.

Here's what happened. A fellow student at your school, Simon's Rock of Bard College, shot you. His name is Wayne Lo and you didn't know each other. He bought a gun from a store in a nearby town. Buying the gun was because of reciprocal gun laws. He bought the ammunition by calling a shop in another state, North Carolina. The shop mailed the box of ammunition to him at the school! The return address was for a weapons store, which gave a clear indication that the contents might be dangerous.

When the package arrived, the school wasn't sure that delivering it to Wayne was the right course of action, but they did it anyway. At the time, Wayne was hearing voices and those voices were telling him to use the gun. He did. He walked around campus, shooting. During the shooting spree, he killed you and the Spanish teacher, Ñacuñán Saez. Four people were wounded. All of you were random victims.

Your circle of people, including our extended Unitarian youth group, celebrated, mourned, and buried you, just a short stroll from home. Wayne went to prison, where he'll remain for the rest of his life.

The lives of many, many other people changed, because of Wayne's actions toward people who he didn't know. There was a void created in our hearts we'll never be able to fill. Your life ended far too early, unrelated to anything you did.

In the last twenty-five years, school shootings and other random shootings have become part of our cultural life in America. They've happened at all levels of school: elementary, junior high, high school, and college. They've happened at a country music festival, an African American church, and yesterday, a Waffle House restaurant.

I wish the collective experience of victims like you resulted in change to make random shootings less frequent, or to make them stop occurring, but it hasn't happened. It must be hard to fathom what happened to you continues to happen to others. Maybe if you could tell your story to others, especially certain legislators and special interest groups, they'd finally understand and change their actions.

I've been telling your story to help change happen. Millions of people across America are trying to change laws to tighten accessibility to guns. Sounds responsible and pragmatic, right? But the NRA and the politicians who they influence believe that the Second Amendment from the 1700s pertains to twenty-first-century weapons. They want reciprocal concealed carry laws. They say "red flag" laws impinge on rights. They want teachers to have guns in classrooms.

This gun issue went mainstream and big in the last two months. A nineteen-year-old shot up his school in Florida on Valentine's Day, resulting in seventeen deaths. Imagine that, only two died at your school! Well, the survivors said "enough," and organized marches and put a lot of political pressure on the government. These savvy, direct, uncompromising kids have been all over the media. They're sick of living in fear and doing safety lockdown drills at their schools instead of learning.

But we've been here before. Will big changes happen this time?

Seven years after you died, two high school students shot up their school in Colorado and afterward, it looked like things would change, but they didn't.

Your dad, Greg, has been helping to lead the charge for gun policy reform for years—he's now a nationally known figure in this movement. You should read his book, *Gone Boy*, about what happened to you. Wayne read it. Your dad went to the store where Wayne bought his gun, met with the administration of your school, found out everything he could about what happened and then wrote about it. He met Wayne, not to grab headlines in a media frenzy, but to try to make some greater good out of this, one way I think of it is that negative feelings don't have to rot people out from the inside. Your dad has been a rock for me when I've needed to talk to someone about mass shootings and making sense of the related issues. Support systems are very important for survivors of gun violence.

For me, well, your death and the random shooting really shook my sense of security. I was worried about other bad things happening, and I found the whole thing really difficult to talk about with anyone who didn't know you. I've become distraught after other random shootings—freaked out at the idea that more friends, families, and loved ones are just starting to go through this loss.

The time I was most distraught was when the anniversary of your death became the anniversary of another school shooting. I visited your grave on the twentieth anniversary of your death. I took the day off from work, went to a record shop along the way, found the stone and sat with you for a while. Popcorn and Moxie were there so I knew that at least someone else had been there earlier in the day. Next, I visited your house, saw your sister and her flowers. Your brother and I talked about basketball. Your dad showed me his new book. I talked about artwork with your mom. And during my visit, word started to emerge about another school shooting. Details became less scant, and we learned that a lot of first-graders in Connecticut were killed.

Shaken, your family and I talked more, and I alternated between wanting to learn more and wanting to postpone the inevitability of getting bowled over by what happened. After we said our goodbyes, I left, turned on NPR in the car, and cried nearly the entire way home as they told of the senseless deaths of six-year-olds at the trigger finger of a very troubled young man and of a town that I knew would never be the same. That town could have been any town. At the time, one of my kids was in the same grade, it could have happened at her school, could have been her. I was a wreck for days. How could another shooting happen? How could it happen twenty years after your death? Had nothing changed in all this time? In private, I talked and talked and talked about it to some of the people closest to me and in public, I acted like it didn't happen, so that I could keep it together and not burst into tears.

I want you to know I'm doing my part. Our family donated money to many groups who support sensible gun policy. We marched last month on the date of the largest-scale marches about this issue in history. I've started to speak out. I told your story and what it's like to be a survivor of gun violence at a forum held by our state senator. I told my kids about you and how much I hope random shootings end, for good, for real. The kids were shocked to learn your story, and that I knew someone who was a victim of a school shooting. My wife and I told them it shows you can't guess what someone experienced. People don't wear signs that say SOMETHING REALLY HEAVY HAPPENED TO ME.

I'll write again in the fall, hopefully, with good news about the midterm elections. And maybe to say your dad celebrated another World Series win by the hometown team.

Love and Moxie,
Mark

CONCEALED CARRY

By Jesse Dorris

Jesse Dorris was a student at Simon's Rock. He was in a play for a friend's senior work at the time of the shooting.

I left high school because I didn't want to die there. I refused to end my life, as a friend had been unable to resist, because I was queer. I figured that when AIDS killed me, I'd have better had a more interesting life than the one available to me on the rocky shores of southern Massachusetts, where I also thought, in my fifteen-year-old way, I might die of boredom. One of the guys who chased me down the high school halls, or threw from behind me a bottle of water, or strategically opened a locker door as I was chased toward it, or who caught me or thought he would or wanted to catch me looking in a locker room—one of these guys with their own murky troubles might kill me, or I might inadvertently kill of them and in that way end my own life. Or The Smiths song's bus. However, I was carrying the trauma of a sexual assault I won't talk about now around town like a shield and something told me it was more likely to attract bullets them stop them. You don't have to pry open a big gaping wound.

I went early to a college on an alienated hill, built to be fled to. Hundreds of us did. One night one of us ordered bullets through the mail; one snowy afternoon, he went to a super-store, and bought a gun. I guess he was wounded in some way, too. He murdered a teacher, a student, shot more. If I had been where I should not have been, I could have been in their path.

When someone nearby whom one doesn't really know— whom one could have, but didn't, and now never will—when someone close is killed and one is at least a certain kind of person, when one at least was me, trauma molds from a shield into a *personality*. One is traumatized; one is traumatic. I became a site of infectious sadness and even proud of it. Pangs of jealousy that I wasn't the one who was killed, that I wasn't the one who did it, were identifiable mirages off in the distance, which is to say I knew I didn't feel that way but sort of wanted to, in the way I generally wanted to be more interesting. Anyone who trespassed onto the site was sorry to have done so. I looked at the ways people found pleasure in the world and was sorry to have figured out this was a way I found mine.

We were released from the school's custody and into our parents'. There was a puce sky and scattering of cameras and reporters and mics. I wanted to say something but wasn't sure what, to say I had been there and why are you. I dropped out and grew Christmas trees, worked in a bookstore, kept quiet. A few years later I was leaving a boyfriend's house in D.C., and a guy with a gun held me up. A few years later, leaving another boyfriend's house, we were held down on the ground. Many years after that I was pistol-whipped and dragged through the streets of Brooklyn. Each time, I mostly only lost time, because that was mostly all I had. Each time became an anecdote, an aspect of a personality. The moments became un-unique. A thousand other kids saw guns in their schools going off, a thousand kids mangled all over the place. A pandemic of trauma shifts into status quo.

What one goes through becomes what one has been through. I was no longer that person, not soon enough. Now, when I think of those moments I don't think of those moments: I think of the weird oil-slick of the camera lens, how footage is *shot*. I frame shots like trophies, like memorials, like spoils.

Of course, somewhere I'm going to die. Wayne Lo is somewhere going to die. Perhaps in prison. I'm not his judge. There's a queer saying and it is to carry. We carry when we are just being too much. There's another saying and it makes me tense and straighten up, it makes me unsure of which shield might work. To carry is to be armed, a proud savior complex, a gun as a shield and personality both. Their protection endangers me even as I'm safe in ways I'll never know. I'm safe in ways I'm already wounded. But then nobody knows. A fifth time could be the charm. And meanwhile we just carry on.

CHAPTER NINETEEN
UNIVERSITY OF IOWA
Iowa City, Iowa / November 1, 1991

KAREIN EMAILS ME photos of her father, Christoph (Chris) K. Goertz. He was the leading theoretical space plasma physicist shot and killed at the University of Iowa on November 1, 1991, by a twenty-eight-year-old former graduate student. These photos are for a book I'm coediting about school shootings. There's a part of me that doesn't want to download them because I struggle with seeing the faces of the murdered after working so closely with the families. But I remind myself I've already committed to the difficult task of assembling both the living and the dead's stories.

So, I move forward. Download the attached images she's sent me. A folder zips about ten photos, some of Chris hiking out into the wilderness, some of him lecturing to a roomful of university science students, and there's two or three happy family photos. But *this* photo. *This one,* writes Karein. *I took this photo of him two days before his murder. It was the last time I saw my father alive.* I fixated on Chris's smile. He looks visibly content, perhaps secure and settled in his life. Happy. But I force myself to stop the conjecture and consider where to place these photos in the essay Karein and I have been editing for weeks now. But I'm hesitant to start, and delay acknowledging her email (or the next round of edits on her essay).

The process of guiding people to speak their truths was isolating. At the end of every brainstorming session with a survivor, I felt powerless. Their family members were murdered violently and suddenly, and I questioned if this was all I could do to help. How will sharing their stories make an impact on schools safety? On gun sense legislation? On bringing awareness to the long-term effects of trauma on the living? I didn't have the right to ask. My family was still alive.

A few days after receiving Karein's email, I finally email her back, acknowledging receipt of the photos she's sent me. It's time to go through her photo essay and insert the images and captions.

Before I start, I text Amye, *Karein sent me the photos of her father.*

Oh boy, she replies.

I feel like the only girl in the world sometimes, I message her.

You're the only one who understands what I'm going through, Amye replies.

I take a deep breath and focus on inserting the photos in her essay as we discussed. Afterward, I give myself permission to cry. I cried for Karein and her family because they live on without Chris as do the many survivors of Iowa. But I hope they will provide immeasurable amounts of hope in the aftermath of so much destruction.

LOREN KLEINMAN, EDITOR

DECEMBER 2018

The following students and staff were shot and killed at University of Iowa (not all ages are known):

T. Anne Cleary, 56, associate VP, academic affairs

Christoph K. Goertz, 47, professor of physics and astronomy

Dwight R. Nicholson, 44, chairman, physics and astronomy department

Linhua Shan, 27, post-doctoral research investigator; winner of the Spriestersbach Prize

Robert A. Smith, associate professor of physics and astronomy

FRAGMENTS: MEMORIES OF MY FATHER
By Karein Goertz

Karein Goertz is the daughter of Christoph K. Goertz, professor of physics and astronomy at the University of Iowa. Dr. Goertz was killed during the shooting at the University of Iowa on November 1, 1991. He was a renowned space plasma theorist, and the top in his field as noted by his colleagues.

Long before school shootings became an almost routine part of the American experience, a student with a legally purchased weapon and no prior criminal or mental health record went on a premeditated rampage through the University of Iowa, killing five, paralyzing one, and then turning the gun on himself. My father was among them. He was forty-seven years old, in the middle of his life and an illustrious career.

The author with her father Christoph K. Goertz in 1969.
Photo provided by the author.

My father and I were very close: we shared the same birthday and people said I took after him. He was a role model, confidant, and mentor who supported and challenged me, talking me through problems and piercing through my self-deceptions with scientific precision. Even after leaving home, I would consult him on personal matters and his brutally honest opinion generally guided my decisions. After his death, I realized to what extent I depended on his sage advice.

I loved my father's adventurous spirit, his inquisitive and critical mind, and his great capacity for enthusiasm. He was interested in so many things and his passion was contagious. My fondest memory is him telling stories. He was a masterful storyteller who could transform a boring highway into a monster's endless tongue, pulling our family car into a treacherous adventure. My father was also a fabulous reader who introduced us to *The Hobbit*, *Watership Down*, and *The Call of the Wild*. He gave each character a unique voice. I can still hear his lisping version of Gollum in Tolkien's trilogy. My father could be very funny, both sarcastic and goofy. He was a big Monty Python fan and came up with his own silly walks or hilarious outfits and hairdos to make us laugh. He knew how to throw a party, loved cooking and entertaining. We would often assemble in the kitchen to watch him make a bechamel sauce or his unbeatable *zabaglione* dessert.

Now at fifty-two, I am older than my father was when he was killed, and I have lived more than half of my life without him. In the years following his death, as I tried to forget what had happened to him, I feared forgetting him. Sure enough, he is not as present as he once was, but as a parent myself now, I find his ways coming back to me and I recognize bits of him in my own son. I know that if I ever need to summon him, Keith Jarrett's soulful *Kölner Concert* recording can transport me right back to the concert hall where my father and I heard the jazz pianist play more than forty years ago. Or I sit down at the piano myself and imagine him listening, urging me to play just one more piece.

Photo of aurora borealis, November 8, 1991.
Photo taken by the author.

As close as I felt to my father, I didn't share his fascination with science. I'm more of a humanist, but I respect the scientific approach and recognize that science is key to solving our planet's most urgent problems. In retrospect, I regret not having listened more to his explanations of the natural world. While he described the aurora borealis, the "northern lights" he witnessed on research trips to Alaska and Norway as highly charged particles released by solar storms colliding with the earth's atmosphere, I would envision a paintbrush sweeping across an enormous canvas.

Finally, I experienced this auroral display myself—exactly a week after the shootings and a day after the memorial service for the victims. As my mother and I were taking an evening walk down an alleyway in our neighborhood, several cawing crows drew our attention up toward a fabulous spectacle of reds and greens in the sky. Our first reflex was to laugh and to interpret this lightshow as a cosmic farewell. Undoubtedly, my father was smiling down at us, mocking us for being so superstitious.

However, I recently read that the Inuit saw a connection between the northern lights and the dead: "A narrow and dangerous pathway leads across an immense abyss to the heavenly regions. Only the spirits of those who have died a voluntary or *violent death*, and the Raven, have been over this pathway. The sky-dwellers light their torches to guide the feet of new arrivals. This is the light of the aurora." To the mind of a nonscientist like myself, my father's auroral departure was an extraordinarily kind message: he was using his scientific vocabulary of the skies to reach out to the magical thinker in me, recalling our lifelong bond of storytelling. Although I have often thought about this strange experience, I didn't find a language for this unconscious realization until now.

Even the scientific community drew a connection and regarded the aurora over Iowa as a "fitting tribute" to colleagues who had spent years studying the phenomenon. Today, a plaque outside the so-called "Aurora Room" in the physics department is dedicated to the memory of its four victims: Christoph K. Goertz, Dwight R. Nicholson, Robert A. Smith, and Linhua Shan.

Christoph K. Goertz in Alaska, 1980.
Photographer: Captain Bull Moose.

My father was such a strong intellectual presence and accomplished in his field that following his path into the sciences would have been intimidating. Both my brother and I chose professional directions that weren't in competition with his. My brother became an architect, whereas I pursued an academic career in language and literature, earning advanced degrees in comparative literature. I'm continuing in his footsteps as a teacher, though, and perhaps living out some of his more literary ambitions. He was always an avid, critical reader and had once considered studying film instead of physics.

The mass shooting of November 1, 1991, happened while I

was in graduate school in Austin, Texas. I had just been home a week earlier for the Thanksgiving break during which my father and I had a long, difficult conversation about my studies. I was having doubts about continuing beyond a master's degree, and he was very frustrated by my desire to give up. It was a heated discussion to be continued over the Christmas holiday which, of course, never came to be. That unfinished conversation may have been part of the reason I continued my studies; I couldn't let him down. The experience of his murder and its psychological aftermath had a profound influence on my subsequent studies. In the years to come, as I worked toward my PhD, I became more engrossed in Holocaust literature and the study of trauma's impact on memory. I think I found a perverse comfort in reading about life experiences that were far more traumatic and far-reaching. It put my own pain into perspective and provided a language to articulate what I was feeling. Sudden violent loss was not an anomaly, but rather an experience many have had to endure. At the same time, the intense preoccupation with this subject matter may also have prolonged the grieving process. It took me several years to complete my dissertation because, in a way, it was connected with my father's death, and completing it would also mean moving on, which I still wasn't ready to do at that point. One night, however, my father came to me in a dream: I was following him through ruins of a charred city, hurrying to keep up with him. I would lose sight of him whenever I stopped to type a few pages on a typewriter in my trench coat pocket and would then rush to catch up with him again. This happened several times until my father finally said, "Karein, you don't need to follow me. Just stop and finish writing. Don't worry, you will always find me." I completed my dissertation a few weeks later.

Since then, I have been a full-time lecturer at the Residential College, a small liberal arts college within the University of

Michigan in Ann Arbor, teaching language and literature courses in German, as well as freshman writing courses and seminars on a wide range of topics that have interested me over the years— Holocaust literature, cities, the art of walking, multiculturalism, modernism, film, literary translation, Berlin, memoirs. I love teaching and often feel very connected to my students. They keep me hopeful about the future. Perhaps my father would be disappointed that I never pursued a tenure-track position with a long list of academic publications to my name, as he had, but I have preferred a more modest path.

A remembrance published in the journal *Physics Today* (October 1992) relates how the beginning of my father's career coincided with new advances in the field of space plasma physics and how he quickly became "one of the world's leading theorists" in this area. He was also senior editor of the peer-reviewed scientific *Journal of Geophysical Research* and a visiting scientist at different laboratories in the United States and Germany which our family experienced as a series of frequent transcontinental moves. At the time of his death, he was elected as an external scientific member of the Max-Planck-Institut für Extraterrestrische Physik in Garching, Germany. He had also just accepted a directorship position at the Institut für Physik in Berlin and Potsdam, newly configured after German unification, and would have moved back to Germany had he not been killed. Over the course of almost two decades, he published more than 150 scientific articles and continues to be cited today.

I wonder sometimes if my father's "brilliant career" made him a target and that subsequently, unconsciously, I have chosen to exist more under the radar. But then I hear my father's voice chiding me to be more rational.

The Goertz family, 1976. Photo provided by the author.

My father was also known as an "outstanding lecturer" and "popular teacher," and after his death, we received beautiful letters to this effect from his former students. I, of course, only knew him as a father, but growing up with him meant growing up with a born teacher who always engaged us in intellectual inquiry. When my brother and I noticed a rainbow, he would encourage us to observe and describe what we saw, and then asked us questions to usher us through an explanation of how the different colors came to be.

Now, as a mother, I catch myself trying to do the same, just not as well. My father, it seemed to us, always knew a lot about everything and had such a wonderful way of sharing it. He believed that even the most complicated of phenomena can be explained in a clear and simple manner. If you truly *know* a subject, you should be able to talk about it so that both a specialist and a child can understand.

I heard about the killings on NPR news as I was driving home: "Gang Lu, twenty-eight, a graduate student in physics from China, reportedly upset because he was passed over for an academic honor, opens fire in two buildings on the University of Iowa campus. Five University of Iowa employees are killed, including four members of the physics department; two other people are wounded. The student fatally shoots himself." It was the top story on the five o'clock news and just over an hour after the shootings, so they hadn't released the names yet. When I heard that it had taken place in the physics department at the University of Iowa and that several were dead, I experienced momentary panic, but calmed myself down with rationalizations: the department was large, I reasoned, and the chance that my father would be among the victims was more unlikely than not. I tried calling home and initially no one answered. Eventually, a stranger picked up and called for my mother, who didn't come to the phone. I could hear a lot of people in the house and began suspecting the worst. I don't remember who told me that my father had been killed, maybe it was my mother. When I broke down at home, my dog came and did a wonderfully primal, protective thing: she quietly lay down on top of me. Her weight eventually calmed me. Years later, when I had to put her down, I remembered that moment.

I then became extremely calm and methodical, calling the German department, where I worked as a graduate teaching assistant, letting them know that I would not be coming in the next week. Then I called the airlines to book a flight to Iowa City. When they said they would need a death certificate to warrant a special airfare rate, I told them to check the front page of next day's newspaper. Then I called close friends, asking them to come over as soon as they could. Eventually the apartment was filled with people. I don't remember much about what was said that night, but I remember feeling immensely soothed by these friends. They cried with me, but we also laughed. In the middle of the night, we all took a walk. It was a clear night and I felt calmed by the sky and familiar Orion. For a moment things were in perspective: no matter what happens down here, whether we feel like our world is falling apart, the stars and planets are there, unmoved and unchanged.

My time in Iowa immediately following the shooting is a blur of fragmented memories. Lots of flowers, cards, people stopping by the house. A huge memorial service organized by the university which I attended wearing my father's oversized shoes. Seeing his body in the hospital morgue and amazed to find hardly a sign of his violent death. Touching him to comprehend what "dead" meant. It must have been much later, my brother and I going to the room where the shootings took place to search for traces. Sorting through my father's belongings in his office, finding poems he'd written, letters, notebooks filled with mathematical formulas.

My mother, brother, and I retreated into our separate emotional orbs. We were each too wrapped up in our own shock to be able to take care of each other. My mother responded with much more anger than I did, wanting to find who was to blame for what happened and launching herself into lobbying for stricter gun laws. I vaguely remember the two of us appearing on the local news, making a statement against the easy accessibility of handguns. She organized a successful boycott against local sporting goods stores that sold handguns. My grandmother, recently widowed, had been staying with my parents at the time. She was inconsolable about losing her youngest son and went around the house asking, "Why didn't he just kill me?" Half a year later, she committed suicide. This was something I have never really processed.

I went into counseling shortly after returning to Austin and graduate school. The sessions were immensely helpful, although I do not remember much of what went on. It was just comforting to have a safe, familiar place to talk about all of the things that were coming up inside that I didn't understand. I often could not remember what year it was or completely phased out and the therapist helped me understand that this was okay, that my mind was taking its time to sort through thoughts and feelings, blocking things out and letting them back into my awareness slowly and incrementally. Since I will never know, I forced myself to believe that my father died immediately: no pain, just a mere instance of surprise, hardly enough time even for regret. I wondered, did he see his life "flash before his eyes" or did the bullet too quickly destroy that part of the brain that stores memories? Was the explosion inside his head enough to drown out the sound of the other shots fired?

I also thought about the killer and wondered how someone could be so filled with hatred to kill another human being. How could he convince himself that he was, in his words, "doing what he was supposed to be doing" which was "making right what was once wrong." The idea that he spent months premeditating this murder while continuing to interact with his future victims was extremely disturbing to me.

Christoph K. Goertz giving a lecture in the 1980s. Unknown photographer.

At the time, the University of Iowa was one of the nation's top five universities in space physics. When Gang Lu, my father's doctoral student, went on his shooting spree, he took out three core faculty members in magnetospheric physics, thereby wiping out that part of the department. How my father's death impacted the science community is probably best answered by people in his field, but considering that colleagues described him as "extremely innovative and imaginative" and as "one of the most outstanding space plasma theorists of our time" (*Physics Today*, October 1992), I can only imagine that it dealt a significant blow to the community. He helped interpret data from space missions to Jupiter, Saturn, Uranus, and Neptune and, at the time of his death, was "pioneering an entirely new area of space plasma physics concerned with the interaction of dust with hot plasmas." Famed professor James Van Allen, who first recruited my father to the University of Iowa in 1973, is said to have considered him his favorite theoretical collaborator.

Christoph K. Goertz in the summer of 1991, just
a few months before his death.
Photo provided by the author.

To confront these recollections again, I opened a box filled with documents I hadn't looked at in well over twenty years: letters, photographs, newspaper clippings, scientific papers, a death certificate, my grandmother's suicide note, program notes from the memorial service, my dream diary, the murderer's statements, Jo Ann Beard's story "The Fourth State of Matter" from *The New Yorker.* I've long feared this Pandora's box with its blunt truths: "Manner of Death: Homicide. Date of Injury: 11/1/1991. Describe How Injury Occurred: Shot with .38 Caliber Revolver. Immediate Cause of Death: Gunshot Wound to Head. Signed by Johnson County Medical Examiner."

I wasn't sure if opening the box would unleash things I couldn't put back in again. And although the notarized Certificate of Death filled me with a renewed feeling of dread, I was surprised by the overall sense of quiet I experienced in revisiting these remnants from what seems like so long ago. The many beautiful condolence letters I wasn't able to fully appreciate back then have allowed me to buttress the image of my father with memories of others. I am reminded that my father did not believe in heaven or an afterlife; instead, he always said we live on in the memory of others.

SONYA ON THE IOWA SHOOTING AND MIYA'S RECOVERY

The following was based on a phone interview between Sonya Rodolfo-Sioson, mother of Miya Rodolfo-Sioson, the only survivor of the University of Iowa mass shooting, and Loren Kleinman, editor, on Monday, July 23, 2018.

In August 1991 Miya Sioson returned from Central America. Since I had sold the house where Miya grew up, she emptied the storage space. She and her youngest brother cleaned the house and packed my effects. On August 22 Miya waved goodbye as her brother drove us to her middle brother, graduate student at UC Berkeley. We promised to attend her December graduation.

After shipping my effects, Miya returned to Iowa City. On October 29 I broke into her busy schedule by calling. This Manila native had time to say only that she took the oath of citizenship the previous day.

On Friday, November 1, a police detective rang the doorbell.

"Are you the mother of Miya Rodolfo-Sioson?"

"She doesn't use that name! Why are you asking about her? She is 1,900 miles away!"

"She was injured."

"Road accident?"

"Shot."

"WHAT? They don't shoot people in Iowa!"

I called family members and Miya's friend. Made a reservation on the earliest flight from Oakland, California, to Cedar Rapids, Iowa, the next day. One brother, his wife, and daughter drove through the blizzard, arriving at the University of Iowa Hospitals and Clinics (UIHC) as Miya was wheeled out of surgery.

She mouthed her greetings over the endotracheal tube. The next afternoon my brother drove me from the airport to the ICU. Some Palestinian students were sitting on the hallway floor, eyes red from grief and sleeplessness. Their solidarity: "Miya is our sister," consoled me.

The blinking instrument lights, Miya in a Stryker frame on a rota-bed tilting back and forth, endotracheal tube in her neck, nick on her lower lip, upper face like her dad's, hit me between the eyes. As I reeled, my brother said, "Collect yourself, she can't see you like this."

When I bent over her, she mouthed "Mamma."

"I'm here, sweetie."

The next day her youngest brother was equally shocked.

Miya's friend said she had been a caregiver for a young man whose neck was broken in a wrestling match. His mother paid caregivers from his insurance settlement. In mid-October she gave Miya a bad check before going on holiday. To meet her November rent, Miya applied to Manpower, which placed her in the UIC academic affairs office.

Ironies: Miya was safer in a war-torn area than in the ivory tower of an American university.

On Monday she became a new U.S. citizen; on Friday she became a nearly dead U.S. citizen.

Because she wasn't paid for working with a quad, she became a quad.

After this grand finale of 1991's disaster series, her uncle called the shooting "our personal Pinatubo."

After Miya was upgraded from critical to serious, she was moved to the neurosurgery ward. Since the bullet hit two vertebrae in her neck, her diagnosis was C4-5 quadriplegia; no mobility below the shoulders.

The neurosurgery team coordinated the other services assigned to her care. Whenever the five-member white-coated team entered her room, I greeted them: "Ahoy, a flotilla of neurosurgeons!"

Since Miya could not press the regular call button, a "shrug" button was placed on her shoulder to pinch with her jaw to summon help. Since the button kept slipping, two friends and I took turns on the overnight watch.

The ward had a particularly rancid psychiatric nurse who accused Miya of manipulating us to socialize with her instead of getting her sleep. Her saying this to the least manipulative person on the planet, further saddened Miya and infuriated me into battle mode: I get up every morning to confound our enemies!

I told this virago that, since the ward had no reliable method for Miya to summon help when alone, her people would ensure that help. One night the respirator started to fail. As her blood oxygen fell and carbon dioxide rose, Miya's panicked tongue click sent her watcher scurrying to the nurses' station before calling me at the Union. Livid, I warned the ward staff that, if sloppiness undid the initial care that saved Miya's life, her family would be glad to contact the media to give the university a second black eye!

As Thanksgiving neared, Christoph Goertz's widow Ulrike and daughter Karein stopped in. I reported our conflict with the psychiatric nurse: her care produces psychosis. Indignant, Ulrike volunteered to contact Dean Judith Anderson, who had befriended Ulrike after Christoph's murder. Dean Anderson supervised the medical school and teaching hospital. The next Monday the hospital staff received the Dean's memo: Leave the Sioson family alone!

Our nemesis entered Miya's room, barking, "You went over our heads!"

I smirked, showing a hundred teeth, "No, your attitude motivated Mrs. Goertz to report to her friend Dean Anderson. SHOO!"

Miya accepted the nursing staff's invitation to offer input as they set her care schedule for the week. Shortly the problem of getting her released to rehab came to a head. Her doctors had declared her infection-free, but her costs had to be paid in full. The donations she received fell far short. Manpower and the University remained deadlocked. So, her boyfriend resorted to their activist tactic: Call the media!

Almost overnight, Manpower acknowledged that Miya's being shot at work in a state university qualified her for Iowa's workers' compensation. The insurance arm ordered a Learjet to fly Miya and me to Midway airport. We left on December 9 and caught the ambulance from Midway to the Rehabilitation Institute of Chicago (RIC). Luckily, my brother and his wife's condo was near the L stop opposite the Chicago Circle campus, where they were professors. We deeply appreciate their hosting me during Miya's three-month RIC program, as well as Miya's visiting brothers and Iowa City friends.

SONYA ON GANG LU

Though Lu's family idolized him, he didn't stay in touch. He began to feel that he was bamboozled to sign into the physics program. He wanted to shift to business, to stay in the U.S. to earn dollars instead of returning to China to earn yuan. His counselor's saying that changing his major would lose him the scholarship angered him. Linhua Shan's receiving both the

Spriestersbach Dissertation Prize of $20,000 and the post-doctoral position fueled Lu's rage. All his job applications were fruitless. Lu made a list of administrators and physicists he blamed and applied for a gun permit in May 1991. Johnson County Sheriff Carpenter said that he denied Lu's application because he was not a U.S. citizen. Lu applied to Iowa's Attorney General's office, which issued him the permit to own (not carry), "because he had no criminal record."

After buying the .38 Taurus, this jobless man had all day to spend at the shooting range, aiming at dummies' heads. As the summer passed, he wrote fruitless letters to the University of Iowa grievance officer and the *Des Moines Register*. Fed up, he awaited a Friday-afternoon opportunity to carry out his final act.

On Thursday, October 31, Lu learned that President Hunter Rawlings III would leave the next morning for Columbus, Ohio, for the Hawkeye–Buckeye football game on Saturday, November 2. Vice president of academic affairs Peter Nathan was at a regional meeting. Only the associate vice president of academic affairs/grievance officer Dr. Anne Cleary, Miya's supervisor, was in town. As midnight neared, the frustrated Lu wrote to his elder sister: "By the time you see this letter, I will no longer be in the land of the living. You should not be sad, because I earned the PhD, and I found some companions to accompany me to the grave."

Friday, November 1—a howling blizzard blew into Iowa City. TV news showed whited-out landscape. The weather and the "weekend mode" distracted people on campus, giving Lu the advantage of surprise.

At 3:30 p.m. Christoph Goertz, internationally renowned space-plasma physicist, convened his group's weekly meeting in a conference room in Van Allen Hall. No one reacted when long-time attendee Lu looked in. Goertz, Lu's major professor, sat at the table's head, flanked by Spriestersbach winner/post-doc fellow Linhua Shan and Bob Smith, Lu's PhD committee member. Lu ran downstairs to check on physics chair Dwight Nicholson: at his desk facing the door. GAME!

3:40 p.m.: Lu ran upstairs to the conference room and shot Goertz and Shan in the head. As Smith ducked, Lu hit his shoulder. As people scattered to call the police, Lu ran downstairs and shot Nicholson in the face, then returned to the conference room where Smith moaned, "Someone tried to kill me." Lu administered the coup de grâce to Smith, then shot the dead Goertz and Shan again. Within five minutes he had dispatched some of the world's best plasma-physics researchers! Since Lu's whereabouts were unknown, police urged people including emeritus professor James Van Allen, to lock their doors. As the stopwatch in Lu's head ticked on, he raced to complete his mission before the police arrived. He ran to Jessup Hall, where Dr. Cleary was holding a meeting. Receptionist Miya was proofing a document on the computer. Later, Miya said Lu seemed nervous as he asked for Dr. Cleary. Miya went to her, and she hesitantly preceded Miya to the counter as Miya returned to the computer. Shortly the gunshot pop triggered Miya's reflex to rise as Lu aimed at her forehead and fingered the trigger; the bullet entered her mouth. *Why did he add her to his list? A sudden yen for a female to accompany him to Hades? An extra bullet?* Since Miya had no role in causing his rage, his bullet's producing only paralysis seems fair. He exited as people ran to Dr. Cleary on the floor, hole in forehead. Someone espied Miya slumped on the floor, back against desk leg, mouth bloody. The police found Lu in a conference room, Taurus in hand, blood oozing from his temple, as he expired.

Within twelve minutes Lu ran stairs at Van Allen Hall, killed four victims, ran two blocks and upstairs at Jessup Hall, and shot two people and himself. Dr. Cleary was in a persistent vegetative state, so her brothers pulled the plug, raising the number of corpses to six.

All hail the American way!

SONYA ON LOSS AND LOVE

The flame that burns twice as bright burns half as long.
—Lao Tzu

The year 1968 began with Miya's birth, followed by Iowa State's offer of a full professorship to her father. The previous August my immigrant-U.S. citizen mother had petitioned for a green card for me. We anticipated a bright future, not realizing that the universe was keeping a ledger. Our credit column had received the birth of our only girl, her dad's job, and the processing of my green card. So, the debit column had to receive Miya's Dad's cancer, Miya's intestinal obstruction, and their surgeries. People who receive great joys should be prepared to pay the price: lifelong sorrow.

I hitched my wagon to the star: a man who was my ideal life partner. I never dreamed that a then-unrecognized melanoma would appear after eight years and cause the star to morph into a comet that would zoom into the cosmos at age forty! I hitched another wagon to the star of his look-alike daughter. Due to the gunshot that paralyzed her, she could not fight an aggressive cancer, so she morphed into another comet and zoomed after her father, also at forty!

People ask: *If you could live your life over, would you do it differently?* While I might envy people in long-term happy marriages, healthy children unmarked by gunshots, I cannot imagine trading places with anyone.

Miya's dad touched the lives of many students for whom he unraveled the mysteries of mathematics. Miya touched the lives of many who benefited from her work against injustice: anti-apartheid, rape-crisis center, battered-women's shelter, Central American *campesinos,* and Palestinians under assault in their ancestral lands. Lastly, her role in Berkeley's 1998 Measure E campaign, that won property-tax funding that started in 1999, for the emergency services of Easy Does It. Any disabled person in Berkeley who needs an emergency attendant can call EDI, whose attendants are on standby. We hope this service will shine Miya's light far into the future.

SUDDEN, VIOLENT, AND PUBLIC: INTO THE CRUCIBLE

By Jane Nicholson

On November 1, 1991, Jane Nicholson's husband, Dwight, was shot and killed at the University of Iowa. Dwight was chairman of the physics and astronomy department, and one of Gang Lu's dissertation committee members.

> **DEATH CERTIFICATE:**
> **DWIGHT** *** ********
> **DIED IOWA CITY, IOWA**
> **SINGLE GSW TO HEAD**
> **AGE 44**

Jane, he is dead. He is dead, Jane.

I balked at the repetition. The friend and colleague on the other end of the line was speaking as though he had rehearsed. If this was true, I assumed professionals were at my husband's side. I was filling in all the blanks of this improbable story line.

This colleague said something about Dwight's having been *shot.* Somehow, despite how preposterous that was, I knew, knew, knew that it was accurate ... *accurate as an outcome for high school sweethearts, undergraduate lovers, twenty-two-years marrieds? For the pacifist and physicist who had not accepted funding from the Department of Defense?* No, never, not at all— and yet you don't get a call like that from a colleague like that unless things are out of order. Yes, it mattered to me that I knew that man, that he considered my husband a dear friend.

I realized his tone was utterly different—because of the message, because of the task of delivering it. Yet it was him through and through, ending the call with the repeated phrase: *You must call a friend now, as soon as we hang up. Call a friend, Jane, right now.*

Dwight and I could've figured right from the start that schooling would be a basis of who we were. We met in high school. I strolled into the homeroom we shared till graduation. I was not thrilled to be a new girl. I can't think how I didn't jump out of the family Buick as my father drove out of Beloit for Racine. As it happened, two months into year two, the boy in homeroom asked me out. That's when I really met him, a boy who didn't come from the same sort of place I had but would take a chance on a guarded new girl.

Where you come from makes quite a difference in schooling worlds. I learned that by being the new girl in a larger, more class-conscious high school. I might have guessed he, too, was an outsider because he presented himself as different. My odd and powerful attraction to him was my unique desire in that new place and it was elemental. You see he was muscular, and he wore his hair in a way that had no name that I knew of. I didn't yet know that he was an outsider because he was bussed in from his rural home. As a student who had attended two large urban high schools, I couldn't fathom this. *What?* The buses really whisked them off directly after school so that they never attended or participated in after-school activities!? I learned that his circle of friends existed outside our high school, a group from his earlier school days. Maybe some of them also wore their hair in a flattop with fenders rather than the more usual rural buzz cut.

Undergraduate days taught us other lessons in pecking order; there were so many students from New York City at Wisconsin.

Madison enjoyed a great reputation and was less expensive for out-of-state students than Ann Arbor. The two of us marveled at the cosmopolitan views and academic advantages of our East Coast friends. We just had more to learn, that's all. We called it our edge—we were only laughing at ourselves.

When we headed to the University of Iowa, we were both new kids on the block, with high stakes—for him in a tenure-track position in physics and for me in the program in comparative literature PhD studies. We were intrigued and enthused about Iowa City. We bought our first house, a modest place. It sat on a heavily wooded ridge and across the street, our neighbors all had properties that dropped off, too, and the terrain did not level off until it hit the floodplain for the Iowa River. If our campus, that straddled the Iowa River, could represent the quintessential Midwestern campus, then our place similarly called to mind the proverbial serene neighborhood.

On that same campus, gunfire from a .38 Taurus semiautomatic pistol rang through Van Allen Hall where a dedicated and respected faculty, student corps, and staff pursued or supported the study, experimentation, or theoretical exploration of physics. Physics explains the universe and its workings and has a philosophical side to it although physicists are all mathematicians to a degree. You understand why his colleagues would say about their department in Van Allen Hall, anywhere but here. You comprehend that their understanding of the beauty of the world's workings was torqued and so were their beings. And one of them called me at about 4:00 p.m. on November 1, 1991.

What happened after the shootings, beyond the detectives and record-keepers, which come into most homicides, was unique to an educational institution. Whether an elementary school or a high school or university, these are institutions that house a meaningful number of people who have roles, goals, and shared expectations—and preparedness for various endeavors. Yet the size of a Big Ten university campus makes a small city unto itself. That large body makes a self-regulating community which is prepared many times over to serve its members' needs. However, crises do not allow for preparation. Imagine the intrinsic capacity for mass disruption in an ordered place with common purpose; gunfire is amplified, ringing through ears, halls, media. This orderliness had placed people in the right place, right time—knowledge that offers to an insider his possible human targets.

These institutions are made up of sizeable buildings that resemble a maze—for a shooter to follow or to get lost in. These institutions also are home to halls and auditoriums that can be turned to the purpose of memorial services. At Iowa, the disproportionate shock waves that rocked the campus and town, launched many public memorial services. These answered needs to do right by those killed and their survivors, the desire to show that "this" was not who we are, and the outright desperation to take stock of who was left. Eyes locked and arms reached out.

But who were the dozens of people who sprang into action by mobilizing equipment and space for people to mourn in large numbers? It comes to me just now, a jogging of the memory, that I have met a few of them and in very disparate circumstances so that I had to work a piece into a fuzzy puzzle. And in the moment of meeting them, I felt their readiness and availability. The presence of each of them was solid and unswerving. Could my gratitude all these months and years later strike a chord?

I have mentioned that it matters in schooling where you come from. In one sense, it means your academic records and experiences, but also where you call home and what that place offered. Although information is gathered by institutions, it just lays there. Despite the records, academe is unlikely to foster foreign students as it should; the welcoming campus does likely not know how much preparation any student is given before heading there. I, too, was a foreign student and though in a place not so strange, remember horrendous headaches from concentrating on how my hosts did things. Later, I viewed a film that counseled foreign students to the U.S. always to leave a dime near the coffee cup—a pedestrian but revelatory clue to larger scenes unfolding awkwardly in a new life. I had witnessed a foreign student do just that when much more would have been an appropriate tip. *Why this lapse? Do we mistakenly feel that Americanness is fully available everywhere through pop culture and increasingly so with ubiquitous webs of media—though access to these is not democratic?*

There's unimaginable propinquity at work in the Chinese graduate student meeting the professor from Wisconsin: both were farm boys and each likely already knew how much it matters where you come from in schooling. There is likeness here, but not equivalence. Knowing that gun violence strikes virtually every community, I know that this propinquity, too, is not an equivalence: some murders are hardly investigated and others receive the disproportionate amount of publicity. This is unjust and unsettling as both too little scrutiny and too much of it are intolerable.

My resistance to hearing his story, our story told by others led me to want to know people in their own words. I have spent nearly two decades in peace or talking circles, in universities, high schools, and community centers. Each person tells the story they need to tell and want others to hear. Each of us claims the moral authority to speak for ourselves. "A family of strangers," one student declared—a young man who hadn't dared to speak on day one. I've sat with joy and sorrow, with those who've lost someone and those who have taken life. Each circle values safe listening and telling and honest connection. In circle, it matters who we are; it matters where we say we've come from. As little of an idealist as I am, I assert that I can live with what has happened and this in part by granting some symbolic immortality to my beloved together with others and their beloveds. A bullet makes a straight-line trajectory, grief makes a circle.

COWBOY JUSTICE

By Mary Allen

Mary Allen was working in Van Allen Hall at the time of the shooting, where the physics department is housed. She was an editorial assistant to Christoph Goertz, editor of the *Journal of Geophysical Research*.

It's November 1, 1991, Friday afternoon, the day after Halloween. I'm sitting alone in an office on the fifth floor of Van Allen Hall, where the Physics Department at the University of Iowa is housed, when I hear a loud noise on a floor below: **POP POP POP.** What I heard must've been a staple gun. There must be construction somewhere. This seems plausible, especially because after the **POP POP POP** I hear what sounds like heavy furniture being rearranged. Later I'll learn this was the sound of people scrambling to get under desks, shoving tables aside, and rushing out the door.

But at the moment I don't have a clue what's going on and I sit there at my desk and continue working, printing out labels for envelopes and folding a pile of letters signed by my boss, Christoph Goertz, editor of the *Journal of Geophysical Research*, before he left for the Friday afternoon theoretical space physics meeting downstairs where he has just been shot along with two other people. When I finish sealing the envelopes, I go down a long dark hallway to the bathroom where I stare at myself in the mirror, then stop at the water fountain outside the bathroom door and fill a little plastic tube with a removable pink sponge on the end, which I plan to use to seal the envelopes.

As I'm wandering back down the hall to my office a young woman, a secretary I know, appears at the top of the stairs and says, **"DWIGHT'S BEEN SHOT! HE'S DEAD."**

Dwight Nicholson is the chairman of the physics department, who, I will later learn, was shot in the back by the gunman while he was working at his desk facing the wall. The gunman was Gang Lu, a recent PhD recipient angry his thesis didn't get an award he thought would increase his chances of getting a job, and not having to return to post–Tiananmen Square China. After he killed Dwight, he went back up upstairs to the meeting room where a few minutes earlier he shot Chris Goertz and two other people: Bob Smith, another professor, and Linhua Chan, the young man who won the award. Chris and Chan died immediately—Chris was the first victim, shot in the head at close range at the front of the room; in the first few seconds, before reality sank in, some people thought it was a Halloween prank—but Bob Smith was only wounded.

Two men were kneeling on the floor beside Bob when the gunman came back. Gang Lu told them to leave the room and then he shot Bob again, finishing the job. Then he left the building, walked over to the university administration building and killed Anne Cleary, the university's grievance officer, who did not respond favorably to his complaints. He also shot Miya Rodolfo-Sioson, a first-day temp worker who got in the way. She was an activist, a dancer, a beautiful spirit, as we learned later, the only survivor and Gang Lu's only impromptu victim. She spent the rest of her life in a wheelchair, paralyzed from the neck down. Afterward Gang Lu found an empty schoolroom on the second floor, took off his tan jacket and folded it neatly over the back of a chair, and shot himself in the head.

I go back to my office and call my friend J., who shares this job with me. Her line is busy, so I hang up and sit there wondering what to do. There is nothing to do, so I keep working, sealing the envelopes containing the letters that will never be sent. I'm confused instead of scared. I'm too confused to be scared. I don't close the door. I don't do anything about the fact there could be a murderer somewhere in the building. I seal a few more envelopes, then I get up and stand in the doorway, looking down the hall. I see a Chinese student with a backpack emerge from the stairwell and I run back into my office. Nothing happens. I try to call J. again. This time she answers, and I tell her that Dwight's been shot and he's dead. She's shocked and stunned. We don't even know yet that there are other victims, people we work with directly; she knows them better than I do—I was hired four months ago but she's been working here for years—one of them is our boss. She tells me to close the door of the office.

But soon, someone comes running down the hall, pounding on doors and yelling, "Everyone get out of the building! They're evacuating the building!"

I go all around the room, turning off the postal meter, the Xerox machine, the computer, the printer. My hands are shaking so hard I can hardly press the buttons, and that's when I realize, the first time I realize, how scared I am. I walk down the long dark fifth-floor hallway to the elevator. All the doors are closed and I don't see anyone, there's no one to share this terrifying moment with. I hold my breath in the elevator, all the way to the first floor, worrying it will stop and a graduate student with a backpack full of guns will get on. That doesn't happen. On the first floor I see flashing lights beyond the exit and policemen by the door waving guns and shouting, *Everyone out! Out of the building!*

It's snowing outside, large white flakes whirling madly in the air. I don't have a car, and during my entire twenty-minute walk home, up a long straight sloping tree-lined street, I feel like a murderer is following me.

I go to J's house. News drifts in over the radio about the shooting. The ten o'clock news confirms five people are dead and someone was wounded but is still alive. They announce the victims. The first face that appears on the screen is Chris Goertz's face.

The aftermath is more or less predictable. There are memorial services, articles in the paper and then editorials, the whole community grieves. Everybody talks about where they were when the shooting happened. Things come out about Gang Lu. He bought his gun at Fin and Feather and target practiced for months. He wrote a long rambly letter to his sister in China, single-spaced on white typing paper, and mailed it the day of the shooting. It was intercepted by the authorities at the Iowa City post office; it says he'll be quantum leaping through the universe and tells his sister not to be sad for him because he's going to take a few traveling companions with him to the grave. On an old Greyhound-bus-ticket envelope the police found in his apartment, he had scrawled, "Cowboy justice is the only action against corporate crime."

People continue speculating about why this happened. There's talk in some circles about how hard life is for graduate students, suggesting that Gang Lu was pushed to his limits by the pressures of academia. A group of us forms to take action on gun control and we meet for about a year. In 2009, a movie is made loosely based on the story; it shifts the onus of the bad guy onto the graduate adviser Chris Goertz character and casts the Gang Lu character in the role of the underdog.

The whole story is rife with misunderstandings. Gang Lu thought Chris ignored his thesis in favor of Linhua Shan's: Chris actually recommended both theses for the award and an outside award committee made the choice. Gang Lu told the grievance officer, Anne Cleary, that the UI space physics group had unfairly passed him over for the award; Anne Cleary didn't do anything because Chris reported that Gang Lu had been recommended for the award.

I learned the truth is subject to shape-shifting and misinterpretation, that the farther you are from a public event the more mythical proportions it assumes, that popular mythology—the illusion of cowboy justice, for instance—can be deadly, that there is no rational reason for murder.

CHAPTER TWENTY

CLEVELAND ELEMENTARY SCHOOL

Stockton, California / January 17, 1989

FIVE CHILDREN BETWEEN the ages of six and nine were killed in the Stockton schoolyard in under five minutes. *These were the children of refugees,* Julia Schardt, a second-grade teacher at the time of the Cleveland Elementary School shooting, told me on June 5, 2018. *Their parents came here from Cambodia and Vietnam to escape persecution only to have their children murdered in America.*

When Julia submitted her essay, I was fixated on the red shoes. I reread the lines *Oeun loves jump rope. So close to the door. The police officer uncovers the little girl and I look at a still, beautiful little face marred by blood from a wound to her head. I see the red shoes she loved to wear.* I see them, too. When I go shopping. On random people's feet in the city. I see them walking alone on the side street where I walk my pup. These shoes fill my mind. They come for me in the night, before bed, at early rise.

Oeun . . .

I never knew beautiful little Oeun Lim. But I know she is still eight years old, wherever she is. She is there with her skipping rope in her red shoes. No blood on her face. No holes. No pain. Whole, again. Returned. The children Julia describes in her essay are not silent, anymore. They laugh. Play hand slaps. Run. They continue to play through the bullets. They don't fall. Instead, they jump rope. Cheer each other on. Rathanar, Ram, Sokhim, Oeun, and Thuy. All their smiles lighting up the sandy schoolyard. I pray for this after hearing, reading, and rereading Julia's story.

Loren Kleinman, Editor
September 2018

**The following students were shot and killed at
Cleveland Elementary School:**

Sokhim An, 6

Ram Chun, 8

Oeun Lim, 8

Rathanar Or, 9

Thuy Tran, 6

THE RED SHOES
By Julia Schardt

Julia Schardt was a second-grade teacher at the time of the shooting.

JANUARY 17, 1989

On a mild winter day the quick, sharp sound of firecrackers broke the quiet of my classroom. It was recess for my second grade students. Ordinary because the routine of teaching can make some minutes ordinary. The firecrackers made it unusual.

Then it became extraordinary because the sound breaking the silence was not firecrackers. It was gunshots. Distant but loud, sharp, shredding the peace of my classroom.

CHANDRA

Chandra had a cold, and her mother didn't want her to be outside. She was sitting in the quiet of my classroom, reading a book. The gunshots were on the playground where my other twenty-eight students were jumping rope and playing tetherball or kickball. I grabbed Chandra's hand to rush her out the back door of my classroom, to where it should be safe.

Her mother didn't want her outside.

And where are my other students?

We stayed inside.

There was complete silence after the shooting stopped. Was it five minutes? Ten minutes? Longer?

Children began filing in from the playground in a single-file line, just as they would on any ordinary day, walking behind or beside me. I wasn't there to lead them, but they came in quietly, silently, unable to process what had just happened. Their safe place was the classroom. What must I have looked like to them? What did my eyes say?

I met them at the door, and they came in and sat down

VANN

Vann is a class leader. Such confidence, intelligence, charm, wit . . . So much promise. He's the last one to walk into the classroom, and he says nothing.

Another child says, "Teacher, Oeun is dead."

Vann still says nothing.

I say, "We don't know that," honestly believing that an eight-year-old announcing another child's murder can't happen. The murder can't happen. A child can't be telling me this.

I don't want them to think about this.

They all sit down on the floor around my chair. This is the routine whenever we come in from recess.

I take roll and two of my students haven't come back from recess.

I look at the faces of my second graders after they've seen their friends mowed down by bullets and all I can think about doing is reading a story.

They say nothing. They look. They trust me to do what's right, and I read them a story.

And Vann still says nothing.

I pick up *Two Bad Ants* by Chris Van Allsburg, which they always ask to hear. I'm a fan of Chris Van Allsburg, so they are as well. He writes with the kind of imagination I want my students to feel free to express. What can they imagine after this?

MALINN

The children are quiet, but in a way, I've never seen them. Their faces are almost expressionless, there's no squirming. I look for any kind of expression, for any typical wiggling or movement from them, but there's nothing. Their eyes are all on me. What must I look like to them? What do my eyes say? I wonder where my two students are, but they must know.

Our principal's voice comes over the intercom to ask if all my students are in the classroom.

I have to say that two of my students are not in the classroom. I didn't know that other teachers are having to say the same thing, that not all of their students have come back from recess. Thirty-five students and a teacher have not come back into the school building from recess.

Then, "Teacher, Malinn is bleeding." A little boy is pointing at Malinn's backside.

Malinn is bright, adorable, charming, sitting in absolute silence. She's been hit by shrapnel from the bullets that broke the innocent silence of our school on that mild winter day.

The reality of this day begins to cast its cold, quiet horror on me.

Malinn is bleeding, but only a little and she's carried up to the office by my classroom aide.

I don't remember the sounds of the sirens or the helicopters, but they came.

OEUN

A fireman walks into my classroom, and I think he's ill. The color has drained from his face, and he is sweating. I want to offer him a place to sit down or a glass of water.

But he is there to check on us, my students and me.

He has been on the playground, bringing the sound of the sirens I didn't hear.

When he leaves, we go back to the book.

Someone's voice comes over the intercom telling the teachers to walk our students up the inside hallways to the multipurpose room.

My students line up in silence, an extraordinary silence that is cold and surreal. The hallway carpet is splattered with blood but no one says anything. We step outside to the short walkway between the classroom building and the multipurpose room where—dozens, hundreds?—of parents are waiting to find their children in the lines making their way from the safety of the classrooms to the large open meeting place where they can unite with their children.

Unless they can't.

We have roll sheets, and one by one we let stunned, silent children and their frantic parents meet in relief.

Unless we can't.

My principal pulls me aside and says she needs to speak to me.

She needs me to come onto the playground to identify my student whose name is not on the list of thirty children given over to the sirens to be taken to a hospital.

Oeun's name is not one of the thirty.

Oeun's name is one of the five.

We step outside, my principal and me, only the two of us. The sun is shining, harsh and unreal in the cold.

The playground an hour ago was full of beautiful, busy, noisy, playful children. Now there is only a police officer to meet us as we take the long walk toward my part of the building. The tetherballs are still, there is no sound other than our steps.

The principal tells me only that I must look at a child lying on the playground, and I must say whether or not she is Oeun, my student. The principal holds my hand and I see a small, almost shapeless form covered in a blanket on the blacktop near the tetherball and close to the door into our part of the building. This is the space where my students play jump rope. Oeun loves jump rope. So close to the door.

The police officer uncovers the little girl and I look at a still, beautiful little face marred by blood from a wound to her head. I see the red shoes she loved to wear. And I say I'm not sure it's my student, Oeun. I can't bring myself to make the final call about this loss, but I know it's Oeun.

My friend who is Oeun's reading teacher must come help and we know it's Oeun.

The walk back to the room where some of my children are still waiting, where some of the parents are still waiting, is long and cold and I must walk by myself.

TOKLA

Tokla is a quiet, studious little girl. She doesn't come into my classroom from recess. She lies bleeding on the playground where a bullet shattered her leg at the hip. An ambulance takes her to a hospital forty miles away. She is one of the thirty, plus a teacher, who don't come back into classrooms that day.

ROBBY

Robby is a first grader, and he is one of my son's best friends. They climb, run, ride bikes, make up games. Robby lies on the playground with a bullet wound in his left foot and a round in his chest. He is carried inside by a teacher and almost dies before an ambulance takes him to a hospital nearby.

MIKE AND RATHANA

Mike is a third grader who runs to his classroom door when the shooting starts. By the time he gets there, the door is locked because the teacher fears the shooter will come into the building. Mike is uninjured and watches as Rathana, his playmate and family friend falls to the ground. Rathana doesn't come back from recess, and he isn't taken away in an ambulance. His teacher must identify his body on the playground.

AMY

Amy is in sixth grade. The older students are in their classrooms waiting for their lunchtime to start when the sound of the firecrackers become the sound of bullets for them. Amy's classroom is a portable building with a window facing the playground. She and her classmates see the shooter use his weapon to spray bullets back and forth across the playground. The bullets hit tetherball poles, leaving holes, or ricocheting back toward the playground. The bullets go through the school building, causing a flurry of cottony soundproofing from the portable walls to float in the kindergarten classrooms.

The bullets go through children. Amy and her classmates watch as the bullets explode through children.

Amy and her classmates watch as the shooter puts a bullet through his own head.

After the shooting stops, Amy's teacher lines up her students to walk them to the multipurpose room to be reunited with their parents. Amy grabs a pair of art scissors to take as protection because she's not sure there's a safe place waiting for her. She's left-handed and worries because the scissors she picks up are right-handed scissors. Can she make them work if she needs protection?

We learn the shooter hated our population of Southeast Asian children and specifically targeted our school. We learn that five of our children are killed—two first graders, a second grader, and two third graders. Thirty others are wounded. A teacher on the playground trying to protect the children was wounded.

We learn much later the survivors will carry the awful memory of this day for the rest of their lives. We also learn we can find ways to live and raise families and be with friends, although it doesn't come easily for some of us.

VANN

The confident, intelligent, charming class leader came to school the day after the shooting, as we all did, except for those who couldn't. He said then, and he said many more times throughout the school year that he should have helped the children who were killed. He should have gotten them inside to safety. He felt the burden of true leadership and he was only eight years old. The promising young leader became an alcoholic and can't keep a job.

MALINN, ROBBY, MIKE, AMY

Malinn's family moved away from Stockton to Southern California. When her older sister graduated from the University of the Pacific (Stockton), Malinn could not bring herself to return to the town where she was wounded and where she saw her classmates and playmates die. Malinn was able to come back twenty-five years later to visit the school site and her classroom, but it was an uneasy visit for her. She is still the bright, charming person she was as a second grader and has a successful career as a writer and fashion blogger.

Robby stayed in Stockton, and although he recovered from the bullet wounds, he still carries the round that entered his chest. He is a police officer for a local school district and an inspirational leader for youth, including his two children.

Mike is still seared by the memory of the murder of his friend, Rathana. It informs his work as a senior program director of the YMCA, and as the father of three sons.

The weight of the memory of the shooting still weighs heavily on Amy, but she is stronger than the challenges and hurdles life has sent her way. As the mother of two teenagers and two toddlers, she finds time to take care of other family members as well.

Chandra and Tokla have slipped away to other places, to live and raise families and be with friends. To me they are still little girls who like to read or play jump rope.

Like Oeun. I don't think about who she might have become or what she might have given to all of us. That is too painful.

Instead, Oeun is forever an eight-year-old little girl, jumping rope, wearing red shoes.

CHAPTER TWENTY-ONE

UNIVERSITY OF TEXAS AT AUSTIN

Austin, Texas / August 1, 1966

WHILE PHOTOGRAPHING THE *[Tower shooting] I was so intent on finding and recording it that I wasn't really feeling anything,* survivor Kent Kirkley told me through text message. But he admits that after he put down the camera for the day, the enormity of what had happened settled in: *after Whitman was killed and the "all clear" was sounded and people emptied out of the buildings and ambulances [which at the time were hearses from the funeral homes] pulled up to remove the dead, the enormity of what happened began to dawn on me.*

The University of Texas at Austin was considered one of America's most horrific public shootings. *This was 1966 before there were any police SWAT teams or EMS units. Nobody had mobile phones, there was no Internet, no way to contact anyone about the situation in front of us. If anything was going to be done, it was us that had to do it,* wrote John Fox (a.k.a. Artly Snuff) who was seventeen when he took his first college semester at the University of Texas at Austin. But he and his fellow classmates were afraid of going out to help, thereby exposing themselves to gunfire. And this is something that John recalled to me in our first phone call.

In our conversation, John remembered the bodies piling up, including one of a pregnant woman, Claire Wilson. *I could see her twitching, and I knew if I didn't move, she might get shot again. But I knew.* John paused. *I knew if I went out there to help, I could be shot too.* But John took one of the biggest risks of his life and ran out from his sheltered space to take Claire out of the line of fire. Claire did survive, but her unborn child did not, and neither did her boyfriend.

As of today, January 18, 2019, it's been fifty-two years and five months since Charles Whitman killed fifteen people from atop the Clock Tower at the University of Texas. But the impact of that day remains. *I still feel guilty*, John told me. *I feel like I could've done more. I could've helped more people. I feel I was*

430

a coward. That day is always with me in my mind. Every day. But I know now that I did the best I could, but there is always a worm of doubt.

Though the biggest takeaway from John and Kent is the power of voice. John continues to write in his essay that *today, when there is a mass shooting, there are a flood of therapists available to talk with the victims. Nothing like that existed in 1966. Nobody knew how to mentally process such horror. I didn't talk about it much for decades. I now know I should have.*

By watching survivors today speaking about their guilt, known as survivor's guilt, has helped survivors like Kent and John to fight their own trauma. John adds in his essay that learning about the term *has helped me fight the loneliness that accompanied my trauma.* But he asks an important question, despite the legacy such trauma leaves in its aftermath, *when will it stop?* This question is being answered every day through marches and survivor support groups, and through personal stories and eyewitness accounts, through sharing the stories of what it's like to live as a survivor of gun violence. Texas proves that *time doesn't heal all wounds*, and how important it is to share our stories of grief in order to begin the long, painful, and often hopeful journey of healing.

Loren Kleinman, Editor
January 2019

**The following students, staff, first responders,
and Tower visitors were shot and killed at
the University of Texas at Austin:**

Thomas Aquinas Ashton, 22, Peace Corps volunteer

Robert Hamilton Boyer, 33, mathematician

Thomas Frederick Eckman, 18, student

Martin (Mark) Gabour, 16, high school student

Karen Griffith, 17, high school student

David Hubert Gunby, 23, student*

Thomas Ray Karr, 24, student

Marguerite Lamport, 45, aunt of Martin Gabour

Claudia Rutt, 18, student

Roy Dell Schmidt, 29, electrician

Paul Bolton Sonntag, 18, student

Billy Paul Speed, 24, police officer

Edna Elizabeth Townsley, 51, observation deck receptionist

Harry Walchuk, 38, PhD student

Baby Wilson, unborn child of Claire Wilson

*Gunby was initially shot at age 23 and survived a surgery to repair his damaged intestine. However, during surgery, doctors discovered that Gunby had one functioning kidney. The gunshot wound damaged this one working kidney, and as a result he received dialysis, which he eventually stopped. He died in 2001 after stopping dialysis. His death is ruled a homicide.

THAT DAY ON AUGUST 1, 1966
By Kent Kirkley

Kent Kirkley was on campus at the time of the Tower shooting at the University of Texas at Austin. At nineteen years old, Kent ran toward the campus and Tower, his 400mm telephoto lens capturing Charles Whitman's destruction both during and in the aftermath of the shooting.

I was born and raised in Austin, Texas. I was artistic, which I attribute to my great grandmother.

In the sixth grade, I won a contest to draw the Austin Symphony program cover. The prize was oil-painting classes at the University of Texas (UT) on Saturdays. I was also beginning to play with photography. I got interested in astronomy and built three telescopes and adapted my father's camera to take photographs through them. I set up a makeshift darkroom in one half of my closet. In junior high, I became more interested in science, entering and winning awards at science fairs. I took a photograph of the asteroid Vesta and submitted it to *Sky and Telescope* magazine, which accepted and printed it. I was fourteen. And in junior high I was on the paper and the annual photographer. I got to use an early electronic flash unit. It was so different from flashbulbs that I'd flash it while walking down the halls and earned the nickname of "Flash."

Kent Kirkley, age thirteen, with his father Ralph Kirkley in
1960. © Kent Kirkley 2019

There was never any doubt I'd go to UT, and I started the fall
of 1965 with the intention of becoming an astronomer. I also
began working in the photography department of the University
Co-Op, which was the primary store for books and school supplies. After my freshman year, I continued to work at the Co-Op
the following summer.

That Monday, August 1, 1966, was much like any other Texas
summer morning, hot. I drove my 1956 Thunderbird down 19th
Street (Now Martin Luther King Blvd) turned up San Antonio
Street, and parked not far from the Co-Op.

A photograph of Kent Kirkley taken a few days before the UT shooting.
© Kent Kirkley 2019

The camera department was located on the second level to the left of the stairs. About ten minutes before noon a guy came up the stairs and toward the counter. He says, "someone's been shot outside." Incredulously, I responded, "and what have you been smoking?" He repeated himself, and I walked halfway down the stairs to a landing. Through the windows, I could see people crouched behind cars parked on Guadalupe and someone lying on the grass of the West Mall. I quickly retrieved my new Nikon F camera and "borrowed" a 400mm lens from the display case. I grabbed several rolls of High Speed Ektachrome film and made my way down the employee stairs.

This was the first image Kent Kirkley took at 12:15
p.m., not showing the observation deck.
© Kent Kirkley 2019

Thinking that going out the front doors would be a bad idea, I went out the loading dock door into the alley behind the store. I had no idea where the shooting was coming from. I walked across the Hemphill Bookstore parking lot behind the Co-Op toward San Antonio Street. At first, I couldn't see the UT Tower as the Co-Op blocked its view, but I could hear gunshots.

Eventually, I got to a point where the Tower began to emerge above the building, and I saw a puff of smoke near the observation deck. I realized the shooter was shooting from the observation deck and that if I could see him, he could see me, and I retreated into the "shadow" of the building. I took a chance and backed up again, exposing the first of several frames timed with the puffs of smoke. Still in the shadow of the buildings, I made my way north down the alley toward 23rd Street. At the corner, I peeked around the corner toward Guadalupe Street. also referred to as "the drag" to see an ambulance speeding down the street.

Kent took this photo at 12:45 p.m. Charles Whitman's (UT Shooter) gun barrel can be seen on the ledge. © Kent Kirkley 2019

Looking west on 23rd Street, I noticed a parked car with two young men crouching behind it. Two co-eds were walking past the car unaware of the men who suddenly jumped out and pulled them behind the vehicle. At almost the same time I saw a bullet strike the pavement near the car, kicking up asphalt. I realized, this was serious.

How to get closer and on campus?

I reversed direction and walked south down the alley passing the Co-Op's dock door. In about a hundred yards was a slim passageway between two buildings. I took it, then proceeded to the sidewalk on the drag. Glancing toward the Tower I couldn't see it as the architecture building blocked its view. I sprinted across the street onto the campus as fast as I could. I walked toward the Inner Campus Drive taking a few photographs of the Tower as it presented itself above the buildings. I was still hearing sporadic gunshots but couldn't tell where they were coming from. A couple of ambulances entered Inner Campus Drive and I photographed their approach. Looking east toward the South Mall, I could see small groups of people hugging the wall beneath where the Jefferson Davis statue was located (it was removed in 2017).

Kirkley took this photo at 1:05 p.m. Smoke or dust from Charles Whitman or local riflemen firing back. © Kent Kirkley 2019

As I approached that area, I could see a body covered in a bloody white sheet. I took a few frames of it. At this point I felt I could go no farther without exposing myself to the sniper as the South Mall and its steps were wide open. More gunfire and I risked a glance up at the Tower, its clock showing close to 1:20.

More gunfire, but it was slackening. Soon, I saw a few people tentatively emerging from the building across the mall and the one behind me. Someone yelled out that the sniper had been killed. It was about 1:35 p.m. More doors opened and people streamed out onto the sidewalks and up the stairs to the paved South Mall.

The covered body of Austin police officer Billy Speed who was killed at the stairway of the South Mall. © Kent Kirkley 2019

I followed and took a few frames of the Tower after ascending the stairs.

By this time there were probably a thousand people on the mall milling around with somber if not horrified faces. I took a few photographs of them. Ambulances pulled up and opened their rear doors. Austin police were there still holding their shotguns. I photographed them, too. After a while, I could see the crowd parted by several men carrying a gurney. On it was a body covered by a bloodied white sheet. Several were carried out to the ambulances. I photographed them.

Kent Kirkley photographed this image about 2 p.m. after Charles Whitman
had been killed and bodies were being removed from the UT Tower.
© Kent Kirkley 2019

Now between 2:30 and 3:00 p.m. I felt I needed to return to the Co-Op and work. I shot some more images of the Tower clock with its bullet-pockmarked face. Crossing Guadalupe, I saw a group of people standing in front of Sheftall's Jewelry store on the other side of the Co-Op. I could see bullet holes in their window and blood on the sidewalk in front of the door. I quickly went up to the camera department and exchanged the telephoto for my 50mm normal lens and returned to Sheftall's and photographed the window and bloodstained sidewalk. I clocked back in and was informed that my father had called asking where I was. They told him I was out photographing. I called my parents back and assured them I was all right.

The front window of Sheftall's Jewelry Store, next door to the Co-Op.
These bullet holes were used by photographer Shel Hershorn for his
Life Magazine cover of the tragedy. © Kent Kirkley 2019

The front door of Sheftall's Jewelry store next door
to the Co-Op. © Kent Kirkley 2019

About 4:00 p.m. I got a call from *Life Magazine*. They'd heard I had photographed the incident and wanted the images. I explained that I had shot color transparency film and wanted to have it processed and see what I had before sending it. He said they couldn't wait because of the production schedule and needed the film sent that night. Again, I explained but we couldn't agree.

Close to 5:00 p.m. I got another call, this time from *Paris Match* magazine and they requested the same thing but had more time. I wrote down the necessary contact information and what they were going to pay. Very little work was accomplished the rest of the afternoon. There was a constant buzz from customers and employees. The rolls of Kodak High Speed Ektachrome were shipped to Kodak in Dallas that evening.

Before work the next morning, I went back to the campus and photographed whatever was happening and evidence of what had happened. This included reporters, the curious, and bullet marks. The processed film was returned, and I was pleased with the images. That afternoon, I shipped the little yellow boxes to *Paris Match*. I didn't hear much from the magazine except that they had received the film. Several weeks later I received a check in the mail and the slides were returned a few weeks after that, each one labeled in French, "Kirkley crime d' Austin."

The afternoon of the shooting and the next morning campus was swarming with news reporters from all over the country. © Kent Kirkley 2019

Some of Kent Kirkley's UT Sniper slides on a light box. © Kent Kirkley 2019

During the shooting, I was focused on photographing who-ever was shooting. I didn't know anything about who or why or the killed or injured.

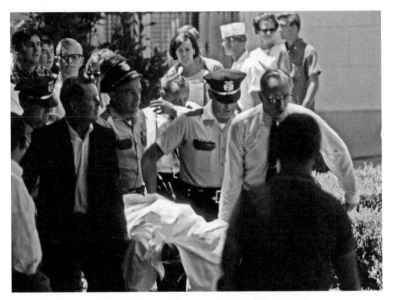

Removing the dead. © Kent Kirkley 2019

I had seen images by Robert Capa, David Douglas Duncan, Joe Rosenthal, W. Eugene Smith, and other war photographers, and perhaps they influenced me. I know that might label me as insensitive but that wasn't the case. I realized the gravity of that day when I saw the two co-eds get pulled behind the parked car and Whitman's bullet strike the pavement, and when I saw the covered body of the dead police officer. When the bodies were being removed from the Tower, that was an *OMG* moment. That evening after listening to the news the magnitude of what hap-pened descended on me. I was astonished at how accurate Whitman had been and how far away he had hit people. Hearing the list of the wounded and killed was tough. Although I didn't personally know any of them, I did know of a few.

Fiftieth Anniversary "Reading of the Names." © Kent Kirkley 2019

I never experienced anything like PTSD or had bad dreams.

I think this was because it was such an isolated incident. To my knowledge it had never happened before and probably wouldn't happen again.

How wrong I was.

The "new" memorial to the victims of the UT Sniper shooting.
Photograph provided by the author. © Kent Kirkley 2019

View of the University of Texas at Austin campus grounds from the top of the Tower, AR.2000.002(002), Austin History Center, Austin Public Library.

Bullet impressions in the Tower, PICA 37424,
Austin History Center, Austin Public Library.

AND SO IT BEGAN
By Monte Akers and Nathan Akers

Monte Akers was sixteen and living in the Texas Panhandle at the time of the UT Tower shooting. He is the coauthor of *Tower Sniper: The Terror of America's First Active Shooter on Campus.*

There are many firsts in a person's life, and in that of a nation. Some are milestones to be celebrated, and others are hung with black crepe. For the United States of America, the school shooting that occurred on August 1, 1966, in Austin, Texas, was definitely the latter.

Because it was the first of its kind, because of various unique features, and because a few decades would pass before mass school shootings became painfully commonplace, the University of Texas Tower shooting by Charles Whitman imprinted on the American psyche as a singular, highly unusual, even interesting event. Today mass school shootings have become so frequent and common that people have trouble remembering their chronology, their details, and the names of those involved. Not so regarding the "Tower sniper."

It is not accurate, however, to describe the Austin event as the first American "school shooting." As early as 1840 there was a shooting on a campus—The University of Virginia—in which a student shot and killed a professor. Dozens more killings occurred at American schools over the next 125 years, but each was more in the nature of a murder than a mass shooting. In 1898 in Charleston, West Virginia, six people were killed when the equivalent of a riot broke out during a student performance at a local school. Four of the victims were killed by gunfire and another was wounded, but the deaths were not the result of a lone gunman targeting anyone who ambled into his gunsights. On February 2, 1960, the principal of a school in Hartford City, Indiana, shot and killed two teachers in their classrooms, then fled to nearby woods and killed himself. However, the death toll from such school shootings never surpassed that from 1898 until August 1, 1966, when the body count reached a shocking seventeen.

And if such tragedies are to be measured only by the number of deaths at a school location, one must include what happened at Bath, Michigan, on May 18, 1927, when a farmer who was unhappy about the amount of property taxes, he had to pay used a bomb to kill forty-five people at a rural school, including thirty-eight children and his own wife.

Still, it is the Tower sniper incident that gets the "credit" for the being the first of a phenomenon that has become horribly ordinary during the first quarter of the twenty-first century. The names of other tragedies—Sandy Hook, Virginia Tech, Columbine, Parkland—are still open wounds on the American psyche, but they were part of the pestilence rather than the initial infection.

The story of the Tower sniper is as follows: a nice-looking, seemingly happily married, former Marine who was about to graduate from the University of Texas with an engineering degree first killed his mother, then stabbed his beloved wife to death as she lay sleeping. Early the next morning he packed his military footlocker with over a hundred staples, from a pipe wrench to toilet paper to a snakebite kit, rented a dolly, and then trundled the locker, three rifles, one shotgun, three handguns, and a battery of ammunition onto the elevator to the eighteenth, or top, floor of the University of Texas Tower. After killing the receptionist on that floor and two members of a family who came up the elevator, he went to the walkway that surrounded the top of the Tower and began shooting students and others on the campus below. For a little more than an hour and a half he blazed away, felling some forty-three more people, during which time dozens of students and civilians blazed back with deer rifles and other personal firearms. A half dozen Austin police officers, a Department of Public Safety officer, and a civilian ascended the Tower, forced the door from the reception room to the walkway that Whitman had barricaded, then crept out and around until they saw the shooter, at which point two of the officers opened fire and killed him. Whitman's body count, including an unborn child, a man who died from his wounds in 2001, his mother, and his wife, was seventeen killed and thirty-one wounded.

An autopsy was performed, and a small brain tumor was reported to have been found. Even though later analysis cast doubt on the effect and even existence of such a tumor, it provided everyone with a degree of relief, or at least an explanation for why such an abomination could occur. Everyone knew that nobody in his or her right mind, and nobody in a land as civilized and enlightened as the United States would ever dream of committing such a horrible, senseless crime.

It was, in other words, the good old days.

There were hundreds of students and people on or near the campus that particular Monday, and in the research and writing of our book about the incident we interviewed several of them. A few were victims, others were participants in one way or another, and most were observers. Their experiences were imbedded, preserved, mayflies in amber. For some it was a personal brush with history, for others it remained a fresh wound, for a few it was still a source of outrage. More than one refused to speak the name of the shooter. Two victims refused to talk to us out of concern we might glorify either the man or the act.

We also learned that the University of Texas took a completely understandable but totally misguided reaction to the shootings. The incident was so contrary to, so much the antithesis of what the school stood for that its leaders set about immediately to divorce itself from it. Classes resumed, victims were not honored, histories of the school and the Tower failed to mention the killings, an attempt to place a plaque where an Austin police officer was killed by Whitman was rebuffed, guided tours of the Tower included no mention of what happened or explanation for the numerous patched bullet holes along the walkway. This rankled many who were there. Loyal Longhorn alumni still grumbled after fifty years that their school had let them down. We know now, based on an overabundance of learning experiences that people touched by such tragedies need a place to mourn, a site to gather, leave messages, flowers, and stuffed animals, and to commune with others. It is part of the grieving process. Truth must be looked in the eye from which tears must be allowed to flow.

Decades of being the poster child for mass school shootings also generated a plethora of myths about the UT Tower shooter and his motives. Because two of his victims were pregnant, he was said to have hated women, or babies, or that he believed his purpose was to spare children the agonies of life and send them straight to Heaven. Even though there is significant doubt that the tumor, if it existed, played a role in Whitman's behavior, (the reasons he did it are more complex) its proximity in the brain to his amygdala has been characterized as proof of the far-reaching, horrifying control exercised by that part of the limbic system.

The truth is that a brain tumor almost certainly did not cause Charles Whitman to go on a shooting spree. What led Charles Whitman to commit the unthinkable is multi-faceted, multi-layered, and complicated. Much of his "rationale" could only be known to him, and some of it is unique to his own experience.

There is no one-size-fits-all profile of a mass shooter. They have varying socioeconomic backgrounds, ethnicities, and belief systems. However, there are certain themes and commonalities that seem to be prevalent in the majority of school/mass shootings, all of which were present and a part of that tragic August day in 1966, namely:

- MALE. USUALLY WHITE;
- MOTIVATED BY A PERSONAL GRIEVANCE, REVENGE, OR DESIRE FOR NOTORIETY;
- FASCINATION WITH GUNS AND/OR THE MILITARY;
- EASY ACCESS TO GUNS;
- USUALLY YOUNG, IN THEIR TWENTIES OR EVEN YOUNGER;
- INTERNALIZATION OF ISSUES AND PROBLEMS;
- A SENSE OF "OTHERNESS" OR EXCEPTIONALISM, DELUSIONS OF GRANDEUR;
- CRIES FOR HELP THAT WERE MISSED;
- DEPRESSION OR SOME OTHER FORM OF MENTAL DISORDER;
- A SENSE OF LOST PURPOSE; AND
- AN ATTACK THAT WAS METICULOUSLY PLANNED; NOT RANDOM; THE SHOOTER DID NOT "SNAP."

Many people's fascination with such horrible events, like the university's reaction to it, is misguided. Rather than as curiosities they should be studied for the purpose of preventing similar outrages. It is the experience of the survivors that are most instructive, and how their grief, anger, pain, and even silence have impacted their lives and provided guideposts for what society must do to construct obstacles and detours for such events in the future.

I HAD THE MISFORTUNE OF BEING PRESENT FOR AMERICA'S FIRST MASS SHOOTING

By John Fox (a.k.a. Artly Snuff)

John Fox (a.k.a. Artly Snuff) was seventeen when he took his first college semester at UT-Austin.

At seventeen, I entered UT-Austin for my first semester. I enrolled in two classes, one in the morning and another in the afternoon. I lived close to campus and often took advantage of the short distance by playing chess with a fellow AHS graduate, James Love, in his room on Rio Grande Street between classes. On the day of the shooting, while we were playing, a bulletin came over the radio saying someone was on the University of Texas (UT) Tower with an air rifle and we both jumped up, thumping over the chessboard, and rushed back to campus.

When we arrived, we heard shots and were waved off the Inner Campus Drive by a stranger who was shielded by a building several hundred feet closer to the Tower. James and I went into the Education Building and scurried up to the top floor, into the office with a view of the Tower. We saw bodies lying on the mall and knew they needed help. So, we left the building and made our way closer. We hunkered down, out of range from the Tower and protected by a large wall covered with massive hedges. As we got near, we crouched under a statue of Jefferson Davis, adjacent to the stairs that led up to the main mall.

From there, we could see the bodies laying out under the hot sun, only about a hundred feet from us. I could easily see that one of the people was a very pregnant woman, alive and twitching her legs. I worried the shooter might see her move and shoot her again. By now, I could hear shots being fired on a regular basis, and I knew that anyone who ran out there to help the fallen stood a good chance of being shot.

On the sidewalk next to me, I saw a fresh pool of blood staining the concrete. I found out later that the blood was from an Austin police officer named Billy Speed. He had been shot at the very place I crouched, killed by a bullet into his chest that went through a six-inch opening in the stone balustrade in front of him. I stared at his blood, thinking about the people bleeding on the mall just a hundred feet away. The carillon of bells on the peak of the Tower chimed every fifteen minutes and reminded me of the people still lying under the blazing sun for another fifteen minutes more. The pressure to do something rose slowly within me.

We crouched there for a long time, unsure of what to do. I was wearing black pants and a short-sleeved dark blue shirt, a choice I would regret long before mid-afternoon. Exposed to the full glare of the sun, I was hot and sweating, but could not leave while those people were out there on the concrete of the mall with no help. I could see people gathered across the mall in a gallery at the base of the Tower and they, like us, were afraid of going out to help, exposing themselves to gunfire.

This was 1966 before there were any police SWAT teams or EMS units. Nobody had mobile phones, there was no Internet, no way to contact anyone about the situation in front of us. If anything was going to be done, it was us that had to do it.

I looked across the street to the English Building and saw a police officer at a window firing a shotgun toward the top of the three-hundred-foot-high Tower. I knew that was futile. I can only assume he was firing out of frustration. And at some point, the heat and my adrenaline combined gave me a case of mild heat-stroke. I became nauseous and dizzy, with a strong headache. For relief, I crawled under the hedges next to the Jefferson Davis statue and stayed there in the shade until I felt recuperated.

When I emerged from the hedges, it was with a new purpose. I had the opportunity to get out of the sun and help myself, but the people in the middle of the mall didn't have that option. Something needed to be done to help them. The Tower chimed again.

I focused on the pregnant woman. It was unthinkable that she remained out there with no form of relief. It became essential to get her and the others out of the sun and out of the line of fire. It was a mission more vital than my self-preservation.

So, I did it. I ran from safety into danger, James at my side. I ran fast, even though time seemed to move at the speed of cold molasses. A man in a suit had been helped to his feet and was running toward safety, but when he got to the stairs, he rolled down, and was now lying awkwardly one step up from the sidewalk. I ran to him first, the closest victim to me. I was now far from any cover, feeling quite naked. I looked toward the people on the mall, now directly between the Tower and me. I focused on the pregnant woman and sprinted up the stairs toward her. At that point, my decisions were being made in nanoseconds since the shooter could start firing at any moment if he sighted us from his perch. I was now at the very spot where he had chosen to begin his killing spree.

I grabbed the pregnant woman's legs, and James grabbed her wrists as we turned to carry her across the mall and down the stairs to safety. Back then I had big, thick-lensed eyeglasses that I thought looked cool because they resembled the pair of glasses Buddy Holly wore. As we ran down the steps, the heavy glasses slipped down and off my sweaty face. I was legally blind without them. James and I set her down, then I had to run back out from cover in a blur to find my glasses. By then, another group of students had run up, carrying her to an ambulance. I looked down at her boyfriend, who had bled out over the last hour. His face was still, white as alabaster. I helped carry him to an ambulance.

When I watch that old grainy black-and-white film, footage taken while the shooter was firing from atop the UT Tower, it reminds me of footage taken in a third-world country. It seems out of place to have occured in the heart of Texas.

We only keep photos of the happy moments of our lives: weddings, vacations, birthday parties, laughing children. No one keeps photographic images of the most terrible moments: deaths, fears, and moments of gore. Yet, with me, the day the shooter was on the UT Tower comprised all these themes, and I cannot forget them as I age. I saw death fall from a clear blue sky. The film of that horrible day keeps being shown over and over on television for anniversary specials and historical retrospectives. I try to move on but can't leave that day behind. It's always there. People seem so fascinated by an event that was the most horrific day I've ever known.

I now know what the stain of evil can do to an individual psyche and how everything in and around the world that one considers safe and comfortable can be instantly shattered without warning. I'd never been more frightened in my life as when I consciously ran out from cover.

The university was closed the next day to clean up the blood and then the school reopened as if the shooting hadn't happened. Today, when there is a mass shooting, there are a flood of therapists available to talk with the victims. Nothing like that existed in 1966. Nobody knew how to mentally process such horror. I didn't talk about it much for decades. I now know I should have. Guilt has followed me incessantly. Why did I leave that woman and those others out there baking in the searing sun? If not for my cowardice, might more people have lived?

I wonder how my life and the way that I perceive things now would have been altered if I'd not kept seeing the broadcasted images of that rampage. The vivid scenes have become part of this nation's video library, trotted out for everyone's casual viewing. During melancholy moments, my mind inevitably goes back to that horrible day, and I review what I endured. I resurrect those dark thoughts normally buried deep within my mind and concealed from all but myself.

I know now that I did the best I could, but there is always a worm of doubt. That worm has been a part of my psyche for over fifty years now, and we are inseparable. Over time, I learned to live with my guilt, the guilt that few knew I felt. I have discovered that survivor's guilt is a normal condition that occurs after a traumatic event. That knowledge has helped me fight the loneliness that accompanied my trauma.

Now there is no reason to name the shooter as everyone knows who it was. I see no reason to stain this page with his name. He did, however, leave a legacy in the form of a template of violence. This template has taken the lives away from thousands of innocent victims and traumatized thousands of family members, friends, and witnesses to senseless bloodshed. When will it stop?

COORDINATING TRAUMA

Activists and Survivor Coordinators Recount Their Paths to Supporting Survivors in the Aftermath of School Shootings

GUN VIOLENCE NEVER TAKES A DAY OFF
By Hollye Dexter

Having experienced gun violence in her own family, Hollye is a dedicated activist for gun reform, using her voice and her writing to advocate for change. She has worked for Women Against Gun Violence, Everytown for Gun Safety, and the No Notoriety campaign.

I was fourteen years old that summer morning when I woke to my mother's screams. I ran to the living room to find my seven-year-old brother Christopher covered in blood. He'd just been shot in the head by a neighborhood teen playing with his dad's gun.

Christopher was in first grade. He was a skinny, towheaded boy missing his front teeth. I held him as my mother tore through stop signs and red lights to the hospital.

"Please don't let me die," he said before losing consciousness.

His eyes fluttered and rolled back as his little body twitched.

"Drive faster," I screamed at my mother. His blood stained my arms.

My brother survived, but the life meant for him was taken with one bullet. With brain surgery and a year of physical therapy, Christopher learned how to use a fork and walk without dragging his leg, talk without slurring, write with his left hand to compensate for loss of motor skills on his right side. He attended school wearing a helmet.

As an adult, Christopher lives with epilepsy and all the effects that come with traumatic brain injury and PTSD: emotional outbursts, rages, depression, self-medicating. Lead poisoning. The bullet remains in his brain.

On the morning of December 14, 2012, three decades after my

brother's shooting, the Sandy Hook massacre unveiled repressed memories, and I relived Christopher's shooting in vivid detail. I'm one of the unfortunate people who knows what a first grader who's been shot looks like. I watched the news with that horrific image in my mind, and in that moment, I became an activist.

Since then, I have worked as a writer, speaker, communications director, and social media manager for several national gun violence prevention organizations. My job requires me to be informed up to the minute of any breaking gun violence story.

EACH DAY AT 7 A.M., I BEGIN:
I Google "Gun violence," "shooting victim," "mass shooting," "domestic violence shooting," "accidental shooting."

Over coffee, I research the stories:

Where did the shooter get the gun?

What are the gun laws in the state where the shooting occurred, and is there a law on the books that could have prevented it?

I type out my daily reporting on child shootings: family murder-suicides, police shootings of unarmed black men, neighborhood drive-bys where children are shot at their breakfast tables.

Then there are the god-awful days of school and mass shootings. The days that we activists get on our national conference calls to rally and plan an action, and later, retreat to our private Facebook groups where we grieve, rant and fall apart, prop each other up again. Because this is my paid job, I don't have the option to "just take a break from it" or "get off social media for a few days" as my friends suggest.

In 2013, most Americans thought Sandy Hook and the Aurora theater shooting were a "fluke." I tried to organize meetings and rallies in Los Angeles and was hard-pressed to get thirty people to show up. Politicians wouldn't dare utter the word "gun violence." President Obama didn't mention it in his State of the Union address. Legislators ignored and brushed past Sandy Hook parents in the halls of Congress, crying and pleading for expanded background checks, which the GOP Congress members cruelly voted against. And so, we, a small scrappy group of pissed-off women, were saddled with a full-time occupation: protesting NRA conventions, marching in D.C., rallying at city halls, boycotting businesses, screaming at the top of our lungs to be heard twenty-four hours a day. No days off. No benefits.

I tried to take time off. For instance, in the summer of 2015, I was in a seaside resort celebrating my wedding anniversary, drinking coffee in my fluffy white robe on the deck of our hotel room, when an alert popped up on my phone. Television reporter Alison Parker and her cameraman Adam Ward had just been shot dead on live television. My husband, Troy, got the alert, too. He looked at me and said, "It's okay. I know you have to work. I'll go get us some breakfast."

And then there was the Sunday when I had a big family event but was woken at 6:00 a.m. by a call from my activist friend, Suzanne. She was crying.

"Forty-nine people," she said. "He shot them all dead in a nightclub."

We started making calls and planned a #LoveToOrlando vigil in West Hollywood that night. We rallied activists, religious leaders, musician, and press, who showed up with our last-minute notice. Instead of family day, my husband and children held signs and candles on Sunset Blvd., talked to press, hugged and cried with gay men now fearing for their lives.

But it was the day of the 2015 San Bernardino mass shooting that broke me. I was walking down the stairs in my house to tell Troy what happened, and my legs collapsed beneath me. He found me in the stairwell, sobbing uncontrollably, unable to move. The mass accumulation of grief had paralyzed me. I realized, then, that no matter how strong I thought I was, I couldn't inundate myself with tales of grief, injustice, and violence at 7:00 a.m. every day and still be sane. So, I took weekends off, joined a meditation group, and made yoga a priority. I took walks during my lunch break rather than working through lunch, turned my phone off in the evenings. I tried to find balance and continued the work.

When I got the alert about the Valentine's Day massacre at Marjory Stoneman Douglas High School in Parkland, Florida, there were scant details. They weren't yet reporting fatalities in the news alerts, but I felt it in my bones.

"I have a bad feeling about this one," I told Troy.

Sadly, I was right. But that same night, something else happened: the Parkland kids rose up. They were filled with righteous anger at the adults in positions of power who failed them. There was a grim determination in their words as they vowed they'd fight, and above all, that their generation would vote. Suddenly, legislators sat up and took notice. An empowered youth movement that votes is a force to be reckoned with, and I sensed a tipping point in our movement. But I know what it is to carry the weight of this movement, and now that the weight has shifted, I worry it's too heavy for their shoulders.

As I write this, we are days away from the horrific anti-Semitic shooting at the Tree of Life Synagogue in Pittsburgh. I'm on the phone, writing reports, and organizing calls to action. And I'm sure that by the time this book is published, there will be another shooting, another #hashtag on Twitter, another violent chapter in American History. I will weep, break, feel hopeless. But after a few days I'll get back up and work.

GUN VIOLENCE NEVER TAKES A DAY OFF.

A TREE BRANCH FALLS AND AN ACTIVIST RISES

By Jennifer Ostrega

Jennifer Ostrega is a Sandy Hook Promise Leader and Founder of Kind Hearts Theater.

One morning in December 2012, shortly after my husband and I moved to the suburbs, I was watching my 4-year-old perform with his classmates in his school pageant. What I could not know—and what I later could not comprehend—was that only a few miles away, in a small community called Newtown, Connecticut, children were being torn from this world and their dear parents. My husband and I wept the entire weekend, feeling the loss of those parents as if it were our own, and we asked ourselves *what can we do?*

The road to my activism started when on June 30th, 2015, a tree branch fell from the sky onto my head while I was typing grades for my college students into my laptop at the end of summer session. I was immediately instructed to rest my brain and abstain from all screen use. Doctor's orders gave me permission to avoid the nonstop flow of bad news I was accustomed to consuming online.

A few days earlier, the nurse at my son's school phoned me at work to report that my kindergartner's head was bleeding; a bully had admitted to pushing him into a bus window. I had already been wrestling with the lack of control that I had to protect him, but I guess that's just what it was to be a mother. Kiss your kid goodbye in the morning and hope for the best. But now I had been injured by another event beyond my control—leaving me with a growing sense of vulnerability living in a world that could be very cruel and indiscriminate. There had to be something I could do.

After my concussion had healed, I welcomed screens back into my life again, gradually. But the screens I watched brought news of more school shootings. I Googled "Sandy Hook parents." *How were they able to go on?* Finally, a Google that provided a glimmer of hope: Sandy Hook Promise (SHP) decided to create a grassroots operation called Promise Leaders. It was at that time I became a Promise Leader for the amazing, impossibly strong people at Sandy Hook Promise. I realized the incredible connection between all my worlds converging—I would be a mother to only one child, age 6 at the time.

Those twenty first graders were killed by an adolescent in pain from social isolation, and what could I do to ensure that my kid would be safe? I am grateful for the ability to recover from what could have been a fatal accident and even better, I gradually started to heal my own traumas by healing others. I became active in the organization and signed up to a grassroots initiative that now has trained over 7.5 million youth and adults to create inclusive and safer communities.

Before I knew it, Sandy Hook Promise invited me to run in the New York City Marathon as part of their team, which for me, was a risk. I did not come from a family of runners, and we were not risk-takers. As I trained each day for the marathon, I had the space to think about how I would blaze a trail. I had a lot of things working in my favor. I had my job teaching youth from foreign lands to help themselves amid a confusing environment. I had my history working with children; just before 9/11, I had been a child coach on *Sesame Street*. I'd studied and performed improv and mastered the ability to create a partnership in seconds that carries the weight of a relationship of twenty years.

And most important of all, I had dissatisfaction. I had an absolute certainty that the world could be better, must be better, and that I could contribute to better our world. So, I started a class called Kind Hearts Theater at an after-school program. It all began with a question: *What if I could bring improv skills and a sense of social partnership, generosity, and community to kids in schools? Could improvisation reduce violence and mitigate the social isolation this young generation is experiencing so profoundly?* Just like the tree branch that had been flagged for removal but was not pruned in time to prevent my injury, so too is the socially isolated student, who has not yet received help and poses a potential threat to others.

First, I worked on pilot programs developing a curriculum that would be easy to teach and adopt to different grade levels. What I quickly observed was that teaching eye contact, agreement, and yes AND had a clear and positive impact on the kids I was teaching.

With the NY Marathon date approaching, I reached out to my local school district about the free programming available to them when it wasn't popular to speak about gun violence, in those months before Parkland. Today, over 6,300 others like me have become volunteer Promise Leaders. I've worked in schools to help spread their message, hoping to mend the underlying circumstances and social isolation that lead to school violence. Sandy Hook Promise has programs like "Start with Hello," that encourage interaction, listening, and support to stop violence before it can ever take root, and "Say Something," which enlists our young people in recognizing and reporting at-risk behavior, catching it at a level where adults sometimes can't see. To date, these programs have helped avert several school shooting plots and threats, as well as teen suicides and other acts of violence. This work has such potential to grow and recently, there has been interest from many more school districts. With each new success, we can spread to another school, and with each school we add, we carry the banners for "Say Something" and "Start With Hello." Just like 70s slogans like "Give a Hoot, Don't Pollute" or "Only You Can Prevent Forest Fires," we can enshrine these steps to end violence and promote fellowship as common knowledge. Our Common Core standards teach math, science, language arts, and critical thinking, but what if one of our national Common Core standards included social emotional curriculum with a learning outcome based in empathy? If children grew up with this staple, then imagine how that would impact the playing field in a positive way within our corporate structure and our schools and communities.

This requires a shift in our thinking. It is something more that I do in addition to my job as a teacher. I push myself because I believe our kids deserve something better. And I know, I can't be comfortable with how things are currently. When video games that simulate school shootings are making money, I'm not willing to be dissatisfied. When anti-bullying programs only last a week, or a day, and we turn on the news and there's yet another mass shooting, it's time for us to realize that what is necessary is to change the fabric of our school culture. What keeps me persisting to be a Promise Leader is that social emotional skills should be ingrained into our heads in the same way we recite the pledge of allegiance every morning.

When I first introduced the Sandy Hook Promise programming in my community, several administrators really understood and supported the idea. These administrators understand that closing the gap of social isolation isn't a one-day activity or wearing a special shirt. It's a mind-set, and it must be taught 180 days of the school year. So, year after year, I keep trying until we all can teach all our children to

"Start with Hello."

AFTER TRAGEDY, GIVE BACK

By Charlene Mokos Hoverter

Charlene Mokos Hoverter is a former middle school teacher and principal of a Catholic Grammar School. Presently, she's a volunteer for Moms Demand Action for Gun Sense in America and is a Survivor Membership Lead and Fellow for Everytown for Gun Safety.

I've never been involved in a school shooting. Nor have my children. Nor have my grandchildren. And here I'm tempted to include the word "yet." Because, I fear, this is a real possibility. Because I know what it is like to be a survivor of gun violence.

Let me share a bit about me family.

We were seven children. My parents had unusual nicknames by which they were always called. *Pickles* for my Mom for the obvious reason of liking pickles as a young girl. My Dad was *Bing*. He looked like Bing Crosby and had a beautiful singing voice. Some of my most endearing memories are of my dad and his sister harmonizing to "Heart of My Heart." While my parents were children of the Depression who dropped out of high school, they were determined we would receive the education denied to them. And so we did. Blue-collar folks with a stay-at-home mom when a stay-at-home mom was the norm, we didn't have extra money. But somehow, through hard work, scholarships, and plain ol' grit we all made it through education beyond high school.

Diane, my oldest sister and firstborn in my family, was a nurse who held a master's degree in midwifery. She was in charge of the delivery unit in Cook County Hospital in Chicago, our hometown. Diane assisted the doctors, mentored the new nurses, and loved the little babies. A mother of four girls, Diane was able to take a few days away in June of 1986, specifically to plan out parents' upcoming fiftieth wedding anniversary. We went to the beach, had ice cream on the boardwalk, and did all those shore activities we locals take for granted. And we came up with a plan for the party. Hall, music, food, drinks, family and friends, and lots of fun.

Diane never attended that anniversary festivity. On the early morning of July 19, 1986, she stopped off at her church on her way to work, as was her habit. On that day she was apparently accosted as she exited her car and was shot in the head.

Later that morning, the police came to the door of our home where my youngest sister was home. Melanie had to look at a picture and identify her sister, Diane, who had a bullet through her head. Then she had to call all of her brothers and sisters with the news that one of us had been murdered.

My parents were traveling in the West and had spent the night of July 18 in Estes Park, Colorado. The morning of July 19 they were heading to my sister's home in Nebraska. In those pre-cell-phone, my sister, Linda, waited all day knowing she had to impart the worst possible news to her mother and father. I don't know how she did it.

I had just arrived in New Orleans for a conference when the desk attendant told me to call Melanie.

"Diane was in an attempted robbery this morning. She was shot and she didn't make it," said Melanie through the phone.

"What?! What?! Are you telling me my sister is dead?" I yelled back.

My mother and Diane's former husband had to go to the morgue to identify Diane's body. My mom returned with Diane's glasses, thick with her blood, and asked my brother and me to clean them. How could I have her glasses in my hand but not have my sister? Why wasn't she here? And the recurring thought: I never got to say goodbye. I love you.

The news carried the story of her murder. We watched as Diane was carried away on a stretcher, as her leg slipped off and dangled, wearing the clunky sandals she loved.

Prior to Diane's murder, I had seen my mother cry twice. Now I feared she would never stop. And my dad? The years passed, but my dad never sang again.

During that intense grieving time, I was outraged at the *lack of outrage* over the killing of Diane. This was not a normal death by illness or old age. This was not an accident. This was an intentional killing that took away the mother of four young girls, the daughter of hardworking parents, the aunt to multiple nieces and nephews, the beloved sister of six siblings, the good friend of many many people. We should be outraged. We should be outraged at every single one of the ninety-six deaths by gun that occur daily here in the United States. We should be outraged that our children are not safe in school. That we are not safe in church, in the mall, in the office, in a concert hall.

Diane never saw her girls get married. She never held a grandchild in her arms. Because in an instant someone with a gun shot her in the head.

As the years have passed, the most intense pain has lessened. My great anger diminished, but not my outrage. Somewhere in my thoughts, in the corner of my mind, was the wish to do something so others wouldn't go through this grief. The thought that I needed to tell people about the anguish that barely lets go. To help make all this STOP!

And then Sandy Hook happened.

And Shannon Watts started Moms Demand Action for Gun Sense in America. And eventually joined forces with Everytown for Gun Safety in America. My Minnesota brother, Bob, found and reached out to Everytown. He and I had spent time talking to each other about trying to do something about this dangerous access to guns in our society; trying to talk through tears as we shared our continued grief and desires. Bob was excited and elated to tell me about Everytown.

So, I picked up the phone and became active with these two organizations that now give me strength, compassion, and unconditional support. Through the training I have received by Everytown, I reach out to other survivors in New Jersey. We help them feel empowered to have a voice in the movement to end gun violence. We share a network of survivors who support each other, talk with each other, and help each other. We speak at community events, club meetings, churches, vigils, religious observances. We author letters to the editor and to our congressional representatives and senators, compose editorials, call our legislators, testify to the members of our governing bodies. We motivate people. We change people's minds. We make changes.

Everytown has given me the path to teach others about this personal heartbreaking experience. Everytown has also allowed me to connect with other survivors who understand my pain, my need. They understand me. The volunteers with Moms Demand Action has given me the joy of seeing others committed to this cause who have been blessed not to have been touched by violence personally but are passionate nonetheless. They are my inspiration and faith in a greater and wiser future.

I do this in Diane's honor. I hope she knows that thirty-two years after her murder, she is missed daily. And how this is my way of saying,

"Goodbye. I love you."

MY PROMISE

By Marcel McClinton

Marcel McClinton, seventeen, is a Houston-based gun violence prevention activist, and gun violence survivor of a 2016 shooting outside of his church. Marcel has traveled the country protesting, speaking, and lobbying with a number of different organizations in an effort to urge lawmakers to enact change, and encourage other young people to get involved.

In 2016, a gunman went on a shooting rampage with an AR-15 outside of Memorial Drive United Methodist Church in Houston, Texas, while I was co-teaching Sunday school inside to our many toddlers. We watched him while crouched under a window, listening to the police scanner. No one felt safe, yet we knew we would be the first line of defense if he came into the building. The shooter circled the parking lot, and then walked the neighborhood streets while shooting at police, church members, joggers, and cars. His intent was to kill. He wanted to instill fear, and he did just that.

Because I didn't get shot, I never considered myself a "survivor," and I didn't immediately get involved in activism. I also hadn't realized how our lawmakers were failing us when it came to gun violence prevention. It wasn't until the Parkland shooting two years later that I felt empowered enough to demand change alongside hundreds of thousands of other young people. I first co-organized March for Our Lives Houston, and worked with over eighty organizers to hold an event where 15,000 Houstonians marched, chanted, and cried together. I found my voice in this movement after two years of silence. Speaking to the massive crowd was exhilarating, and empowering.

As the weeks went by, I noticed Houston's energy and interest around the issue dwindle. Our team was working hard to re-energize our city when I received notifications of the Santa Fe High School shooting. I texted my mom immediately and told her we needed to drive the fifty minutes to Santa Fe after school. I didn't have a plan, and I didn't know what crisis outreach entailed, but I wanted to be there for anyone who needed someone to hear them, hug them, or tell them they're loved.

I've now protested, spoken, and lobbied around the country. In June, I spent four days each week in Washington, D.C., lobbying for gun violence prevention legislation. I also had the incredible opportunity to meet with lawmakers leading on this issue, as well as some who greatly oppose the work we're doing. I spent two weeks on Road to Change, a summer cross-country bus tour with students from Parkland, Chicago, Milwaukee, and St. Louis. On Road to Change we met with survivors of gun violence, and were tasked with working toward empowering each community we visited. We listened to stories, shared our own, and discussed ways to combat an issue every community faces. Each day was a new experience, and I went home in July feeling emotionally drained, but also reminded about exactly why I do the work that I do.

I never want another person to experience fear, trauma, or death when our lawmakers have the ability to end these senseless tragedies. I serve on Houston's thirty-seven-member Commission to Prevent Gun Violence, and work with local, state, and federal leaders on ways to best tackle this issue. Our focus before the midterms has been education, outreach, and registering folks to vote. I'll soon be exploring solutions to gun violence with global leaders, as I've been invited to spend four days in November in Costa Rica with former Costa Rican President Óscar Arias and Nobel laureate Jody Williams.

The countless speaking engagements, travel opportunities, and network-building have been amazing, but the root of my work will never change. I've missed school, quit football my senior year, and even had to leave my sister's graduation immediately after she crossed the stage, because gun violence doesn't take a break from society, and neither can those of us working to prevent it.

Before I sleep at night, I think about the twenty-six toddlers in my Sunday school class for whom I continue this fight. I will remember the sounds of those gunshots outside my church for the rest of my life. I will forever remember the look on the kids' faces as we hid. I've known most of them their whole lives, and I would do anything to protect them. Through my activism, I hope to help create a better America for them to grow up in.

THE ROAD TO HOPE

By Natalie Barden

Natalie Barden was ten years old when a gunman entered Sandy Hook Elementary School and killed twenty-six people on the morning of December 14, 2012. He murdered six educators and twenty first graders, including her seven-year-old brother, Daniel. In this essay, Natalie recounts how Daniel's death shaped the years that followed and recalls some of her favorite memories of her brother.

It's been almost six years years since I've been able to make a memory with my little brother. My brother Daniel was an old soul. He was four years younger than me, but in my mind, we were always the same age. He was constantly holding the door for others and talking to kids who didn't have many friends. Daniel made sure no one was alone at school. He even helped worms cross the hot pavement so that they wouldn't cook in the sun. Daniel was full of light and energy. He radiated positivity.

Daniel Barden. Photo courtesy of the Barden family.

December 14th was a Friday, and I was excited because my school, Reed Intermediate, was having a movie night for the fifth graders. Daniel's bus for Sandy Hook Elementary School came later than mine, but that morning he woke up early to be with my older brother, James, and me as we got ready for school. I was annoyed by how much Daniel was hugging me, unappreciative of his affection. The morning ticked on, ushering us out the door to school.

Not long after the first bell, we went on lockdown. Assuming it was a drill, we huddled in the corner of the classroom. Quietly, we studied for our scheduled science quiz. But that silence was interrupted by the announcement of an "incident" at Sandy Hook Elementary School. Incident. I assumed there was an animal near the school or an accident in a neighboring town. We stayed in lockdown for the rest of the morning, needing escorts even for the bathroom. By lunchtime, we were allowed to sit in the hall and eat, students swapped theories of what went down. I, too, was wrapped up in the drama of it all, not expecting it to mean anything.

By the time we boarded our buses to go home, helicopters were circling above. The parking was lot filled with news vans and people recorded us as we drove by. Still, none of this meant anything to me. I couldn't consider the possibility of something terrible happening at Sandy Hook that day, yet for some reason all I could think about was Daniel. I wanted to get home to him and my parents as soon as I could. I imagined myself wrapping him in a big hug.

It's been almost six years years since I've been able to make a memory with my little brother. As a family, we loved to play games, board games, card games, whatever. One of Daniel's favorites was Sorry. Every time he pulled a Sorry card he would exclaim "Sorrrryy!" And when the card was not usable, he would yell "Sorrrryyy!" followed with a quick "can't use it," almost as if it was one word. These were his iconic lines in the game, that we all started using every time a Sorry card was pulled. I can still hear the sound of his little voice saying those words, even though its been years since I've actually heard them.

That day the bus didn't go to my usual stop, but to Caroline's house down the street. There were three families in my neighborhood that were extremely close, the Malins, the LaBancas and my family, the Bardens. That day the kids from all three families went to the Malins. Maggie and Kyle were there, the youngest from the other families. We all seemed to ignore the fact the only people missing from our usual crew were Daniel and my parents. We didn't acknowledge the weird energy in the air. I found out later the parents in that house already knew what happened and were trying their best to hold it together for James and me.

I sat in the Malin's playroom as Maggie, who'd been in the elementary school, recounted what happened. She talked about hearing gunshots. Kyle was quiet. I don't remember thinking of the story as reality or connected to Daniel. It was bizarre, a fabricated drama. I don't know how long we just sat, eating cookies, and watching a Christmas movie.

It's been almost six years years since I've been able to make a memory with my little brother. James, Daniel, and I all had our own rooms. James had a bunk bed, and I had a single, but for some reason Daniel lucked out and got a queen. So of course, most nights the three of us would all sleep in Daniel's bed. Some nights my mom or dad would climb in and the four of us would squish together to read a book. When it was finally time to go to bed, we didn't really sleep. My brothers and I'd stay up talking and joking around. James would tell Daniel and me some bizarre stories about underwater gummy bears or whatever popped into our heads, and we would giggle like crazy until we fell asleep. We'd do this most nights out of the year simply because we loved being together.

Soon, Mrs. Malin announced she would drive us home. The short car ride was silent. I can only imagine now how impossible that day must've been for her. Mrs. Malin was like a second mother to all three of us, and she was with James and me when our world changed as we knew it. My parents greeted us at the front door and told us to go upstairs with them. I peered into the kitchen and saw other family members sitting at our table. I followed my parents and brother up the stairs, silently crying. Somewhere deep inside of me, I was acutely aware of what was coming. Inside my parents' bedroom, my brother and I screamed and cried. Cried and screamed. There was nothing else to do after learning our seven-year-old brother was dead.

In the days and weeks after, there was a constant stream of friends and family in my house. People were always bringing food and cards and presents. I talked and cried with the people I loved the most. Yet, I still was in denial of what happened. I remember sitting in my basement with my friends weirdly making bracelets with Daniel's name on them, as if he was going to wear them someday. I didn't want to acknowledge his absence was permanent, and I don't think I allowed myself to do so until I got to high school. I started to think about Daniel on a daily basis, crying more often than I did.

It's been almost six years years since I've been able to make a memory with my little brother. On weekend mornings, James,

Daniel, and I would turn the TV on and all snuggle up on our cozy red couch. Whenever we got bored of Disney or Nickelodeon, or could no longer agree on a show, we would play games and wrestle. When I think of Daniel, I see him in his New York Yankee pajamas, getting ready to tackle James. James would put our big green blanket over his head and be the monster. Sometimes Daniel and I would take turns being the monster and James would get a turn at jumping on the green figure. We'd wrestle until someone was crying and then find a new game. Daniel loved running around and tackling each other so much that we invented a special game called "Wild Daniel" where he'd just go crazy on us, and the three of us would laugh uncontrollably.

Shortly after Daniel's death, my father and some of the others who lost loved ones that day, founded Sandy Hook Promise, a nonprofit organization dedicated to preventing gun violence. I've grown up with Sandy Hook Promise (SHP). I have watched my dad, Mark Barden, become a voice in this movement. The formation of SHP is a blur to me, as it was so soon after Daniel's death. There's a picture of me at some meeting in the very beginning of the Promise with my head on my mom's shoulder looking absolutely destroyed. And that's how I felt.

As time went on, my family continued to stay involved in the fight for gun violence prevention, and SHP continued to grow. I remember coming off the bus to news vans in my driveway or coming home from swim practice to eat dinner with cameras surrounding the table. I learned the drill: you introduce yourself and say hello, and then pretend they're not there so they can capture your "normal life." I hated being recorded and hated interviews because it reminded me I was different and made the loss of my brother feel all the more real. However, I was never forced into it any of it. I remember my parents giving James and me the choice, while encouraging us to allow the media into our lives because of the powerful voice we had. So, I suffered the cameras and questions because I knew it was my duty to prevent a tragedy like ours from happening to anyone else.

As I grew up, my dad became more and more involved in gun violence prevention. In the earlier days of Sandy Hook Promise, the focus was legislative. My dad was learning every detail of gun violence and how to prevent it. He was writing speeches and visiting with lawmakers. I remember standing next to him the first time he introduced President Obama. In front of my friends, I would pretend to think it was cool, and even brag that my dad was getting to meet these important people. However, I never enjoyed it. I didn't like the constant conversation in my house. In all honesty, it probably wasn't that constant, yet every time I heard the word "gun," I wanted to scream because it made me think of what had happened to Daniel.

It's been almost six years years since I've been able to make a memory with my little brother. We got our Christmas tree the Sunday before my brother died. My family always loved Christmas. There's a beautiful picture of Daniel putting an ornament on the tree from that night. He didn't decorate the tree just to decorate it and get it over with. He took his time and savored the moments. In the picture, Daniel's already put the ornament on the tree, but he's standing and looking at it appreciatively. When we decorated that tree, we all talked and laughed, spending time together as we listened to Christmas music and drank eggnog. I remember making Christmas cookies. The three of us went into the kitchen and started a recipe for sugar cookies. We got every sugary and colorful thing we could find in the pantry and put it all on the counter. We spiced each cookie up with something different. Some had sprinkles, or chocolate. I think I put some Heath bar in there. I remember Daniel really wanting to make a cookie with gummy worms in it, so he did just that. When we brought the cookies into the family room, Daniel picked what he suspected to be his special cookie. We all laughed so hard as Daniel bit into the gross cookie and made a face of disgust.

Daniel decorating the Christmas tree. Photo courtesy of the Barden family.

In 2013, senators Joe Manchin and Pat Toomey co-sponsored a bill that would've closed the loophole in the federal background check system. This means every purchase or transfer of a firearm would have had to be accompanied by a full background check and entered into the National Instant Criminal Background Check System (NICS), effectively closing the loophole that mostly exists at gun shows and on the Internet. The Manchin-Toomey Bill would have prevented convicted felons from attaining a deadly weapon legally. After this bill failed at the federal level, SHP decided they could be more effective in stopping these massacres by focusing on prevention.

Now, the nonprofit organization trains schools in programs to recognize the warning signs of someone who is at risk of hurting themselves or others and provides them with tools to get the help they need. They have four effective programs that achieve this in different ways and have already saved so many lives. Even though it was difficult at times, seeing my dad work for gun violence prevention for so long and so tirelessly is amazingly inspiring and makes me proud to be part of this family. My parents showed me that when things are wrong you stand up and you fix them.

Gun violence prevention has always been something I've felt strongly about, for obvious reasons. When you know the terrible, life-shattering pain gun violence causes, I think it's only human nature to want to prevent others from experiencing the same pain. Even in middle school, I got into an argument with another kid over gun safety to the point where he ended up blocking me on social media. Despite my belief in the cause, when I was younger, I never wanted to be a big part of this movement, and left that work to my dad. I tried not to listen to the news because I couldn't handle hearing about shootings. I had difficulty thinking about the shooting for long periods of time, and still do, even with the practice I've now gained. I didn't want to have that conversation every day, because it's so emotional and hard for me to deal with, even more so when I was younger, because for a long time I was in denial over what happened to Daniel.

It's been almost six years years since I've been able to make a memory with my little brother. Daniel and I got to be in the same school for one year. Sandy Hook Elementary School went from kindergarten to fourth grade. Daniel didn't even make it through first grade. But while he was in kindergarten, I was in fourth grade. Every morning we'd get off the bus together. His classroom was on the way to mine so we would walk together. I didn't mind walking with Daniel because he was so cute and we got along very well, so I wasn't embarrassed like some fourth graders might be. Sometimes we would even hold hands down the hall. Once we stopped at his classroom he would hug and kiss me, always saying, "Don't wipe away my kiss!" As he turned into his room, he would look back to make sure I obeyed his instructions. Daniel was a wet kisser, so a lot of the time I would wipe my mouth, and he would fake his anger.

My own path in this movement began in early 2018 when I heard an announcement in homeroom referencing a gun violence prevention group called Junior Newtown Action Alliance (JNAA). As I listened, I realized there shouldn't be a gun violence prevention club in this school that I haven't joined, let alone never even thought about. Of all people in this school, I should be a part of advocating for such change. After talking to my friends and getting a few of them to join with me, I went to the meeting. That first day I felt so uncomfortable. Everybody in the room knew who I was and looked at me every time Sandy Hook was mentioned (or so it felt). Still, I joined the club and continued to go to the meetings because I knew the importance of me being there.

Not long after I joined JNAA, seventeen students were shot and killed at Marjory Stoneman Douglas High School in Parkland, Florida. When I first heard about the tragedy, as terrible as it sounds, I honestly didn't want to think about it. I think this is something a lot of people do, maybe without even realizing. School shootings are such a horrific thing that it can be easier to just ignore them. But that's no longer an option.

I realize now we can't allow ourselves to become comfortable with the murders that are happening every day. I had to acknowledge the horror that happened in Florida, and it brought up emotions and thoughts that usually don't surface. I knew where that town and those people were on this painful journey, and it connected me to them. I no longer had a choice in speaking out for gun violence prevention. I knew I needed to do this—not only for Daniel, but also for victims of gun violence everywhere.

It's been almost six years years since I've been able to make a memory with my little brother. Every year, the five of us would pile into our van and make the journey down to Florida to visit our family. Some might not enjoy an eighteen-hour car ride in close quarters with their family members, but I always loved that trip, and I think my brothers didn't mind it, either. We'd listen to books on tape, and when we got the new van, we'd even watch movies. My mom always had lots of snacks for us and we'd go through every road trip song we knew. Another thing we did to pass the time was make "forts" in our car seats. Really, we'd just drape a blanket over our heads and tuck it into the seat in front or behind us. For a kid, there's nothing more magical than being in your own little fort, even if it's just a blanket. I can still see Daniel bouncing around under his red blanket, singing along to the song "Dynamite." It was one of his favorites and he knew every word. Whenever I hear that song now, I can't help but tear up, remembering how full of life he used to be.

Daniel and Natalie. Photo courtesy of the Barden family.

After Parkland, I started to notice these remarkable young survivors who were becoming the voice of those lost to mass shootings. Their strength and determination inspired me, as it did people across America, young people in particular. They showed us the power of our voices and encouraged people everywhere to stand up and say, "no more." These students gave me the strength to become more involved. Since the shooting at Marjory Stoneman Douglas, our group, JNAA, held a vigil for Parkland at our high school, we planned and participated in the national walkout, and we traveled to D.C. for the March for Our Lives. I've been trying to navigate my way through this new activism while still knowing and respecting my own limitations. Gun violence is an extremely difficult topic to talk about for me, and probably always will be. I force myself to open up when I think projects are worthwhile and will be effective in reaching people.

In early 2018, I was featured in *Teen Vogue*, where I shared my story very publicly for the first time. This experience introduced me to powerful and inspiring student activists from Parkland and across the country. I now know so many kids who have selflessly committed their lives to activism, some of whom I stay in contact with, and know are always there for me. I also traveled to Parkland to meet with some of the survivors. I spoke with people who were going through what I did. Knowing their long road ahead, it was heartbreaking to be there and feel their pain.

But from all our pain, a movement emerged. The activism coming from young survivors and people across the country has given me hope, and they give me the strength to continue this work because I know I'm not alone in the fight. When we stand together, we can accomplish change. That's why I believe everyone, young and old, needs to be involved and actively talking about gun violence. I don't want this momentum to fade. I see the work my father has done over the years combined with the new energy from young activists, and it fills my heart with something I haven't felt in a very long time: hope.

Daniel's last letter to Santa. Photo courtesy of the Barden family.

ACKNOWLEDGMENTS

We send our deepest thanks to the following individuals and organizations for their support and nurturing during this collection process.

Max Sinsheimer, our incredibly supportive and hardworking agent and founder of Sinsheimer Literary, LLC, www.sinsheimerliterary.com. Thank you for believing in this project and sticking out the whole process with us. We are forever grateful, and we couldn't have brought this project to life without your help, direction, and advice.

Nick Magliato, our superhero editor at Skyhorse. Thank you for understanding the nature and sensitivity of this project as well as your patience, counsel, and endless support. We are grateful for this book and project to find a home with Skyhorse.

Jaime Bedrin, Moms Demand Action, Essex County Local Group Leader

Kristina Anderson, Koshka Foundation

Jennifer Lugar—Moms Demand/Everytown Survivor Contact

Elizabeth Lee—MOMs PA

Julia Spoor—MOMs PA

Stephen Nolt—Author of *Amish Grace*

Donald B. Kraybill, Coauthor of *Amish Grace*, Senior Fellow Emeritus, Young Center Etown College

Martha Frankel, Woodstock Radio

Beverly Donofrio, writer

Dr. Bonnie Culver, Wilkes University MFA

Tammy Kreznar, Survivor Program Support Manager, Everytown

Sandy Anglin Phillips, www.survivorsempowered.org

Mike Miller, Manager & City Archivist, Austin History Center/Austin Public Library

Prof. Joan Neuberger, Department of History, University of Texas at Austin, Editor of *Behind the Tower*, behindthetower.org

Eve Fox, Author and Principal, Fox Strategies

Herman Bontrager, West Nickel Mines Community

Madeline Moya, Media Archivist, Austin History Center, Austin Public Library

Mike Miller, CA, Manager & City Archivist, Austin History Center/Austin Public Library

Nell Carroll, Director of photography/Editorial, *Statesman*

Dr. Judy Redling, Associate Provost; Ginny Reiner, Academic Coach; Diane Moscaritolo, Accessibility Director; Tara Dilkes, Tutor Coordinator; and Nora Boyer, Math and Science Director; Nazlin Shakir, Master Tutor and ELL Specialist; Dr. Max Orsini, Graduate Writing Specialist all from Drew University for listening and offering their support of the project.

Alyssa Waugh for offering her Chicago skills and bringing together the bibliography and resources for the digital archive.

Brian Bull from KLCC for generous use of his Thurston photograph

Gail Bradney, NY, for use of her beautiful farmhouse in Woodstock

Oscar Lindermuth, PA, West Nickel assistance

Mike Herbstritt, father of Jeremy Herbstritt, West Nickel assistance

Aaron Esh, West Nickel assistance

Keith Maitland, Director, *The Tower*, www.towerdocumentary.com

Thank you to *The Rumpus* for publishing Loren Kleinman's essay "A Friend in the Dark" on February 11, 2019, which included previously unpublished sections and excerpts that now appear and have been republished in this book in the following introductions: West Nickel Mines, University of Iowa, Virginia Tech, Marjory Stoneman Douglas High School.

Loren would like to personally thank her family for their support, love, and encouragement during this process: her loving husband, Joseph Wade; Linda and Brian Kleinman; Jenny, Kyle, and Kyle Jr. D'Agostino; Dana, Dan, and Ryan Hanks; and Betsy D. Sauther. Thank you to friends Annette Damato-Beamesderfer, Kitty Sheehan, Monique Lewis, Claudia Serea, Roseann Torsiello, David Juarez, Christina Seeber, Jaime Ekkens, Susan Shapiro, Jessica Ciencin Henriquez, and Jaime Lubin. Thank you, forever.

Amye would like to personally thank her family for their support, love, and encouragement during this process: Timmy, Penelope, and Samantha Archer. Sam and Doreen Barrese, Donna Kopicki, Jennie Barrese, Bill and Carol Archer, and Stephanie McLane. She'd also like to thank her supportive coworkers who let her cry in their office more than once. And to her fellow writing friends, thank you for the love, support, and hand-holding when needed.

NOTES

FOREWORD

1. Akers, Monte, Nathan Akers, and Roger Friedman, PhD. *Tower Sniper: The Terror of America's First Active Shooter on Campus.* Houston, TX: John M. Hardy Publishing, 2016.

HEATH HIGH SCHOOL, WEST PADUCAH, KENTUCKY, DECEMBER 1, 1997

1 and 8. "Analysis | More than 220,000 Students Have Experienced Gun Violence at School since Columbine." *The Washington Post.* Accessed November 16, 2018. www.washingtonpost.com/graphics/2018/local/school-shootings -database/?utm_term=.e7edaf99eff7.

2 and 4. "Analysis of Mass Shootings." EverytownResearch.org. April 11, 2017. Accessed November 16, 2018. everytownresearch.org/reports/mass-shootings -analysis/.

3 and 5. "New Poll of NRA Members by Frank Luntz Shows Strong Support for Common-Sense Gun Laws, Exposing Significant Divide between Rank-and-file Members and NRA Leadership, Mayors Against Illegal Guns." PR Newswire. www.prnewswire.com/news-releases/new-poll-of-nra-members-by -frank-luntz-shows-strong-support-for-common-sense-gun-laws-exposing -significant-divide-between-rank-and-file-members-and-nra-leadership -163592606.html. July 24, 2012.

6. Parker, Kim, Juliana Menasce Horowitz, Ruth Igielnik, Baxter Oliphant, and Anna Brown. "Views of Gun Safety in the U.S." Pew Research Center's

Social & Demographic Trends Project. June 22, 2017. Accessed November 16, 2018. www.pewsocialtrends.org/2017/06/22/views-of-gun-safety-and-the-key -responsibilities-of-gun-owners/.

7. Sanger-Katz, Margot, and Quoctrung Bui. "How to Reduce Mass Shooting Deaths? Experts Rank Gun Laws." *The New York Times.* October 05, 2017. Accessed November 16, 2018. www.nytimes.com/interactive/2017/10/05/upshot /how-to-reduce-mass-shooting-deaths-experts-say-these-gun-laws-could-help .html.

BETHEL REGIONAL HIGH SCHOOL, BETHEL, ALASKA, FEBRUARY 19, 1997

1. "Evan Ramsey's Tattered Life Filled Him with Rage. Then He Brought a Shotgun to School." *Anchorage Daily News.* Accessed November 16, 2018. www.adn.com/alaska-news/2017/02/18/evan-ramseys-tattered-life-filled-him -with-rage-then-he-brought-a-shotgun-to-school/.